MY PERSONAL STORY

IN AND OUT OF

EUROPE

MY PERSONAL STORY
IN AND OUT OF
EUROPE

ANDREW PEARCE
Former MEP

Matador
9 Priory Business Park
Kibworth Beauchamp
Leicestershire LE8 0RX, UK
Tel: (+44) 116 279 2299
Fax: (+44) 116 279 2277
Email: books@troubador.co.uk
Web: www.troubador.co.uk/matador

ISBN 978 1783060 177

British Library Cataloguing in Publication Data.
A catalogue record for this book is available from the British Library.

Typeset in Aldine401 BT Roman by Troubador Publishing Ltd
Printed and bound in the UK by TJ International, Padstow, Cornwall

Matador is an imprint of Troubador Publishing Ltd

This book is dedicated to the memory of my dear wife, Myra, who died in 2006.

I am very grateful to Hilda Weissfloch for the enormous amount of valuable advice she gave me in the preparation of the text. I also thank Suzie Woodward for her help.

Contents

Preface

I was a Member of the European Parliament (MEP) from 1979 to 1989. This book is about what I myself did, saw and heard during that time. Part I is chronological, telling how I became an MEP, from early life, school, university and national service and then five years as an official in the European Commission. Part II deals with my time as an MEP, topic by topic, activity by activity. Part III is an account of my work as a member of the European Parliament committee concerned with aid and trade with developing countries. Part IV tells my story after I came out of the Parliament, working in a British retail company on European affairs and then back in the European Commission for a further eight years. Part V is a series of reflections looking back over my time involved in the European Union (EU) in one capacity or another. At the end is an appendix which gives a simplified explanation of how the EU works.

When I applied to be a candidate in the first direct elections to the European Parliament in 1979, I could not have foreseen the places I would visit, the people I would meet and the actions I would be part of. I had no knowledge that I would be arrested "at gunpoint" on a ferry on the Zambezi, would be bitten by a monkey in Sierra Leone and spend a night in a former Portuguese Army brothel in Angola. I did not foresee speaking on Spanish national radio about the bestialities of a Spanish bull run which I had witnessed. I expected to be debating with some of the big figures in European politics but could not know that they would include Barbara Castle, Ian Paisley, former French premier Pierre Pflimlin, Otto von Habsburg, French right wing leader Jean-Marie Le Pen and British European Commissioners including Leon Brittan and Roy Jenkins.

I could not have imagined the depths to which the British media would sink in reporting on the EU and the damage this would do to the British people's understanding of its activities. Likewise I was unprepared for the absence of effective means of co-operation between our MEPs and our Conservative "colleagues", the MPs (Members of Parliament i.e. Members of the House of Commons). I could perhaps have foreseen having milk poured over my feet by a Cheshire farmer, given the sensitivity of milk quotas at the time! But I did not anticipate being instructed to "Sit" by Mrs Thatcher during a briefing session in Downing Street! Yet this was the life on which I was embarked.

The book is a set of personal recollections and impressions – perceptions, if you like – not a definitive history. We all make most of our decisions on the basis of personal recollections and impressions. These are some of mine.

Andrew Pearce
2013

PART I

How it All Began

School, Russian and Newcastle Brown Ale

I am frequently asked how I came to be an MEP. Was I from a political family or background? Did I undergo special training for it? No, to both! Here is how it really was:

My family lived in a leafy road in Aughton, near Ormskirk, ten miles north of Liverpool. My father, Henry, was a cotton broker in Liverpool. Owing to an attack of poliomyelitis in childhood, he walked with the aid of two sticks and leg splints. The broking firm in the Liverpool Cotton Exchange which he inherited, buying cotton in America and selling it in Finland and Sweden, was moderately successful before the Second World War though it was not one of those which made some of the Liverpool brokers immensely rich. Blockades of the sea lanes during the war and the shortage of dollars afterwards brought his business more or less to a standstill. A fraud by a member of his staff made things worse.

His mother, who died when I was five, was reputedly a difficult woman. In pre-war days she had a gardener, a chauffeur and two country cottages in North Wales as well as her house in Aughton. My own mother, Evelyn née Andrew, daughter of a railwayman, had stepped up from the Liverpool working class and must have struggled to gain acceptance by the middle class family into which she married. She read the *Daily Mail* and minded stalls at local Conservative bring-and-buy sales.

My time at Rydal School in North Wales, preparatory and senior, gave me an interest in history and geography but that was as near to politics as it went.

I was called up for two years' National Service in the Royal Air Force (RAF). I underwent basic training – mainly parade-ground drill, designed to subordinate recruits and instil military discipline – at Bridgnorth in Shropshire. A part of our training which I really disliked was taking a Bren light machine gun to pieces and reassembling it in so many seconds (and praying that it did not collapse afterwards because I had fitted the pieces together wrongly!) The camp there has since been completely demolished. A highlight of the training was being sent out to camp on Wenlock Edge on a frosty night with a groundsheet and blanket but no tent, obliging us to collect sticks in the darkness to support the groundsheets.

After initial training, I was sent to a fighter station in East Anglia for a month. There seemed little to do there and I felt I was wasting time. However, one day I was told to prevent the squadron leader's boxer dog running across the wings of the Meteor jets in the hangar, these jets being part of Britain's instant response to threats of Soviet incursions into our airspace. I cycled to the village post office each day for the station's mail. This camp later became an open prison.

Then I was sent for nine months to Crail in Fife, on the east coast of Scotland, to be taught Russian. The tuition was excellent. Because familiarity with numbers in Russian was critical to what we were being trained to do, we were made to play Bingo in Russian for ha'pennies. The purpose of the course was to teach us to translate, on paper, Russian material which was put before us. The work for which we were being prepared was of extreme secrecy and the training for it was almost equally so.

We had to take turns on security duties. We helped to guard a million pounds worth of naval stores in hangars at the camp and I formed part of a security detail several times in company with six other conscripts. We were each armed with a pick handle. On one security detail, I threw a *Daily Mirror* reporter out of the camp by the seat of his pants. He was trying to get a story about food poisoning there. It was perfectly true that the kitchens, run by civilians, were filthy and that a good deal of the stores delivered to it were surreptitiously spirited elsewhere without getting anywhere near our plates. Trainee cooks from the Highland regiments were drafted in to replace the civilians. Several of them ended up in police cells within a week as a result of disturbing the peace of local villages.

Those of us who wanted to go into the village at the weekend for a drink had to face the Scottish licensing laws. Pubs were closed on Sundays but inns could serve alcohol to people who had travelled three miles or more. The Scottish bus industry was mobilised to transport the drinking population of village A to village B, three miles away, and then the drinking population of village B to village A – and of course the reverse at closing time.

We underwent a limited number of military drills at the hands of a naval chief petty officer, a corporal of horse from the Life Guards and an RAF sergeant. Their badges of rank were understood by members of their respective services but not always by others. A little drama was played out on numerous occasions.

'You horrible little man!' bawled the duty non-commissioned officer.

'Yes, Sergeant,' would say an inoffensive RAF trainee.

'I'm not a f★ ★ ★ing sergeant; I'm a chief petty officer,' would come the riposte.

'Yes, Sergeant,' the RAF man would reply.

One day, the general officer commanding the army in Scotland came to visit. An RAF squad including me was turned out to march up and down for his delectation. We were put in the charge of an army sergeant whom we had not seen before. Now, the drill routines of the three services are not the same; a simple instruction to come to "Attention" was performed to different commands and with different timing in the three services. On our normal parades we had come to an inter-service arrangement to avoid a clatter of heels at the command to come to attention, instead of the hoped-for single nice clean thud. Soldiers, if my memory is correct, respond to "'Shun!", airmen to "Atten-shun!" and navy people to "Hands Ho!". The sergeant in charge of us on this occasion knew nothing of all this. Not wishing to cause ourselves or the sergeant trouble, the squad decided, by some kind of telepathy, to march up and down our own way, taking little notice of the sergeant's commands. The sergeant got the idea. The general was very pleased.

The camp at Crail was used years later partly as a pig farm and partly for go-karting.

I then spent three months undergoing further training at Pucklechurch near Bristol, which, years later, became a young offenders institution. Then, having acquired sufficient ability to translate from Russian into English and knowledge of certain radio techniques, I was sent to work in Government Communications Headquarters (GCHQ) in Cheltenham. This was after passing a rigorous security vetting. I worked with other RAF national servicemen, army personnel (both officers and non-commissioned ranks) and civil servants in a unit of about a dozen people. We occupied half of a large office which was divided down the middle by tall filing cabinets. I had no idea what the people on the other side of the filing cabinets – or anywhere else in the complex of buildings – did, such was the secrecy of the place.

The security at GCHQ was intense. To leave documents out at night would have resulted in strong disciplinary action – except for when the titular head of the department, an upper-class type, was concerned. I'll call this official Grenville. Grenville managed to have meetings in London, where he effectively lived, every Monday and Friday so that he was only in his Cheltenham office three days a week. He was rarely entrusted with the nightly locking-up ritual. On one occasion when he was in fact so entrusted, he locked all the filing cabinets but left the keys on his desk. The Head of Security, a very senior personage, who would have been incandescent if anyone else had done this, merely said: 'Look here, Grenville, old chap, you really must be more careful in future.'

My application to go to Cambridge University, which I submitted while at school, was not successful. The problem was that I had not taken Latin at O level. It had been my intention to become an engineer and I didn't need Latin for that, but I had later changed my mind and decided to go for an arts degree. I thought I could take my O level Latin while in the RAF, but as my brain was totally occupied with having Russian hammered into it, the idea of studying Latin went by the wayside.

After finishing National Service in 1958, I began a degree course at King's College, Newcastle, which was part of Durham University at that time. Here I learned the basics of economics – thankfully not of the socialist kind. I enjoyed myself, learned to understand Geordie, drank Newcastle Brown Ale and gained a love of Tyneside and Northumberland which is with me to this day. I wasn't involved in politics there. However, I did know a fellow student of the emerging left wing who said he would assassinate the then Prime Minister, Harold Macmillan, if he ever got the opportunity. The nearest I got to student politics was to be a minor official in the Annual Rag Week celebrations. This raised some £20,000 a year for charity from generous and tolerant Tynesiders. The Rag involved such antics as playing hockey round the feet of policemen on point duty in the main shopping street; pushing along a bath full of green water, with a supposedly naked girl in it, for people to throw pennies into, and singing the *Blaydon Races* in pubs. One of my jobs was selling raffle tickets around the shipyards and this task gave me my first impression of the antiquated state of that industry. Several of the yards did not even have a notice board outside bearing the company's name or logo; their management seemed to have very little pride in themselves. My other job was to chauffeur the Rag Queen and Miss Camay – sponsored by the firm which made this soap – who had both been "kidnapped". I had to drive them from the luxury hotel where they were supposedly being held for ransom to a gala performance of the Rag Show at the Empire Theatre. There was in the Rag, as elsewhere in student life, a noticeable difference in maturity between the "men" who had done national (military) service and the "boys" who had not.

The bar, known as the Bun Room, in the Students' Union building at King's College, was so crowded on Saturday evenings that the best way to get beer was to go to the pub down the street and bring back some pints on a tray. I heard that female students sometimes danced bare-breasted on the top floor of the building on Saturday evenings. Drug-taking was rare, but a café in the city was said to be used for smoking opium though I was never aware of this when I was there. Politicians and other VIPs, dressed in smart suits, came to Union debates at King's College Union on Saturdays and were treated to vigorous but courteous intellectual scrutiny. All types of dress for students were acceptable, from jeans to city suits. When I revisited King's College ten years later, it seemed to be compulsory for all students to wear Chairman Mao style clothing. A friend and I in city suits were glared at with hostility. I later visited this friend's *alma mater* in London and the same trends in student attire were apparent there.

Just before my final exams at university, someone stole all my study notes from my briefcase. I passed nevertheless, thanks to some friends giving me access to their own notes for some last minute swatting. What sticks in the throat is that the thief must have been someone I knew, since the notes would have been of no use to anyone else.

I obtained my degree in economics and although I never became an economist, much of what I learned stood me in good stead later in life. As final exams came to a close, representatives from many large companies visited the university to recruit new graduate staff. At that time, all graduates could find jobs without much difficulty; there was little risk of becoming unemployed. Nor was there much chance of becoming rich either. People in managerial positions seldom earned much more than skilled manual workers. The jobs and salaries offered by the various companies and public organisations tended to be similar; I only knew two students whose starting salaries were significantly better than mine. One went to Nigeria for a few years, leading a life cut off from life's ordinary pleasures, and saved a lot of money. The other went to work for the BBC, which offered what seemed an enormous starting salary. He later became a regional newsreader. The prevailing business climate, the attitude of the banks and the rapaciousness of the taxman – levying a ninety eight per cent income tax, in some cases – meant that running one's own business was a non-starter – except for those with family businesses to inherit.

Engineering greater efficiency? Maybe

I was taken on by English Electric at their Stafford plant. My parents' next-door neighbour back in Aughton, was very curious to know whom I knew in the firm who had favoured me with a job. I was surprised and disgusted that he thought the "Old Boy" approach was still the only way into industry. This neighbour was steeped in the horrors of the class war then being fought in Britain. He used to tell of trying to speak on the telephone to the editor of a local daily paper about some industrial dispute. The editor said he could not do this because his calls were overheard by the trade union representatives. He would and did, however, meet my neighbour elsewhere outside office hours.

My job at English Electric was in Organisation and Methods (O & M). This entailed giving advice to departments in the company on how to make the work of the plant's 4,000 office staff more efficient. The O & M department had some successes but I sometimes thought that firms like English Electric knew it was a good thing to employ graduates but were not too sure what to do with them. Whether I became an expert in matters of efficiency is for others to judge, but I did acquire some understanding of how offices and the people in them worked, knowledge which seems to have escaped a number of today's politicians!

The firm made large equipment for generating and transmitting electricity. Much of this was sold to the British state-owned power sector on a cost-plus basis. The calculation of the price which the state-owned electricity authorities paid partly depended on an index of current average prices. It was important that this index should be as favourable from the company's point of view as possible; indeed, there was a small department solely concerned with achieving this. Sometimes I accompanied the manager of this department on one of his frequent visits to consult with government officials in London. I'll call this person Dennis. Dennis and I would go down to the company's prestigiously situated London head office by train, contriving to make the journey take most of the working day, before checking into one of the company's apartments in Mayfair. Business the next day took up most of the morning but finished in time to repair to a little private club of dubious reputation in Soho for lunch. This club closed at three o'clock in the afternoon but Dennis knew another one round the corner which opened at three o'clock. This took us through until it was time to catch a late train home.

Attitudes within the firm to saving money were far from rigorous. I was innocently surprised at the reaction of a departmental manager to some proposals I made for changing working arrangements in his department. I calculated that my proposals would reduce the department's costs by £20,000 a year, quite a sum in those days. The manager of the department just laughed; such a derisory sum was not even worth discussing! In any case, the cost-plus pricing system offered no incentive to be efficient, rather the reverse.

I had my first encounter with the world of consultants during this time. My boss, a very sensible former Royal Navy chief petty officer, had proposed a means of reducing clerical costs in a particular department by up to thirty per cent by bringing in more office equipment and reallocating work among the staff. His proposals were rejected as being impractical. Then somebody in head office decided to employ consultants to study the department. Two consultants appeared in our midst. Both were tall, slim and good-looking; one was American, the other French. Both wore expensive suits. The two consultants said they could cut costs in the department by thirty per cent, provided they were given a free hand. They then proposed changes which were more or less the same as my boss had proposed. This time the changes were accepted. I suppose if you spend a large sum obtaining advice, you might as well accept it, otherwise you could be accused of wasting the money spent on it!

On one occasion I had to go into the factory at night to study a particular problem affecting the night shift. The lights were ablaze but it was extremely difficult to find anyone at all, let alone anyone who was working.

In one part of the factory which I passed through frequently, there were a number of women applying smelly, sticky black gum to insulating tape wound around long and heavy copper bars. It was a filthy job. At Christmas time, it was regarded as fun by some of these women to capture an apprentice, undress him, tie him to a pillar and paint his private parts with the black gum.

Purchasing was another area of questionable efficiency. One particular purchasing clerk, who issued the official purchase orders for office furniture and equipment, would be taken out for lunch two or three times a year by his principal supplier. After prawn cocktail followed by fillet steak and chips at a local restaurant, he would arrive back a little late, slightly tipsy, and clearly feeling extremely guilty about such corrupt behaviour. I have often been surprised in later years at how small a financial outlay may be necessary to swing business towards a supplier who offers "sweeteners". But in those days, getting the best price for what a firm purchased was often less important than ensuring that the goods would arrive on time, failure to deliver on time being endemic in British industry.

One middle-aged departmental manager had an office which was approached by a long external iron staircase. He had an equally middle-aged secretary with whom he would indulge in natural delights on the desk from time to time. The couple felt secure in that they would hear the clanging of feet on the iron staircase of anyone approaching and could resume respectability in good time. But there was a flaw in their perception. The windows of this office were opposite the large expanse of windows of one of the workshops. The departmental manager assumed that nobody could see through these windows; they were very high up and the glass appeared to be darkened when viewed *from outside*. However, there was a high level staircase used for cleaning the windows on the inside, and this made an excellent and much-used viewing platform through which those inside could see perfectly well into the departmental manager's office. The departmental manager was for some reason known as "Jumbo".

In 1965, the time came for me to move to a better job. I went to work in succession for two construction firms in West London, again in Organisation and Methods. These jobs took me to many parts of Britain giving me more knowledge of the country in which I lived. I visited an opencast coal mine in South Wales where there were drag-line excavators. A drag-line excavator was like a crane with a bucket attached to its jib by a chain. The jib was thrust forward and then dragged back pulling the cable towards the machine and scraping earth up from the ground below it – 60 tonnes at a time! The caterpillar tracks on which the machine stood were taller than me. I went to a motorway construction site in the West Midlands where truck-loads of surplus soil ("muck") were booked off the site (to authorise payments to haulage contractors). Sometimes the muck was driven round to another entrance of the site and then booked out a second and maybe a third time. The gatekeepers who were supposed to keep a tally of the muck leaving the site were, not unnaturally, unwilling to argue the point with a driver who threatened them with a shovel. At one of the company's offices in West London I was responsible for uncovering fraud concerning an absentee worker. A wages clerk added a fictitious name to the payroll, opened a bank account in that name, paid wages into it regularly and took the money himself.

I often experienced the blandishments of salesmen. One firm supplying office machines used the good guy/bad guy technique. The bad guy implied that if you didn't buy from his firm he might tell your boss that you were taking bribes from another supplier. The good guy then said that this was unfair but why not buy from his firm anyway?

Although based in London, I had to spend a couple of months on secondment at a branch office in Newcastle, where I attended a meeting addressed by Geoffrey Howe (later Lord Howe of Aberavon). In those turbulent times of trade union agitation, he urged all Conservatives to stand up and be counted. "We should not let Labour hog the headlines with its marches and protests" and so on. I asked him what he actually wanted us to do… march down Whitehall and throw bricks or what? He had no answer. Sir Geoffrey was a good thinker and exuded honesty and common sense but the willingness to fight for his beliefs which he later displayed in finally confronting Margaret Thatcher was a long time coming.

First political steps

It was in Stafford that my first involvement in politics took place. I went along to the local branch of the Young Conservatives (YCs) in the party's town centre office. The YCs were then a very strong organisation across the country and the best middle-class "boy-meets-girl" outfit in the land. At the time of my first visit, the Stafford branch was in the middle of a seemingly interminable discussion about the details of its programme of weekly events. Nothing could be agreed, except that I, not even yet a member of the YCs, should be made chairman there and then! I was Chairman for several years and the branch prospered.

I became an officer of the main Conservative Association in the Stafford & Stone constituency and got to know the MP, Hugh Fraser, Air Force Minister at the time. I was invited to join one of the two Conservative clubs in the town – the less prestigious one. (The more exalted club was reserved for people who were more "established" than I was.) Like the majority of the Conservative clubs that I have come across in later years, the club I joined was Conservative in name but gave virtually no help, financial or otherwise, to the party. Most of the members were local tradesmen and skilled workers from families which had been in the town for generations. These local members did not mix with the influx of people who had come to live in the town in the post-war period. I would go into the club, say hello to the barman, order a drink and then stand there. Nobody made the slightest effort to be sociable. After two or three visits, I decided I had better things to do with my time.

I helped in one of the wards for the municipal elections and stood as a candidate for a county council seat. I had no hope of winning this particular seat but it was good experience. For the Tories to run even a "paper" candidate forced the Labour party to put some effort into the ward thereby reducing their resources available for other wards. The resources at our disposal for a typical ward of some 3,500 people in less-favoured Tory areas amounted to three or four elderly ladies and a couple of gentlemen available sometimes in the evening. Journalists, and therefore the public, have little idea how small are the resources of any of the political parties at local level, without which the basic functioning of democracy could not take place.

Lilian Wood (later Lilian Hodgkinson), the party's agent in Stafford, was a friend and a tremendous support to me. She persuaded Hugh Fraser to nominate me for inclusion on the Conservative Central Office list from which constituencies selected their parliamentary candidates. I was the first person for whom he had done this. Hugh was a remarkable man. He was an aristocrat with a great sense of caring and a willingness to support the party workers at grass-roots level. On one occasion he agreed to come from London to Stafford just to sit in a dingy pub and have an in-depth political discussion with me and four or five other YCs before returning to London the same evening. At that time, it was not very difficult to get on the Conservative Central Office candidates list provided that you were not a declared homosexual, a known wife-beater or a member of the National Front. I was interviewed by Jim Prior, then a deputy chairman of the party and later a cabinet minister. He said I looked like a shaggy dog and should get a hair-cut. I was accepted, but the hard part, finding a constituency, was to follow.

The groups of local party worthies, who at that time selected Conservative candidates in their constituencies, inevitably tended to choose people like themselves. Thus, people who didn't wear conventional dress or who expressed views out of line with conventional party thinking were viewed as unsound and therefore rejected. It was the narrowness of their thinking and their distrust of people who came from outside their own circles that tended to produce near-identical MPs in terms of social class. The selection committee preferred public school, middle-class, youngish men as candidates in safe seats.

A result of this was that the party sometimes seemed incapable of understanding the aspirations and problems of ordinary people. Yet somehow it managed to choose, in succession, two outstanding leaders who did not fit the mould at all – Ted Heath and Margaret Thatcher. The history books may show these two as having a great deal more in common than appeared at the time. Both were from ordinary backgrounds. I found no intellectual difficulty in admiring both of them. They each tried to roll back the stranglehold of trade union power and of monopoly forces in trade and industry. Both needed courage in the face of miners' strikes. Ted Heath wasn't helped by the London press disseminating exaggeratedly grim tales and near panic about the effects of miners' strikes during his time at Number 10.

While I was working in Stafford, I acquired an early taste of how to get things done through the press. The issue concerned the commuter railway from Liverpool to Ormskirk, serving Aughton, my home village. British Railways proposed to withdraw all trains on Sundays and the whole service looked threatened. I wrote a letter to the local paper opposing the cuts but suggesting shorter trains to save electricity. As I have learned countless times since, many people in the public sector resent any member of the public suggesting that official ideas may be less than perfect. But I won the argument, and the service runs to this day, attracting far more customers than previously. I saw that being willing to speak out in the press, in defiance of officialdom, was one way to let common sense and justice prevail.

After moving to work in London in 1966, I went into hospital to have my tonsils removed and there met Myra whom I married later that year.[1] Our wedding was in a Roman Catholic Church in Kingsbury in North West London. The priest, who was English, unlike so many who were Irish, later married a nun. The couple emigrated to New York where I visited him and his family some years later.

Myra and I honeymooned in Paris and Luxembourg. I only booked accommodation at the last moment, not being very flush with funds after paying the cost of the wedding. I followed the recommendation of one of Myra's friends and booked a room at the Hôtel de la Trémouille in Paris – quite delightful but at a cost which made my eyes water. I learned a lesson: ask the price first before buying anything!

I have always been fond of walking in cities and decided that on our first day we would walk from the Arc de Triomphe to Notre Dame, taking in the Place de la Concorde and the Tuileries Gardens on the way. Most of the major sights in Paris are more or less in a straight line apart from the Sacré Coeur. This time it was Myra who learned a lesson: always ask the distance before agreeing to go walking with me!

We bought our first house in Croxley Green near Watford, shortly after our wedding. We lived next to a fairly young works manager in the telecoms industry. Nine hundred people worked for him. All of these employees, except for the man who made the tea, had higher take-home pay than he did. That was not untypical of industry at that time. In more recent days of high and indeed excessive executive pay, it is hard to imagine the poor level of remuneration of much of Britain's management at that time. This was a big incentive to emigrate and a big disincentive to take on additional responsibilities at work.

It was while working in London that I was selected as prospective parliamentary candidate for the Islington North constituency, a seat which the Conservatives were very unlikely to win. The sitting Labour MP, Gerry

---

[1] We were happily married for almost forty years until Myra died of cancer in 2006.

Reynolds, Minister for the Army, had a majority of 7,831. My objective was to improve my chances of being selected for a winnable seat by demonstrating campaigning experience. This was not the part of Islington that rich socialists of the Blair generation came to make their own but an impoverished strip of London running down from Highgate Archway, across to Finsbury Park station to the east and Tufnell Park tube station to the west.

I did all the things that prospective candidates do to get publicity in the local papers. Less usual was that I acted as a witness in a prosecution of a food shop which was selling second-hand meat pies – they had remained unsold at the end of their shelf life in one shop and were then offered for sale in another. My constituency chairman, John Hanvey, and I bought a pie which was full of green mould. In the magistrates court the defence changed their plea to guilty when they saw that I was actually going to turn up and give evidence. "When the pie was opened... Tory sleuths got a shock!" cried the *Islington Gazette.*

I tried to help people with housing problems. Many people in the area had dreadful housing conditions. When I became a candidate, Islington Council was one hundred per cent Labour and quite unable to cope financially; it was also thoroughly incompetent. However, during my time there, the Tories were swept into power in a remarkable turnaround. The Tory-controlled Greater London Council, which also had housing estates in the borough, seemed to be similarly incompetent as regards carrying out its housing policy.

Some of the properties in Islington North were appalling, even though people still lived in them. One group of four streets, the Whittington Park project, just off the A1, had been earmarked by the Greater London Council (GLC) for demolition and the consequent re-housing of up to 300 residents. This was scheduled to take twenty years, twenty years of growing dereliction and fear for the residents who remained in their homes there. The *Islington Gazette* published two photos of the properties concerned on 10 April 1967. One was captioned: "Rubbish smoulders in one of the derelict houses. Residents claim a hazard is created by smouldering bonfires left by workmen." The other was captioned: "Several homes in this demolition area are still occupied. Unfenced demolition sites make it difficult for children to play in the street, say residents." Anthony Fletcher, chairman of the GLC's housing committee, described conditions as hideous after visiting the area with me; one woman had seen nine rats in her house. Anthony was quoted in the *North London Press* on 20 September 1968 as saying: "Many of the people are living in a kind of squalor which is intolerable in the modern age." I visited one couple who lived on the first floor of a house where the ground and second floors had been empty for months and had become regular sleeping places for alcoholics. In the summer, the fire brigade had to be called out almost every day to deal with fires in these streets which had been started deliberately. The residents who could not yet be re-housed suffered hell.

I used the full force of being a Tory candidate, which was not much, to try to get the GLC to move them to better accommodation at once. The local GLC office got a verbal dressing-down from me which it sorely needed. When I asked an official there to phone County Hall about the matter she said, 'We do not have telephonic communication with County Hall!'

Many of the residents waiting to be re-housed were handicapped, single or had large families. County Hall was busy building houses with two and three bedrooms but seemed to have not spotted that this did not meet the demands of many of the people on the waiting list.

In another part of Islington, I went to see a blind man in a ground-floor flat in one of the large, circular, Soviet-style blocks of council flats which municipal planners had devised. This was on a plot of land where there had previously been several public streets. The flats could only be entered from inside the circle, access to which was through an archway. The police had no power to patrol inside the estate – although some of the police dogs were not aware of this rule – and good order was supposed to be maintained by council caretakers. But these were mostly too cowed by the threats of hooligans and hot-rod motorcyclists and by money changing hands to have much effect. Nor, it seemed, could anything deter some of the tenants who were using their flats as clothing workshops, even though the thudding of ironing machines destroyed the peace for everyone else. The blind man told me that while his wife was out, some of the local thugs had stuffed burning paper through his letter box and then shouted to him:

'Come on, you blind bastard, see if you can find that.'

The foregone conclusion, which a general election would have brought to my campaigning efforts, changed momentously when the sitting MP, Gerry Reynolds, sadly died and a by-election was called. There was just a slight chance that I might win the by-election called for 30 October 1969. This was not a prospect I welcomed because I would certainly have lost at the general election which was to follow a few months later and my job in the construction industry would have gone. An Irishman, Michael O'Halloran, was selected as the Labour candidate. He was pleasant enough but not even his best friend could have described him as intellectually gifted. He was, however, strongly supported by the Irish republican movement, which had a nasty side to their operations. Another candidate was the Rev. Brian Green, the

Islington campaign leaflet

general secretary of the British Council of Protestant Christian Churches of which the Rev. Ian Paisley was a vice-president. The Rev. Green was also a supporter of the National Front. He said that Britain was morally, spiritually and politically bankrupt, and criticised Michael O'Halloran for travelling on what he termed "a Southern Irish" passport.

Apart from reading the local paper, we had two other means of monitoring what Labour was up to, but neither was very accurate. My resourceful Conservative constituency chairman had some friends whom the local Labourites did not know. We asked these friends to go to a pub on Highgate Hill where the Labour Party workers gathered; they were to stand near them and listen to their conversations. Other information came to us, unasked for, from Michael O'Halloran's neighbour, a Russian immigrant who used to listen through the wall between the houses with a glass pressed against the wall, to her ear!

My party agent was Frank Pike, a very wise man who ran the Tory operation in nine North and East London Labour seats. This being a by-election, Conservative Central Office had said that it would take charge of everything itself. I asked Frank how I should plan for the by-election. I needed to know where I should get the candidate's deposit from, for example. He looked at me blankly and said that I should ask my bank manager about it.

Frank said: 'Let's not wait for Central Office to come up with an election address; let's just do it ourselves. Just write down a few ideas, get a few photos and we'll get it off to the printers.' I then asked him how to get the photos taken. 'You've got a camera, haven't you? Just get some local children or passers-by to take a few snaps of you and Myra close to local landmarks that everyone can recognise,' he said. We had the whole thing wrapped up before the Central Office mandarins cottoned on, somewhat irately, to what we had done. They later circulated the election address Frank and I had produced to all Conservative Associations in Greater London as a model of how these things should be done.

17

One day after being on the campaign loudspeaker all day, I was very tired. My voice had boomed over the loudspeaker saying: 'Hello. This is Andrew Pearce, your Conservative candidate speaking. Support the Conservative government.' Unfortunately, a gremlin got into my brain and I said: 'Hello. This is Speaking, your Conservative government.' After another tiring day, I found myself pulling into the car park of a block of flats called Pearce House. 'This is Pearce House,' I boomed authoritatively over the loudspeaker. 'Vote for your Andrew candidate on Thursday.'

Another evening, I shouted, 'Are you going to vote Conservative, Madam?' to a woman with her head stuck out of the second-floor window of a crumbling house. 'I'll ask her,' she replied, turning round. 'Eeeeedie,' she screeched towards the inside of the house, 'there's a feller 'ere wants to know if you are going to vote Conservative.' Pause. 'No, not today, thank you,' said the woman turning back to me before slamming the window down.

Although unemployment in Islington was not at the level I subsequently encountered in Merseyside, it was a problem which people brought up from time to time. I decided to inform myself by standing outside a Labour Exchange. A young man wearing bangles asked about unemployment benefit. I asked what kind of job he wanted. He wanted to be a guitarist in a pop group. Was he good at playing the guitar? No he couldn't play but wanted to learn. Couldn't he take another job while he was learning? No, he wanted unemployment pay while he was learning. It wouldn't surprise me if he got it, the system being what it was.

Enoch Powell came to speak at a rally in Islington Town Hall. At that time, much of the press and many politicians gave the impression that there was no immigration problem in Britain, despite clear figures showing an increase of new arrivals. Powell had the courage to bring this matter into public debate even if his pronouncements went too far for many people. There was a problem with immigrants – not, at the time, in Aylesbury or Tunbridge Wells, but in places like Islington North. When a couple of old ladies are living quietly in a large, faded house, and the house next door is rented to fifty lusty, male immigrants with a taste for late-night partying, there is likely to be a problem for both the old ladies and the immigrants. Some of the immigrants, sometimes but not always Black, came from situations with different social customs. Such old ladies were not happy to find excreta wrapped in newspaper lobbed over their garden wall after a late-night party. I think Enoch Powell did Britain a service in bringing immigration into the public domain, but that does not make him or me a racist.

On polling day, Labour were out in droves. One of the local Roman Catholic priests had had the faithful praying that the best man should win and arranged for leaflets to be handed out as people left Mass to remind them who the best man was. The priest went round in his car to take a number of women to the polling station. These were mostly Catholic wives of Protestant men who were out at work at the time. We complained about this to the Catholic hierarchy after the election, and the priest was later transferred to a parish in a remote part of Britain. Truckloads of Irishmen descended on the polling stations and were handed slips of paper to tell them how to vote. It was, in any case, the practice in that part of London, unlike most places, for party workers to hand out publicity material to voters as they went into the polling stations from the street. We invoked a rarely-used procedure whereby I nominated agents to stand *inside* the polling stations and challenge people to swear who they were. They would be committing a crime if they did so falsely. Part of the problem was that, in the case of the many multiple-occupied houses with constantly changing occupants in the area, several copies of the forms which people had to complete to get on the electoral register were pushed through the letter boxes and picked up and filled in (or destroyed) by anyone wishing to do so.

I had no doubt that most of the Irish people legitimately entitled to vote would vote for Michael O'Halloran. If they were interested in politics at all, they would tend to be Labour. And Michael was Irish. I looked with amusement therefore at an article in the *Free Press* in County Wexford (where Myra was born), asserting that my 'canvass has emphatically shown that the Irish in the area are committed to the Conservative cause.'

On the day of the election, I teamed up two of my more individualistic helpers who were determined to show their gratitude for my having listened to their problems. These were the Russian lady who lived next to the Labour candidate and a Scotsman who believed that playing the bagpipes in the street would increase the Tory vote. I stationed them outside a polling station where we had no other helpers with a pile of my leaflets.

A black moment was when we found that someone had come into the constituency office on election day and stolen the duplicator on which we were about to run off copies of the last minute leaflet to distribute to people whom we believed had not voted up to six o'clock in the evening.

With the fulsome support of Myra and the Tory prospective candidates for the other parts of Islington – Norman Tebbit[2], John Szemerey and Richard

---

[2] In his book *Upwardly Mobile*, Norman, who went on to be one of Margaret Thatcher's most distinguished ministers, was kind enough to refer to his role as my *Personal Assistant*!

Devonald-Lewis, who were most generous in their support – we fought a good fight, but I lost. Soon after the by-election came a general election, on 18 June 1970. Michael O'Halloran, Labour, got 13,010 votes, I got 7,862 and Brian Green, National Front, 1,232.

Frank Pike wrote afterwards in The *Conservative Agents' Journal* for January 1970: "The candidate was all that an agent could ask for. He and his charming Irish wife spared no effort. He introduced one interesting theory, namely that people today are tired of being talked at by politicians and really want to ask questions and tell us what they think. He therefore reduced his speeches to a minimum and allowed a longer than usual time for questions at which, incidentally, he was very good. I am convinced that his theory is correct."

I changed jobs later in 1970, to work for an engineering firm in Teesside, and whilst there I became chairman of Darlington Conservative Association. At that time Darlington was a bellwether constituency; the vote there went the way of the country as a whole. We had to choose a new candidate. In order to carry out the selection, a number of local Tory bigwigs emerged from the woodwork – people who hardly turned up for anything else and were certainly not known for assiduously knocking on doors or pushing leaflets through letter boxes. I decided that we would begin by creating a sort of identikit description of the person we wanted. Darlington is partly a market town, partly a commuter town for neighbouring Teesside and also a successful engineering centre. We needed someone who could represent the sort of people who lived there, not a country squire or a London lawyer. The selection committee interviewed the hopefuls and gradually everyone who responded to our criteria were eliminated for trivial reasons – one failed because he wore brown shoes with a blue suit; another because he had a pink tie! I determined to reject the whole exercise and start again. The second time round we selected Brian Hord, who *was* a Londoner but who came across as someone who understood ordinary people and the world of industry and commerce. When the election came, he fought a good campaign but did not hold the seat. He later became an MEP at the same time as I did.

An interesting side issue of my time in Darlington was that of party colours. At this time, the supporters of Edward Heath at party headquarters in London had decided to move away from royal blue to a more turquoise shade. But in Darlington we still had some royal blue posters from the previous elections which could be used again to save money. Moreover, red had been the Conservative colour in Darlington and several other towns and cities in the past and some of our "Vote Conservative" bill boards were red. Our publicity was therefore quite a hotchpotch!

One of my best party workers was a butcher's assistant who lived in a terraced house in one of the less grand parts of the town. He and I would have a pint quite often and discuss campaigning. It seemed that anyone with aspirations of advancement in Darlington would drink in this particular pub on a Wednesday evening, that particular club on a Thursday, some other pub on a Friday and so on, in order to be seen by the right people. One pub he took me to was favoured by off-duty policemen. At closing time, I could see the eyes of the customers at the bar looking at each other in the mirror behind the upturned spirits bottles. One of the officers would nod. 'That's the highest ranking officer here tonight saying it was all right to lock the door and carry on drinking,' explained my friend.

After some time working in Teesside, I felt it was time for another career move so I replied to an advertisement in *The Times* of 15 October 1973 for the first group of British people to be selected by examination and interviews to join the European Commission's staff in Brussels. The advert was for Administrators. A net salary of £4,400 a year, after deduction of tax and social security contributions and the addition of an allowance for a head of household with one dependent child, was offered. I took the job title to mean that I would be concerned with administrative or management systems. I thought I would be suited to this in view of my Organisation & Methods experience and the fact that I was a member of the Institute of Administrative Management.

The examination took place in Alexandra Palace in North London on a very cold day. There were not nearly enough exam papers for the number of candidates present and we had to sit there for an hour while extra sets were photocopied. Given my expectations, I was more than a little surprised when I saw that none of the questions related to administration in the management sense but were entirely about European politics. Having been involved in politics and having argued the case for British membership of the EU in various political meetings, I had no difficulty in answering the questions. I pitied those who, like me, had thought that this was about management techniques but had no knowledge of politics. In French, which was then the dominant language of the EU, "Administration" often means *public* administration.

I passed the exam and went for the interview in Brussels.

The advertisement in 1973 which started my career in Europe.

An Irish interlude

After getting married in 1966 and amid the campaigning in Islington North, Myra and I had several trips to County Wexford in Ireland where she was born. Her Dad was the local postman who went round his territory on a little motorbike. He also took on the cleaning of the village hall where dances were held every other week, attended by hundreds of lusty young men and women in search of you know what. Myra's Mum drank vast amounts of strong tea (the aluminium teapot was put on the gas stove to boil the tea) with an endless stream of neighbours and relatives who passed by at all times of day and seemed to have nothing much else to do.

Myra took me round to meet umpteen relatives and family friends. Large and frequent administering of strong tea, soda bread and country butter almost completely blocked my digestive system. However, this did not stop me enjoying the wonderful potatoes her father grew; they went all flaky after being boiled.

Myra introduced me to her former dentist in Wexford who, I was given to understand, had been something important in the IRA in the county and was allegedly still under police surveillance. Having taken on board that I was English, he paused for what seemed like an eternity and finally said he supposed I was all right because I had married into an Irish family.

One day I went out with Myra's father to a pub a few miles away to meet an old acquaintance of his. He gave me a tattered book printed in the 1920s which detailed the activities of the campaign to get the British out of Ireland, and of the civil war between Irish factions in Wexford County, assault by assault, ambush by ambush. We talked in the empty back room of the pub for an hour about his experiences in the independence campaign and in the much more destructive civil war which followed. After a while, another man came into the pub and sat opposite us. He did not speak. My friend turned the conversation to other matters. After the other man left, I asked my friend why he had changed the subject of our conversation when the other man came in.

'You see,' he said, 'one day during *The Troubles*, I was in an IRA raiding party attacking the Royal Irish Constabulary station in the nearby town. Your man here that's just after leaving was the local RIC (Royal Irish Constabulary) sergeant, defending the place. We have never spoken since.'

'Yes', I said, 'but that was forty years ago.'

'That's right,' said my man.

Until the Irish boom of the late 1990s at least, the British could be blamed for anything that was wrong in the Republic. I once asked a man why, in a county where strawberries were grown in large quantities, it was almost impossible to buy such fruit in the shops. The strawberries, in fact, went for commercial jam making.

'It's all the fault of the British,' I was told. 'When the British landlords were here, they bought strawberries so it was worthwhile for the shops to stock them in season. The British landlords were thrown out. The Irish don't like strawberries so it's not worth the shopkeepers stocking them. So if you can't buy strawberries now, it's all the fault of the British.'

The Troubles broke out again in 1969 while I was visiting Myra's family. I decided to go up to The North, as they call Northern Ireland, with her teenage brother, Peter, to see for myself what was going on. At that time the state-run RTE television service wallowed in every crisis in The North, giving the impression that there was nothing but trouble in Northern Ireland. Fortunately, for the sake of balanced truth, people in the east and north of the Republic could get a different view by watching BBC or ITV.

Peter and I went to Londonderry and parked in the outskirts. It seemed a pleasant city situated on the river Foyle with an old city wall round it. Sentries had been posted by the Republicans around the Bogside, to keep out anyone not authorised by the rioters. Peter and I talked to several of them. Among the first dozen or so, none came from Derry; only a few from Ireland at all. At least one was an American who bore recent scars obtained, he said, during a demonstration of some kind in Germany a couple of days before.

Eventually we found a local man among the sentries who proved to be the uncle of John Hume, the leader of the Social Democratic and Labour Party – the non-violent Republican Party. We spent the next hour or so with the uncle in a pub, debating *The Troubles*. I came to know John quite well during our time in Strasbourg and, much later, in 2012, visited him in his house above the Bogside. We talked about Derry being the first UK City of Culture the following year. (Liverpool was Britain's first European Capital of Culture in 2008.)

On leaving the pub, Peter and I went past a gable-ended house completely painted with Republican slogans and insignia. People were standing about in front of it. I asked if I could photograph it. Yes, they said, but not with any people in front of it. So I have this photo of the gable end although there were about fifty people hiding round the side of the house out of sight. In one street, buildings were being torn down to be replaced with new social housing. I later saw these buildings used as a backdrop for a television interview, giving the impression that what one was looking at was property which had been damaged by riots.

After Derry, Peter and I drove to Belfast. In one Protestant street, we were subjected to a high-decibel lecture from a local woman about the inadequacies of the police. Apparently there had been *only* about a dozen policemen in this little street when the Catholics came marching past the end of it!

We went to a small Catholic enclave on the eastern side of the river. A butcher's shop was strewn with bits of meat that had been thrown about when the shop was ransacked during a riot a short time earlier that day. There were two policemen outside. One told me he had earlier served in the police in London. I pointed to a couple of men holding pieces of wood with nails sticking out of them and asked why the police did not arrest them. They said that to do so would probably cause another riot and would make the situation worse. The former London officer said that in his view much of the problem here was simply criminal behaviour and that such riotous behaviour was likely to spread to other UK cities, with or without a political cause to "justify" it. This was 1969: Brixton and Toxteth were still to come. Peter and I arrived home safely, much to the surprise of the family. Not all of The North had been in flames, as a diet of the RTE television would have had you believe.

A Eurocrat

I was interviewed by Henry Chumas, one of the first group of British civil servants who were sent directly by Whitehall to work in the European Commission after the UK joined in 1973. He was one of the two Directors, the second rank from the top, in one of the Directorates-General, the Customs Union Service. Henry had been a bright star of the Customs & Excise at Heathrow. He wanted someone in Brussels who had exactly the knowledge of management techniques, computers, documentary procedures etc. that I possessed and which I had expected to be the basis of the examination I took at Alexandra Palace. He took me on at the Administrator grade and I started work there on 11 March 1974. I was part of the first intake of British staff other than those sent from Whitehall.

One of my first jobs in the Customs Union Service concerned the fixing of import duties which varied from time to time for certain products. The basic idea of customs duties these days is not, as in former times, to raise revenue but to regulate trade and protect home producers. In respect of products for which EU producers could not meet the whole of the demand, a certain quantity was let in duty-free. There could also be seasonal variations. For example, there was a case for discouraging imports of green beans from Kenya during the summer when EU producers could supply the demand, but not in the winter when there was no EU production. Some of the duty-free quotas were expressed in quantities, some by weight and some by value.

I had to check lists, in six languages, of products such as canned pineapple, plywood and complex petroleum derivatives which could benefit from this scheme. Office essentials such as scissors and adhesive tape, for putting official documents together, were hard to come by in the Commission offices. I used to go out to a nearby shop and buy them with my own money. Piles of documents had to be taken to a building elsewhere in Brussels for meetings at which officials from each of the EU countries would approve or not approve every detail of what the Commission was proposing. A senior colleague of mine bought a little two-wheel hand truck to transport the documents down to his car and then up from the garage to the meeting room in the other building where the meeting was taking place.

This system of variable import duties required that customs offices all over the EU should report by telex the level of imports at frequent intervals, sometimes by weight, sometimes by value. I visited the British Customs office in Liverpool one day while on leave in the UK to see how officers there handled the system. I found that they were typing in the required import figures in pounds sterling, pressing the key for sterling on the telex machine followed by the numbers. When I checked what happened to the message in Brussels, I found that a pound sterling sign typed in Liverpool came out as a hash mark in Brussels, appearing to indicate a reference number for the items, not the value!

I attended a meeting of officials of the EU countries when there was a discussion about import duties on beans. As in all Customs work, there have to be precise definitions of the products subject to quotas and duties. Traders try to circumvent import limits for certain products by claiming that the goods they wish to import are in fact not of the type to which limits were to be applied. From the Customs point of view, a *haricot vert,* literally *green bean* in English, did not have to be green; it could be green, black, red, white, yellow or purple. The term refers to the type of plant, to distinguish it from a runner bean or a broad bean. The French official in our meeting knew all about the matter, including how to grow and cook them. The expertise of the official from the British Ministry of Agriculture was embarrassingly poor by contrast. Getting such matters right could be commercial life or death for European (including British) farmers who grew beans.

My next project was to prepare the specification for a very simple computer-to-computer method for transmitting the relevant import information and certain agricultural data between Brussels and the national Customs services. Projects and systems in the EU were usually given code names such as ESPRIT, (French for "spirit"), the name of an information technology programme, and PHARE (French for "lighthouse"), the name of a project to prepare additional countries to join the EU. This was done for ease of identification by people speaking different languages. I wanted a name for my project which was pronounceable and meaningful in all six of the EU working languages. In the bath one morning I came up with "CADDIA", standing for Communication and Automation of Data and Documentation about Imports/exports and Agriculture. If the Germans would permit a "C" where they would normally use a "K", the initials were the same in all six of the then EU working languages.

A bit corny perhaps but better than having everything in French as was the case at that time.

I went to Geneva several times to technical committee meetings on customs topics. Although the UN headquarters is in New York, several parts of the family of UN organisations, such as the Economic Commission for Europe, are based in Geneva. These meetings were held in the huge and splendid *Palais des Nations*. Meetings of bureaucratic organisations, including the EU, are often not very sparkling in terms of speed, lucidity or interest. The meetings I attended were at the bottom end of the scale. A particular objective was to advise on the definitions of types of goods by which the right to import them at this or that rate of customs duty would be determined. The EU and other national blocs set the rate of duty for imports into their territory on the basis of these definitions.

As a junior official I was there to listen and take notes. More senior officials did the debating. Sometimes it sounded like major power play – this was in the Cold War period. There were major pronouncements that "the United States insists that…" or "the Soviet Union cannot agree that…" and sometimes it degenerated into farce. There was a discussion one day about differences in the use of the English language between American English and British English. The different English speakers enjoyed this sort of discussion. It was esoteric and the French speakers couldn't join in. (Nobody would dare to challenge the view of France about how French should be used, not even the Swiss or the Canadians!) One day, however, I heard the Soviet delegate say, 'Mr Chairman, we have heard lengthy opinions on how British English treats this term and equally lengthy explanations of how American English regards the matter. Now please let me tell you about how this word is used in Russian English!'

After a couple of years, I was seconded to a team of European Commission staff negotiating limits on imports of textile fabrics and clothing. The idea was to give the European textile industry time to adjust to the fact that Far East producers could always undercut them on price due to their much lower wage rates. The only future for EU producers was to go for better design and quality and to make use of their ability to respond more flexibly to delivery requirements through geographical proximity to their customers. The issue was of massive importance to EU producers who clamoured for import restrictions. It was important too for EU retailers and consumer lobbies who wanted freedom to buy the cheapest goods. A particular situation to be avoided was where Customs duties kept up consumer prices for certain types of goods which

EU producers could not supply in sufficient quantities. Shell suits, then popular at the cheaper end of the market, were a case in point. While there was a case for protecting EU manufacturers of other types of suits, there was no justification for Customs duty on imports of shell suits because virtually no such garments were manufactured in the EU.

The EU had a MultiFibre Arrangement (MFA) with some thirty countries which exported textiles and clothing to it. The purpose of this was to reduce imports, without contradicting the rules of the General Agreement on Tariffs and Trade (GATT) which made the general imposition of import quotas extremely difficult. The MFA was supposedly voluntary (though that was not the reality of it). Under its terms, the EU could negotiate quantitative limits which exporting countries would apply to each type of product. The EU would check that this was being respected. If these limits were breached, more draconian measures, which the GATT did in such circumstances permit, would be introduced.

The Commission had rented six floors in a tower office block in downtown Brussels for the negotiations. There were five or six meetings each day with the delegations of the various individual exporting countries. French/English interpretation facilities were provided. The Commission officials had a daily morning meeting with civil servants of the EU countries who checked that the Commission was staying within its negotiating mandate. Sometimes meetings flowed over into Saturdays and even Sundays. One Sunday, Etienne Davignon[3], was due to meet high officials from the USA and Japan, who were all involved in the GATT protocols under which the import limitations were applied.

The particular conference room used on this occasion was arranged with two sets of seats facing each other, like choir stalls in a church. The Commission staff sat on one side, the Americans and the Japanese with their respective advisers on the other – a juxtaposition which did not please the Americans who did not like being "lumped in" with the Japanese. I arrived very early for the meeting, due to there being not many trains at that time of day on a Sunday from our home in the suburbs. Davignon was already there, gazing out of the window and smoking a foul pipe which he took everywhere with him. The meeting began. The US delegate, brandishing a sheaf of papers, hectored the

[3] Davignon, a Belgian viscount, was the European Commissioner responsible for these negotiations. He had previously worked for Paul Henri Spaak, a one-time Belgian Minister for Foreign Affairs and one of the founding fathers of the EU.

Commission. American officials liked to suggest that the EU was very protectionist while they ran an open economy whereas in reality the opposite was the case. Davignon, who had no papers with him, listened to the American in silence, with an occasional nod to his advisers. When the American had finished, Davignon systematically but quietly demolished his arguments one by one, leaving the American embarrassed.

The quotas for clothing had to be as tightly defined as those for beans. We had to distinguish, for example, between T-shirts, pullovers, sweatshirts, T-shirt dresses, tank tops and so forth. This was far from just bureaucratic nonsense. Clothing producers in Britain, France and the other EU states were, and still are, very specialised and could not easily change from producing one type of garment to producing another. We therefore had to specify some 120 categories of textiles and clothing for which quotas would be applied. Precise definitions had to be provided to prevent "quota-hopping". I made use of a set of product definitions which one of the international retail chains gave me.

My own job was to design and put into operation a system of export licence forms to be used by the Customs services of the exporting countries and to negotiate with the exporting countries their acceptance of this. The forms had to display the precise information needed to check observance of the quotas at the point of importation.

After several months of negotiation, all the exporting countries accepted my proposals, except Hong Kong, a British colony! The negotiation with Hong Kong proved to be one of the more entertaining negotiations. The European Commission team was headed by Paul Tran van Thinh, a French national of Vietnamese origin, generally known as Tran. The Hong Kong team was led by an Englishman, a member of the Hong Kong colonial government. One day we came to the quotas for women's underwear. The French language version of the European Customs tariff showed *soutiens gorges et bustiers*. The English language version only said *brassieres*. Each time the French-speaking Commission spokesman read out the two terms *les soutiens gorges et les bustiers*, the interpreter thought she should also use two words in the English equivalent. "*Bras and halters*," she said. *What was a halter*, I asked myself – *a rope for pulling a horse?* The Hong Kong team fell about laughing. Tran signalled to me after a while and I asked the interpreters to come out of their cabins to get to the bottom of the problem. It turned out that a *soutien gorge* is a normal bra – a strap round the neck from which the cups are suspended – whereas a *bustier* is, in old parlance, a *bodice* or nowadays a *strapless bra*, a device which pushes the cups upwards from mid-chest. I suppose the term *halter neck* has similar linguistic origins to this second meaning.

In the course of these negotiations, I was part of a European Commission team which went to Malta. The Commission in those days had very few offices outside the EU and did not have one in Malta, so we stayed in a tourist hotel. Each morning at half past eight we had a team meeting in the hotel lounge and the early-bird holidaymakers passed by us in their swim suits on the way to the pool or the breakfast room. There were only four ambassadors from EU countries in Malta. The newly-arrived German ambassador had not yet presented his credentials to the Maltese authorities; the French ambassador was deaf and missed part of what was being said; the Italian ambassador was by far the brightest but had committed some indiscretion (I did not hear what) and was *persona non grata* with the Maltese at that time; the British ambassador was, shall I say, not over-versed in European commercial policy.

When we arrived, the ambassadors, representing the Council of Ministers, insisted that they should be informed about all aspects of the negotiations. So Tran called them as each crisis developed, which was about twice a day, and invited them to our team meetings, starting on the first day.

'Eight thirty in the morning? Good heavens, a bit early, that.' 'Er…actually, I've got another appointment at that time,' said one or other of the Ambassadors. 'Eight o'clock in the evening? Sorry, we've got dinner engagements. Can't get out of them.'

The Maltese did not like the import limits which the Commission wanted to set. They therefore arrested the whole of our team! There was no unpleasantness, no policemen or handcuffs, but a kind of house arrest – or rather "hotel-with-a-swimming-pool" type of arrest. In the end an agreement was reached. The final meeting was in the evening in a government office. Tran could speak English perfectly well. However, he decided to negotiate in French, using the time taken for interpretation into English to gather his thoughts or to whisper to colleagues. As the sense of each paragraph was agreed, Tran would scribble down the wording in French on a piece of paper and say, 'Pearce, Pearce, write this down in English. Quick.' I scrawled it down. 'Give it to me,' said Tran. He passed my translation across the table and it was duly initialled by the Maltese.

In the course of these negotiations I visited companies in Tunisia and Malta where jeans were made, to see for myself what was involved. Most jeans carry brand names which, for many people who wear them, matter a great deal. There are also cheaper, unbranded jeans available; these might be of similar quality to branded jeans or may be of cheaper cloth and made with less attention to manufacturing quality. Jeans are basically an item of work clothing.[4] At one stage, the United States Customs set a lower rate of import duty for work clothing than for other clothing. They ruled that if jeans had a label stitched on, this amounted to a form of decoration so the garment could not be classified as work clothing. One American manufacturer responded by not sewing on a separate badge but by designing the garments so that the brand symbol was used as stitching for the pocket, therefore being a matter of function rather than decoration! The garments would therefore be exempt from the higher rate of duty. These apparently trivial matters could make a big difference to company profits.

The problem of "counterfeit" branded jeans came to our attention. A factory I visited had a contract to make a quantity of jeans for one of the brand leaders. Its client gave precise instructions as to the cloth and fastenings to be used. The manufacturer duly ordered a consignment of the stipulated cloth, the amount required for the client's order – and then the same amount again. It proceeded to manufacture twice the quantity of jeans ordered by the client, attaching the proprietary brand labels to half of them which were dispatched to the customer. They then sold the other half of the production run without the *official* brand labels to other clients. Whether some of these were later passed off as being of the same brand as the first half of the order, I cannot say. The point is that the second half of the production run was in every respect, apart from the brand label, identical with the first part. Indeed, any of the jeans in the run would have been acceptable to the brand holder once the brand labels had been attached. Were the jeans in the second half of the production run fakes? It is a moot point. Customers are willing to pay a premium of twenty-five per cent or more for the branded goods, and not just because of its quality. If alternative goods are of exactly the same design and quality, is the premium justified? Wearing branded jeans is, for many customers, a personal statement, a means of identifying the part of society to which they wish to belong. One manufacturer of branded jeans considered the matter of such importance that it recruited a retired senior military officer to travel the world to try to stamp out the production of "counterfeit" jeans.

---

[4] The word "jeans" comes from Gênes, the French word for the Italian city of Genoa where these garments were first produced. Jeans are usually made from a fabric called denim, originally called *serge de Nîmes*, after the city in the south of France.

One aspect of the EU system for controlling clothing imports had negative consequences for UK manufacturers because the industry, or Whitehall, failed to understand how to make best use of it. The Germans *did* understand it. A process called "CMT" (cut, make and trim) had long existed in the garment industry. A producer or retailer of clothes would send a quantity of fabric to another company, perhaps in another country, to be made into articles of clothing according to a strict specification of design and quality. This practice was used, among others, by German producers especially as wage rates in Germany rose. German clothing firms found it convenient to send German cloth to neighbouring countries such as Hungary to be made into suits or other clothing and then brought back into Germany and put on the market, often bearing a "made in Germany" label. This may look like cheating but the cloth was German, and German quality standards were applied in the manufacturing process. Therefore, it could be argued that there is not much difference between using Hungarian labour in Hungary and using Hungarian and other immigrant labour in Germany, if the cloth and the manufacturing standards are the same. The Germans claimed that the garments imported back into Germany should not be subject to import quotas because the cloth from which they were made was German. A procedure was therefore devised whereby such re-imports could be exempted from import quotas by the Government of the EU country where the cloth had been made. This was known as "outward processing".

The weaving and dyeing of cloth are two industries to which modern production techniques could be applied. The cutting and sewing of the cloth into garments was inescapably labour-intensive and the gap between EU wage rates and those of East European and Far Eastern countries kept getting wider. The German government therefore took advantage of the EU's outward processing scheme. The British government, in response to pressures from trade unions and clothing manufacturers together, refused to do so. Not for the first time, Britain tried to defend industries which would inevitably die in the face of foreign competition at the expense of supporting newer techniques which could survive in the modern market place.

Agreements under the MFA with nearly thirty countries were eventually reached, including the use of the licence forms which I had designed. I then had to ensure that all countries would have a stock of the licence forms ready for use in the near future. I achieved this by having a stock of the forms printed and personally delivering them in my car to each of the countries' embassies in Brussels just before Christmas that year.

Tran sent me on a fifteen-day trip to India, Malaysia, Singapore, the Philippines and Korea to explain the new system to them. At this time, the Commission had no offices of its own in any of these countries. I was given a return economy-class air ticket. I was also entitled to the Commission's standard rate of reimbursement of hotel and meal expenses but nothing to entertain officials of the countries visited in return for the hospitality which they would undoubtedly offer me. Certain legal problems peculiar to importations into Germany were to be discussed. I was therefore accompanied by two men from the German retail sector. One of the Germans was a very senior company director who, in return for being party to all of the discussions, would pay for any lunches or dinners which we felt it appropriate to offer. The two Germans travelled first class. When we arrived at each airport, I descended from the door of the plane's economy class, was given a garland of flowers, did a television interview and underwent passport formalities in the VIP lounge, while the two Germans got out of the first class part of the plane and queued up with the tourists and other passengers for the routine passport and customs checks.

Germany held the Presidency of the Council of Ministers at the time so I was met by someone from its local embassy at each stop. In Delhi a German Embassy official said he had received instructions from Bonn to join in all of the talks. Did I mind? I said that I didn't, but in return he should lend me an office in his embassy for the day, with access to a telex machine. He should also lend me a car with driver. 'No problem at all,' was his response. At the end of the first day, the embassy official said that the matters being discussed were too technical for him to understand properly. Would I therefore mind drafting his nightly report to Bonn? I said not at all, provided it was in English and that he would also send it also to Tran in Brussels. No problem. The same procedure followed at my other stops.

The Indians treated us to a fashion show designed to convince us that current Indian evening wear was actually based on ancient fashion customs and therefore qualified for exemption from quotas under the special provisions in the MFA for folklore products.

While in Delhi, we discovered that a representative of another retail company, a little Belgian man, had been sent to follow us and to find out what we were doing. We agreed to take him on board with our team, provided he paid his share of the hospitality. Whereas the two Germans were delightful and generous companions, the new member of the team was dull and rather mean unless well prompted. In Seoul we were asked to advise some manufacturers on how to categorise their products as shirts, T-shirts, sweatshirts etc, so as to conform to the quota classifications. We were taken into a theatre and confronted with about 200 manufacturers each holding armfuls of garments. The two Germans and I decided that we would let the little Belgian deal with this as his reward for his meanness. We walked out and left him to it.

On these visits a problem can arise due to the copious amounts of alcohol offered. At a dinner in Korea, at which two Ministers were present, toast after toast was proposed, each accompanied by a glass of whisky, intended to be downed in one gulp. Custom had it that I, as leader of the EU delegation, should propose a toast after each toast proposed by the Koreans. Having been warned about this, I managed to pour several glasses of whisky on the floor, into an adjacent bowl of flowers or have it absorbed by a corner of the table cloth stuck into the glass.

The debate between the protection of the interests of clothing producers in the EU on the one side, and retailers within the EU on the other, continued long after I had left the European Commission and been elected to the European Parliament. British clothing manufacturers had to accept the need to adapt to changing market conditions and to respect customer requirements – as I said in a letter printed in the *Midland Bank Review* in February 1981. I wrote that there had to be an end to the old take-it-or-leave-it attitude summed up in the Bradford adage, "If tha' wants tha' wool, tha' can bloody well come and fetch it."

★ ★ ★

I worked for four years in the European Commission. When it was announced that there were to be direct elections to the European Parliament and that I could take unpaid leave of absence from the Commission while being an MEP, meaning that I had a right of return to a job, this seemed to be my big opportunity. In the first direct European Parliamentary Election in June 1979, 410 members were elected from the then nine EU states. An MEP's mandate would be for a fixed period of five years. (Elections for House of Commons MPs were, before application of an Act of Parliament of 2011, held on a date chosen by the Government, *not more* than five years after the previous one, but often less.) In most European countries, votes are cast on Sundays; in the UK, Thursdays have always been voting days, for both national and European elections.

In the European elections of 1979, 1984, 1989 and 1994, a first-past-the-post system was used in England, Wales and Scotland, similar to the system for elections for the House of Commons. Most Euro-constituencies comprised about eight House of Commons constituencies. Each Euro-constituency therefore had some half-million electors. From 1979 Northern Ireland, on the other hand, had a system of electing three MEPs by a proportional representation system similar to that used in the Irish Republic.

I wanted to be a candidate. The key for me was to be not only selected as a candidate but selected as a candidate in a seat which the party could win.

Marcus Fox MP, the Tory Party vice-chairman in charge of choosing candidates for the first direct elections to the European Parliament, adopted what was then a novel course of action. He drew up a list of people who actually knew something about the matters which the candidate would be dealing with when elected. The Conservative Associations in each Euro-constituency would select their candidate from this list. Many Tory Members of the House of Commons wrote off the new MEPs as mere technocrats, unable to follow the rules of party loyalty or wage the warfare of party politics as in Westminster. Some of the MEPs came to believe that many MPs were little more than lobby fodder for the Tory whips in the House of Commons. The difficulty was exacerbated by the apparent belief by some of the MPs that MEPs lived in vastly superior financial circumstances. This was completely untrue.

I applied to eleven Euro-constituencies in the North of England. All but Cheshire East said that they would interview me. I was offered places in the final interviews in two of them, Cheshire West and Lancashire Central, the area around Preston. I turned down the Lancashire seat in favour of Cheshire West which appeared to offer the better chance of victory. There were normally three interviews in each Euro-constituency, the first two being held before fairly small committees where one's personality and general background were important as well as knowledge of Europe.

In each constituency a key question was about willingness to live in the constituency, which the party workers wanted. Many Westminster MPs give the impression that they live in their constituencies but the nature of their job may make this impossible in any literal sense, at least for provincial MPs. It is different for MEPs. I was quite prepared to live with my family in the constituency and travel to Brussels and Strasbourg from there as often as was necessary. MEPs had to be in Brussels for at least two periods each month and had to go to Strasbourg for one week a month. In the fourth week, party meetings were held in Brussels or elsewhere, which, for the Conservatives during my time in the Parliament, sometimes meant London. Only one or two of the British MEPs in my time lived in Brussels. MEPs who lived in their own patch tended to fight for the particular interests of their own electorates rather more insistently than other MEPs.

Another question was whether one's wife or husband would help with campaigning. Myra said she was willing.

The final selection meeting at which Myra and I had to present ourselves was at Conservative HQ in Chester. The room was full with a hundred or more people present. I was given to understand that one of the candidates really had no chance and was only there to make up the numbers. The choice was really between me and an MP for a constituency elsewhere. The MP went in first and I was to be third. While the second candidate was being interviewed, the MP told me he thought he had done well and was clearly confident of victory. He offered to help me to get his old Westminster seat in due course.

My turn came. The size, shape and acoustics of the room suited me and my voice carried well. I spoke well and answered questions successfully. Myra gave the right responses too and looked good. The chairman of the committee was one of the comparatively few men I met in politics at constituency level who judged aspiring candidates on whether they would really deliver the goods, not on conformity to some social or ideological stereotype.

The delegates voted and gave me the job. I was over the moon at my success and conscious that Myra's enthusiastic support had played an important part in it. We honoured the undertakings we had given. After being elected we bought a house in West Kirby and had no other home during my ten years as an MEP. I became a familiar sight in the Wirral – although those of my half million electors who lived at the other end of my constituency in Nantwich or Runcorn, thirty or more miles away, did not see me quite so often.

Myra loyally and energetically supported my political work, helped with correspondence and planning my diary as well providing a home for me and our four children. She accompanied me at many events and went to many others on her own. Various honorary local positions – chairman of this or that – are offered to, and accepted by, politicians and their spouses. Myra ended up being chairman of more voluntary bodies than me as well as undertaking the lion's share of raising our four children.

★ ★ ★

So what did I hope to achieve as an MEP? My objectives fell into three broad categories. Firstly, I wanted to try to ensure that EU actions were in the best interests of Britain as a whole. This included, among other things, opposing any attempt to introduce socialist measures. (In 1979 Mrs Thatcher was only just beginning to rid Britain of the state control of industry and overweening trade union power which had brought Britain to a low ebb and made recourse to the International Monetary Fund (for a bailout) necessary, in order to prop up our currency.)

Secondly, I wanted to ensure that EU activities were of benefit to my own area. I wanted to support local economic interests and the list was long: shipbuilding, shipping, dairy farming, fishing, the chemical and oil refining industries, insurance, small business, car manufacture, fund management, horticulture, engineering, retailing and tourism, to name but a few. I saw then, and have seen since, how much of British public expenditure and how many decisions on national policy are focused on the interests of South East England.

Thirdly, I wanted to use my position as an MEP to improve understanding in Britain of the advantages of our country's membership of the EU. The British public had (and still has) doubts about the matter despite the referendum of 1975 having strongly supported our membership. People suggested that Britain's membership did not justify the political and financial price we pay for it. It was interesting to turn the question around and ask what Britain's place in the world would be if we were not in the EU. I pointed out that we would be very peripheral to the important decisions of world affairs if we stood alone in the face of a combination of French political ambitions and German economic might but that, as part of the EU, we could share in the taking of major decisions which affected us.

As time went on, I became interested in additional policy areas such as the protection of consumers' interests, partly because I was asked to attend the Parliament's committee dealing with such matters and partly because it was one of the fastest-growing areas of EU policy. Also, I was made a member of the Parliament's committee concerned with the EU's programmes of aid for Third World countries. This was viewed by some in Britain as of little consequence but it was of considerable importance in the eyes of the French. For them it was an instrument of national economic policy – captive markets for exports and sources of raw materials and a basis for French cultural influence. I also developed an interest in animal welfare, a topic which frequently came up in meetings in my constituency and was a ready basis for publicity.

Few in politics can truthfully claim that great steps forward were entirely the result of their own efforts. However, some can claim to have given events a significant push in the right direction. I believe that I was one who helped to give that push.

My Patch

In the 1979 election, being selected for a winnable seat was perhaps the hardest part. The next hardest task was to convert the confidence in me of the local Tory hierarchy into a majority of all those electors who would turn out to vote. Half a million citizens in my Euro-constituency were entitled to vote under the system prevailing in 1979, though everyone knew that the turn-out would be very low. Many of the factors that determine the winnabilty of a seat are out of the hands of the local candidate. The popularity, then later the unpopularity, of Mrs Thatcher had far more influence on the outcome in Cheshire West than anything I could do. Moreover, the activities of the Boundary Commission could be decisive and in my case boundary changes eventually sealed my fate.

Professional Conservative Party agents told me that in a typical House of Commons constituency of 50,000 to 60,000 electors, the quality of the local party's organisation can affect the result to the extent of 500 to 1,000 votes. The candidate's personality and individual efforts may be worth another 500 to 1,000. An exceptional sitting MP might do better than that. Frank Field, Labour MP for Birkenhead, was one such MP. But the outcome was mainly the result of national factors. Elections to the European Parliament turned out to be similar, not least because the whole thing was new to the voters.

Every constituency has a large measure of built-in support for one party or another. Insofar as elections produce unexpected results, it is often due to the respective turn-out of voters in the contesting parties. The question was whether those who basically supported a particular party actually go out to vote for it or whether they would just stay at home. Labour voters who actually switch and vote Tory, and Tory voters who turn to Labour have been comparatively rare – though that may be changing. A further point is that, as I saw things, people make up their minds how they vote, *if* they vote, long before election day.

When people asked where was I based, I always replied, with full truthfulness, "in West Cheshire and Wirral". I lived there. My family lived there. My main office and my filing system were there. Most importantly, the voters who put me into the European Parliament lived there.

A Euro-constituency usually consisted of eight Westminster constituencies. However, this did not mean that each MEP had eight times the workload of each MP. An MEP does not deal with the most voluminous types of problems dealt with by Westminster MPs such as allocation of social housing, placement of children in schools or personal problems arising from unemployment – though it has to be said that MPs, of their own volition, take on much casework which is more properly the business of local councillors.

Since my time as an MEP, a system of regional proportional voting has been introduced for elections to the European Parliament. The new system responds to the complaints of Liberal Democrats that the previous system was unfair – the Liberal Democrats had often received a large number of individual votes across the country but did not get a proportionate number of MPs or MEPs. However, the new system has broken the link between electors and the elected. In North West England the regional electorate of nearly six million voters elects a bloc of eight MEPs, instead of a constituency of some 500,000 electing one single MEP, as was the system in my time. The new system creates a territory far too big both geographically and numerically to be properly understood and covered fully by any one MEP within the bloc of eight.

Having been selected I had to satisfy not only a majority of my constituents or at least the majority of those that would vote. I also had to satisfy Don (later Sir Donald) Wilson, the Conservative Euro-constituency chairman. Sir Donald was a millionaire industrialist-turned-farmer who had been chairman of Chester Conservative Association and later became North West Regional chairman of the National Health Service. I also had to satisfy the party's Euro-constituency agent. I was ably and enthusiastically served in turn by several of the Conservative party agents within the Euro-constituency acting in that capacity in succeeding elections.

Sir Don was the driving force who moulded and drove the campaigning support from the beginning. Cheshire West was one of the few Euro-constituency Conservative associations which always had money in the bank, and when the Euro-constituency associations were merged into regions under Conservative Central Office, Cheshire West was in surplus. I saw Sir Don's energetic motivation at the first fund-raising dinner which we organised at the Royal Liverpool Golf Club at Hoylake. We had a room full of paying customers for what was then a very new and unknown venture. The dinner made a handsome profit, all costs being covered in advance by the proceeds of sponsorships! The ability and drive of Sir Donald and his successors set high standards and helped me to make the most of the opportunities which the constituency offered. I am grateful to them all. The British political process could not function without people like these, as well as the dozens of party workers in the local branches. Media pundits have little idea of the importance of the efforts of such people.

The campaigning on which I embarked after being selected was almost continuous over the next ten years. From the time of being elected, I explained my activities and presented my case six days a week and attended as many as ten functions of one kind or another on certain weekends. Insofar as the quality of the candidate and the local campaign count, these two factors do so over the long term, not just in the two or three weeks before election day. The objective of campaigning was to meet as many constituents as possible. I needed to show them that I understood and cared about their hopes and worries and to tell them of my belief that Conservative policies were the best policies for them. During the run-up to an election, making personal contact was the key, being seen, "pressing the flesh" – but not, for me at least, kissing babies! Such personal contact does have an effect. Quite a few people do not vote unless they had actually met the candidate. But I was under no illusion that the effect I could have was minor compared with that of the party leaders through the media.

Campaigning in Hoylake

The boundaries of my Euro-constituency, taking in Wirral and parts of western Cheshire, were changed twice during my time. In 1979 the Cheshire part included mainly Tory areas around Northwich and Nantwich, but later some of the best Tory territory was transferred by the Boundary Commission to other constituencies while strong Labour areas in Runcorn and Widnes were transferred into mine.

Polling day in my first campaign exemplified the contrasts within the constituency. One election day I popped into a party committee room in a large house with a south-facing terrace below a medieval castle overlooking the splendid Cheshire plain. The flowers bloomed, the bees buzzed, the butterflies fluttered and the distant cows looked content. Champagne was served and the faithful who turned out to vote were duly logged. Tory Cheshire was in good order. By contrast, my next call that day was at New Brighton at the mouth of the Mersey – a dilapidated place in 1979 but once a popular dormitory town for Liverpool commuters and day-by-the-seaside trippers from Liverpool. (EU grants have been used recently to bring back some life to the place.)

The Cheshire part of my constituency initially contained Crewe, a town formerly famous for building railway engines and Rolls Royce cars. Crewe was a utilitarian little town but with a considerable pool of skilled labour providing the basis of many successful firms. Nantwich was an old, prosperous country town. Northwich, not far away, had produced salt since Roman times, leaving large areas of water-logged subsidence and large underground caverns in which Cheshire County Council stored some of its archives. When in Northwich, I usually popped in to see a butcher who was a regular respondent to the questionnaires about current politics circulated by the Forum of Private Business. Word would soon spread that I had been there. This sort of contact was a more useful guide to the thinking of the people I wanted to influence than any number of opinion polls.

Also nearby is Winsford, one of the badly-designed residential areas into which several thousand Liverpudlians were relocated in the 1950s and 1960s, in many cases against their own wishes. These people badly needed new accommodation but had little choice about where they were moved to, be it Liverpool or elsewhere. I visited a day centre for unemployed people in Winsford where one young man playing snooker told me he had had a job screwing the tops on bottles of a certain product. 'I just couldn't do that for the rest of my life,' he said. The cost of the bus fare to the factory plus the cost of a canteen lunch meant that he was no better off going to work than staying at home and playing snooker at the day centre.

Runcorn is an old Cheshire town around which major chemical plants had developed. Then another draft of involuntary Liverpool overspill was grafted on to the town in the 1960s. In the middle of this is "Shopping City", set among bewildering expressways and busways. Local people distinguish between the old and new towns as Heaven and Hell but I am not quite sure which is which. Our main campaign worker in Runcorn, a friendly lady with bad feet who always wore sandals but no socks or stockings, lived in a house fortified against vandals and intruders.

Some years ago, the government decreed that Runcorn should be tied with Widnes, across the Mersey, to form the Borough of Halton. One of our party workers frequently said that Widnes was a part of the County Palatine of Lancashire currently occupied by Cheshire County Council. Widnes had been one of the country's greatest concentrations of chemical manufacturing since the Victorian era. When I was a boy, Dante might have recognised the belching smoke and piles of multi-coloured chemicals in Widnes as part of his vision of hell. The Conservative club in Widnes was the most supportive of the Conservative clubs in my area; the members had not seen a live Tory there in decades and I was indeed fêted when I went there.

Halton was later made a unitary authority, separate from the ministrations of Cheshire County Council, and later still included in Merseyside for certain purposes.

The cathedral city of Chester has a historical feeling about it with its "rows" – double-deck shops – some built in medieval times, some in similar style in the nineteenth century. It is now a successful tourist centre and is also the home of several important industrial firms. During the 1980s I visited, among others, two firms manufacturing tow bars for cars. They were having problems with proposals for EU legislation.

Wirral has wealthy residential areas such as Hoylake, Heswall, West Kirby and Caldy. These places were strongly Conservative. Other residential areas varied from solid middle-of-the-road places like Bromborough and Prenton to places such as Liscard, Rock Ferry, North Birkenhead and Leasowe, which had some of the worst social stress in the country, caused by high unemployment and low incomes.

Birkenhead's economy had depended on shipbuilding. The town grew rapidly in the 1800s as Laird's shipyard developed and expanded, but a century later suffered hard times for many years. The British government favoured yards on the Clyde and sometimes those on the Tyne for warship production. The Birkenhead trade unions made matters worse. The docks in Birkenhead, part of the Port of Liverpool, are still active.

I tried to make local councillors see the tourism potential of Birkenhead but the light only began to dawn on them much later. Birkenhead's priory was founded around 1150 by monks who were later given a charter by the king to ferry people across the Mersey. Hamilton Square in the town is one of the finest in Britain, and Birkenhead Park was part of the inspiration for the design of Central Park in New York.

The town has problems common to most inner-city areas, crime being one of them. The son of a friend of ours had his school notes taken from his mother's car in a car park in Birkenhead, just before his A levels. I decided to help and looked around some council flats nearby, choosing a Sunday morning to do so when few locals would have been up and about. The domestic rubbish from these three-storey flats was disposed of down chutes into five-foot-high bins at ground level. The school notes were there! Fortunately the bin was pretty full so I could reach them without having to clamber inside, which I doubt I would have done.

Port Sunlight in Bromborough is the original home of the UK part of Unilever and has a very large research establishment as well as a soap factory. The influence of the Leverhulme family is all around, not least in the splendid Lady Lever Art Gallery.

Neston is currently joined to Ellesmere Port for parliamentary and municipal purposes, but the two places have little in common. At one time, ships carrying coal from local mines set sail from nearby Parkgate. Neston has two points of note: The first was that for some years it became a port as the river Dee silted up at Chester; the second that Admiral Nelson's mistress, Lady Emma Hamilton, was born and brought up in nearby Ness in 1765. (In view of the growing importance of tourism in the area, it was surprising to find that one of the local council's tourism officers did not know this.)

These are just a few of the towns in my patch, their citizens all part of the half a million voters I was to represent. Each part of the constituency had its own individual character and interests.

★ ★ ★

A matter of local interest dogged me at a great many of my meetings, although it had no connection with the EU. People in Wirral complained of having an "L" postcode because they did not like the association with Liverpool. There was some justification in their complaint. It was said that a number of London-based property developers would not undertake work in areas with this code. There was a widespread failure to understand that the only thing a postcode tells you is where your mail is sorted. Years later, the sorting of mail for Wirral was transferred from Liverpool to Chester and the area redesignated with a "CH" post code. All this may sound petty but people take a real pride in where they live and resent the action of some official, probably in London, appearing to try to rename the place where they live. As it turns out, the rebirth of Liverpool in the twenty first century (thanks, in no small degree, to EU money and the European Year of Culture in 2008!) now means that an association of Wirral with Liverpool is an advantage, not a disadvantage, as many people previously thought.

★ ★ ★

My constituency and surrounding areas had its share of gentry and a few aristocrats. Three of their Lordships played a significant part in public life in the area. The Earl of Derby was President of Merseyside Chamber of Commerce. The Duke of Westminster, one of Britain's richest men, lives just south of Chester. Eaton Square, Eccleston Square and Belgravia are parts of the Duke's London property empire named after villages near his Cheshire seat. Lord Leverhulme founded the UK part of what became Unilever, the Anglo-Dutch giant behind Sunlight Soap, Persil, Wall's Ice Cream, PG Tips and so on. He put his imprint on several properties in Wirral and gave the Lady Lever Gallery to the local community, complete with his own choice of paintings (including an excellent collection of pre-Raphaelites) and furniture. Port Sunlight village which he created for his workforce, is an excellent example of what is now known as corporate social responsibility. When socialist colleagues spoke about the evils of Victorian capitalism, I liked to use the case of Lord Leverhulme to prove that some, at least, of Britain's industrial and commercial giants of yesteryear gave their workpeople a much better quality of life than they had had before.

Appealing to those half a million voters

At first, I did not campaign on Sundays so as to have time with Myra and our children and to catch up with correspondence. It was also out of respect for those with strong Christian views, namely that Sunday was a day for religious matters rather than political. I attended quite a few all-party meetings organised by the churches on other days. These offered larger audiences than meetings organised by the Tory party alone but they also gave exposure to the other candidates, some of whom would not have attracted ten people on their own.

These church meetings tended to attract many who favoured greatly increased EU aid to the Third World, which few of them had visited. As I began to acquire first-hand experience of Africa (see a later chapter), I came to see the folly of handing out aid to the corrupt dictators who ruled much of Africa and for the well-meaning but ridiculous socialist farming systems which were then in vogue. The audience did not want to know about these realities.

I was often upbraided about the EU's failure to use more of the "mountains" of surplus food produced in the EU to feed starving people in Africa. I would not for one moment defend the food mountains; they were a scandalous waste of taxpayers' money to placate the farming lobby. Nor did I oppose the use of EU food, whether surplus or not, to feed people suffering from wars, droughts or similar calamities. However, supplying food to a poor country on a long-term basis is not good policy; it puts the local farmers in those countries out of business. The prices they needed to charge to cover their costs could not compete with the free hand-outs. Moreover, some of the food donated may not be suitable as part of the overall diet in such a country.

Another issue which arose at these church meetings was the proposal to permit small shops to open all day on Sundays and for supermarkets to open for up to six hours on Sundays. The protests were particularly strong in the village of Helsby. The English Sunday would be ruined by motorised hoards on their way to the local supermarket, it was loudly claimed. Sunday opening came but I don't think the good citizens of Helsby, nor those of countless other villages, noticed the difference. On Sundays people still go to church, the village shop is still open and all is tranquil.

Sometimes I came across people whose Christian values and honest intent shone through. It was a pleasure to meet such people. Nevertheless, electors with strong religious beliefs present special problems to the canvasser. I risked being drawn into deep discussions for hours on end only to find that the person with whom I was speaking would vote for one of the other parties no matter what I said. I experienced this difficulty in "double" measure at one particular house where two elderly ladies of deep Christian belief lived. They were identical twins and had that extraordinary telepathic understanding of each other that identical twins sometimes have. It's difficult, but stimulating, to debate with a couple when one starts a sentence and the other finishes it. And, of course, if one of them was out when I called and I met one in the street later, I never knew which of them I had been speaking to previously.

The topic of hunting was a problem which arose in meetings with Church groups. I don't hunt, nor do I like hunting, but I do not think it should be banned by law. I argued that one should not ban everything one does not like. While this position avoided the worst criticism, it did not satisfy either side. I could not and still do not understand that for some people hunting generates more fanatical passion than almost any other human activity. Most hunting people are the sort of people who make Britain's countryside what it is: they care. They may be right or wrong in their sporting pursuits, but they care.

The activities of hunt saboteurs are unacceptable. Not only do they try to break up hunts while they are in progress but they pick on particular supporters in their homes. They turned up by the dozen outside the home of one of my helpers who was a hunt supporter and shouted obscenities. Police in rural areas find it hard to deal with this since quite large numbers of demonstrators can be brought together quickly to a location, previously decided in secret. Some of the saboteurs were students. Some demos were subsidised out of students' union funds by such methods as the provision of free buses to take them to the demos. They may have been ban-the-bomb one day, anti-poll tax the next and hunt saboteurs the day after.

Some of my campaigning was frenetic. I had to make myself known in eight separate Westminster constituencies in 1979 – Birkenhead, Wallasey, Wirral South, Wirral West, Chester, Ellesmere Port & Neston, Northwich and Nantwich. The towns in the extreme corners of the constituency, West Kirby and Nantwich, were some thirty or more miles apart. I decided from the beginning of my first campaign that I would visit several different parts of the constituency each day of the campaign so as to give the impression that I was everywhere all the time. Familiar with the campaigns of their MPs, many of the faithful could not understand why I was not as visible as their MPs were during their own UK elections. 'David (or Alastair or whoever) always spends a whole day in my area,' people would say. Why could I not do the same? The explanation that I also had to visit places thirty miles away may have shed light on the situation for them but it did not entirely take away the feeling that I was somehow not doing the job properly.

At first, I mostly drove my own car. Sometimes I was piloted by one of our lady helpers driving another car; this was sometimes a nightmare. Some of these ladies drove like maniacs! Of course they knew the roads well, which I didn't. I managed to keep up with them but they kept giving me that "What was keeping you?" look. It was even more difficult when I had no pilot car. Many of the schedules were tight and one day I arrived at a retirement home an hour late. The residents had been positioned – propped up would be sadly nearer the truth – in the lounge, television sets blaring, waiting for me. The owner was furious at my lateness. (One never knew in retirement homes whether the residents were helped individually to fill in their postal voting forms or whether the owner or staff did so for them and, if so, whose voting preferences were actually expressed.)

One electioneering idea was to drive in a convoy of four or five poster-bedecked cars. One such convoy hurried along the A540 towards Chester from Heswall behind a woman driver for whom electoral imperatives clearly meant nothing. We approached the point where the road became a dual carriageway. 'Now we'll get past this wretched woman,' said the local party chairman. 'Pass me the mike for the loudspeaker.' 'A la chasse, Madame, à la chasse!' ('Tally Ho!') he boomed over the loudspeaker in tones which any self-respecting huntsman would have envied. Even though loudspeaker announcements from moving vehicles are often unintelligible – and serve to boost the ego of the speaker as much as anything else – the lady-driver could hardly have missed the point. I doubt we got her vote but she did get out of the way. As the candidate, I could not of course approve of such behaviour, but it was nice to get to Chester more quickly and was good for the morale of my campaign team.

It was the custom in the Wallasey constituency to have a car cavalcade on the final Saturday of an election campaign. This meant twenty or thirty cars with flags, posters and loudspeakers trailing slowly through the streets attracting good wishes, applause and rude noises in equal measure. I doubt that anyone seriously thought that this converted anyone from Labour to Conservative but it kept our troops in good spirits. Significantly, if I had not agreed to this local custom, it would have provoked accusations from the faithful of not really trying or being too stuck up or not bothering with this end of the constituency. So I agreed to have a cavalcade. Among those wanting a cavalcade were some of those people who come out at election time to carry out some of the more dashing aspects of campaigning, people who didn't do anything else for the party. 'Leave it to us', they said, 'we'll organise everything'. I left it to them.

I turned up at the appointed time to find that I was to stand in the front of a car – the front seat had been removed – and stick my head through the sunshine roof. If you have never done this, you may not realise that the aperture of the sunshine roof comes about mid-belly. The late Barry Porter MP once described me as portly; this was a dastardly slur that I was obliged to reject but I am bound to admit that I was larger round the middle than was ideal for this particular car roof aperture. This meant that once standing in position, I was jammed. Certainly, I could extricate myself gently downwards, but if any respected local elector had happened to hurl anything accurately in my direction, I would have had to take it full on. Fortunately nobody did this. A further problem was that I could not easily speak to the driver to discuss progress, nor hear directions. The cavalcade's journey began badly and deteriorated at every traffic light. The car I was embedded in was in the second half of the cavalcade. The front of our procession soon disappeared from our sight. When we passed through Moreton we met the front end of our own procession coming back towards us in the opposite direction!

My campaigning team in any one electoral ward was usually about four or five people. This was for a ward of 11,000 voters, say 5,000 houses. The other political parties were no better off. The ordinary members of Conservative local branches were stalwart people. They distribute many of the election leaflets, put up the posters, knock on doors and telephone voters to canvass support. They take elderly supporters to the polls in their cars on election day. They do this without pay and for no reward except a measure of recognition by the candidate, MP or MEP. Yet a good many people, including armchair journalists in London, seem to think that the political parties have whole armies of volunteers just waiting to be given jobs to do. Unfortunately, so do some of the voters.

One imperious lady voter said to me: 'Sorry, I can't talk to you now; I'm just drying my hair. I always wash it on a Tuesday. Could you send someone round tomorrow night?' How many troops did she think we had? Should I send old Mrs Brockett, aged seventy two, who had bad feet? Or perhaps Jim Denholme — but then he was on business in Turkey? Or Natalie Carruthers, but she had just delivered 200 envelopes round the council estate'. I hadn't the gall to ask her to go out again that day; her husband would have complained. Or Fred Burns, but he wouldn't do political work except in his own road. (The names are fictitious but the situations very real.)

Delivering leaflets house to house was still absolutely necessary in campaigning. People may not read them but they still complain if they don't receive them. The electoral roll for a constituency is divided up into wards, and each ward further divided into polling districts of several dozen or several hundred houses. Local party workers undertake to deliver to two or three streets or more. If the work has not been properly prepared, it is particularly maddening to slog up and down a road stuffing letter boxes only to find that one half of the road is in another constituency or ward. Not only has time been wasted, but the candidate for the other area complains that his voters have become confused.

Of course, before reaching the letter box, one must first get through the garden gate, if there is one. A garden gate can be kept closed by a vertical or horizontal bolt, a slide or latch (inside or outside), a stake driven into the ground, a hinged piece of metal, a rope loop around the gate, a post or a brick or stone. These are but a few of the mechanisms one encounters. Some garden gates are apparently not opened from one month to the next, there presumably being another means of access to the property.

Having delivered thousands of leaflets over the years, I've also learned a lot about letter boxes! Most letter boxes are waist-high and horizontal but some are high up and vertical and some of these have springs strong enough to trap a wild animal. One has to push the flap right up with one finger, gloved if the weather is cold, and then knock the leaflet in with a swift tap. Then one has to get one's finger – and the glove – out again without sustaining injury. Voters are not favourably impressed by party workers who interrupt *Emmerdale* or *Coronation Street* in order to ask for their glove back because it is stuck in their letter box! Some people stuff horizontal letter boxes with old socks to keep the draught out; others simply nail up the flap. Occasionally there will be a dog which snatches the leaflet and presumably chews it before the elector has a chance to read it. Certain letter boxes are almost at floor level and often have strong flaps; glove problem again! Pushing letters through floor-level letter boxes requires a certain gymnastic ability which is not always characteristic of would-be candidates and volunteers.

These problems may be slight when calling at a friend's house on a sunny summer's afternoon. But come with me sometime on a cold, windy, dark, damp evening along an ill-lit road, carrying in one hand a four-inch-thick pile of slippery leaflets. When you come to open your fiftieth letter box of the evening with one hand, you will share my sympathy for postal delivery staff. This led me to think that, at least in new houses, there should be a building regulation whereby letter boxes should be easy to open and placed conveniently. (In many European countries, every property with a garden has to have a letter box so situated that the mail can be placed in it from the pavement without entering the garden.) I issued a call, by means of a parliamentary resolution, for consideration that standards should be set for letter boxes. A local radio journalist asked to interview me about the problem. I sat next to her on a sofa outside the hemicycle in Strasbourg. I explained the various difficulties about letter boxes and when I got to the part about not being able to get my gloved finger out, she started to giggle and we had to start again. Next time she laughed aloud; then she got hysterics. In the end it all became too much for her and after more side-splitting hilarity, she fell off the end of the sofa!

Attendance at fund-raising events is compulsory for any candidate. Myra and I went to a Tory fund-raising event in a large marquee in someone's garden in a country area. A generous supporter had loaned the use of a tent the day after a wedding for which he had hired it. All the local worthies were there. Myra and I arrived late, this being our fourth and last event of the evening. As we approached the marquee, the decibel level of conversation was high. It was going well!

Alastair Goodlad, the local MP, was there. Alastair did not like making speeches very much and was not enthusiastic about shaking hands or meeting numbers of people in the tent. Myra and I happily went around and spoke to just about everyone but, having regard to the niceties of relations between MPs and MEPs, I did not feel it right to make a speech since the MP himself did not wish to do so. I continued around the marquee and had an obligatory go on the tombola. I don't usually win much on such games but on this occasion I could not lose; every ticket I bought was a winner! Success like this is bad for a politician's image and however jocular the cries of 'Fix! Fix!' are meant to sound, the situation was not one to be encouraged. I needed the votes. I therefore wrote out a cheque for the local branch in order to "repay" some of my winnings. The organisers considered this was a generous gesture. I then went back to where Myra and I had stacked up our booty, only to find that, with the same motives in mind, Myra had given away most of our prizes, leaving us in a decidedly negative financial position for that evening!

A group of voters considered essential for a Tory victory are the farmers. Politicians in rural areas must pander to them. I say "considered" because the proportion of farmers in even a rural constituency is now very small. There was a Farmers' Club outside Chester. Its function was mainly social but with political undertones. Here, as elsewhere, I found farmers as individuals charming, generous and in some cases pillars of the party's local organisation; but put them in a National Farmers' Union (NFU) lobby or give them a piece of NFU material and another side emerged.

With European Commissioner Christopher Tugendhat while electioneering with youngsters on a European Social Fund training scheme

Farmers like to appear to be poor. Some really are poor but it is often those who are not who plead poverty most strongly. I noticed in my meetings with members of NFU branches that the farmers would arrive with dirty bits of newsprint which they would read out. 'On the 14ᵗʰ of March five years ago, *you* said…' I became practised in responding that circumstances had changed since then. One farmer always came to my regular meetings with the NFU county officials wearing worn-out trousers. He would have straw under his finger nails, if not behind his ears. I went to his house once. It was so big it had a mini-telephone exchange so that calls could be passed from one room to another! Another farmer pleaded poverty. I asked if it would mean his wife would have to give up her Mercedes. He looked shocked. 'Oh no, lad', he said, 'It's not *that* bad."

The scandal of surplus milk production in the EU led to large quantities of butter and skimmed milk powder being stored at considerable expense to taxpayers, not least in the UK. This had obliged the EU in the mid-1980s to limit the amount of milk which dairy farmers could produce. Many farmers seemed to think that the taxpayer should just pick up the bill for however much milk a farmer wanted to produce. The NFU never explained why producers of clothing, television sets, golf clubs, chocolate bars etc should not also be paid for producing goods for which consumers were not prepared to pay. They said that shoppers should buy British rather than imported goods where farm produce was concerned, yet were quite content to purchase foreign cars and equipment even when British alternatives were available.

I met angry farmers one day at Beeston market. One of them poured a can of milk over my feet. My socks began to smell later that day. It is ironical that, ten years after milk quotas were introduced, a proposal to scrap them gave rise to even greater screams from the farmers as the quotas had acquired a monetary value and could be bought and sold.

Television reporters liked to visit Conservative clubs during elections to obtain comments from the grass roots on the events of the day. The members of such clubs tended to be fairly old, half way up the social ladder and right-wing – although there was no guarantee that they would actually vote Tory. To think that the members of these clubs necessarily represented Conservative party opinion was completely wrong. But it no doubt made good television and was simple for the TV people to make. Some of the Conservative clubs contributed to Conservative party funds but not all. A few allowed their premises to be used for running the party's campaign on polling days.

The best Tory club in my constituency was the Ellesmere Port Conservative Club. The club committee was splendid, helping at election time and making me welcome whenever I popped in. It was one of only a few which regularly made its premises available for campaign purposes and contributed to party funds. Unlike many other Conservative clubs which were for men only, this one had a mixed lounge as well as the main men's bar. Feathers were sorely ruffled when Beata Brookes, MEP for North Wales, strode into the men's bar one evening after making a speech by invitation in the mixed lounge! However, to be fair, the club did run regular dances and social evenings at which women were welcome in the ballroom.

For the candidate, electioneering is primarily about meeting the voters. In election campaigns, Ministers and other party leaders are dispatched around the country to support the local candidates. This can be a mixed blessing. Organising the logistics is time-consuming – 'The Minister will arrive by helicopter at Chester; will need somebody to type out a short press release; is willing to give an interview to Radio Merseyside and *must* be on the 2.24 train from Runcorn back to London', would say the briefing from Conservative Central Office.

But what if none of the electors had heard of the particular Minister? One such Minister, wished on us at short notice, was a charming man who came to campaign on a day when my previously announced schedule took me to Runcorn. This is the kind of town where one rarely meets someone who admits to being a Tory voter. Nowadays, when the television screens are monopolised by a handful of front-bench spokesmen – and of course long-winded and opinionated media "personalities" telling the viewer what the minister really meant to say – it is not surprising that lesser political lights are hardly known outside their own constituencies. This particular Minister did not expect to be widely recognised. He probably did not want to come at all but had accepted to do his share of the foot-slogging dreamed up by enthusiastic young men at Conservative Central Office.

John McGregor, Agriculture Minister, *was* recognised by several members of the public. He came to Neston, very late indeed, full of apologies, and accompanied by a television crew. He was completely responsive to our suggestions of how to use the half-hour he was to be with us, before being whisked off again in his helicopter. He was very willing to accommodate the television crew who had a deadline to meet. The people whose farm he was visiting had laid on some pigs for the Minister to admire in front of the cameras. It looked good on the regional news.

Peter Lilley was a different kettle of fish. I had striven to increase spending from the European Regional Development Fund to help local industry, so we took him to a trading estate of small "nursery" industrial units in Neston. I pointed out the successes and also some of the current problems before he went over to be photographed with some of the entrepreneurs. He rejected what I wanted him to say to the local press. We should not be talking about problems and about throwing public money at them, according to him. The fact that some of this was European money – a minor European success story – did not go down well with him. Fortunately the pictures in the paper did not reveal his thoughts.

Sir Leon Brittan, then vice-president of the European Commission, came to support me in the 1989 election. We went to Parkgate where members of a family firm sat round a table in the back of their shop taking the heads off locally caught shrimps. We posed for photos of us eating some of these delicious morsels. Sir Leon managed superbly to sample some of them with a cocktail stick, never actually touching the shrimps with his hands. (The odour of shrimps is particularly difficult to get rid of without a thorough washing of the hands.)

Leon Brittan tries shrimps in Parkgate

The big visit was by Mrs Thatcher. She came to a Conservative function at Heswall in Wirral. She arrived very late because an accident had completely blocked the motorway through Cheshire from Manchester airport and her plane had been diverted to an airport in North Wales. The Cheshire police were fully occupied with the accident so the Welsh police escorted her but they had some difficulty in finding the hall where the meeting was being held. Eventually she arrived, immaculate and cool as a cucumber, notwithstanding a small group of demonstrators howling about something outside the building.

'Good afternoon, Prime Minister. Welcome to Heswall,' I said. 'It's very nice of you to come.'

'Good afternoon,' she replied. 'It's very nice of *you* to come!

She spent a few minutes at every table; there were five Tory party workers at each table. An extra chair had been left empty for Mrs Thatcher at each table. Every person in the room felt lit up by her presence.

When you have made a thousand speeches, you know what kind of speech you are good at and what kind you should avoid making. I always avoided using a prepared text if I could, but the organisers of conferences always asked for a copy of my speech to put in the document packs, without which regular conference-goers would feel deprived. A speech has to be relevant, amusing and stimulating or even shocking. I found it useful to listen to the radio on the way to the place where I had to make a speech. Some of the audience would also have heard the latest news and I tried to make a bond with them by beginning with something which was fresh in their minds and relating it to the circumstances of the audience.

In my business life, in pre-"*PowerPoint*" days, I had become accustomed to using flip charts and slides to illustrate lectures I gave. Although it is not usual for politicians to use such tools, I found it useful to explain the EU by showing a few maps and charts. I soon found out that to depend upon blackboards to display flip charts or slide projectors being available was to depend on an Act of God, who seemed not to be always paying attention at the right time. I therefore produced my own device on which to hang flip charts. The trick is to be able to turn over the charts that people have seen, which is impossible if the chart is hanging on the wall rather than over a blackboard easel. I purchased a second-hand bathroom cupboard to which two strips of wood could be attached by bolts and butterfly nuts. The charts, with holes punched at the appropriate positions, could be placed between the strips of wood and secured by the bolts. The cupboard was then placed on the edge of a table – every meeting room has one table at least – so that the pad of charts was hanging down below the level of the table. It was easy then to look at a chart and then turn it over the back to reveal the next one, and so on. Primitive, certainly, but it worked.

There seemed to be a dense fog which clouded most people's minds about the structure of the EU so I used the charts to clear the air and help answer questions such as 'Which countries are in the EU?', 'What is the difference between the Commission, the Council and the Parliament?" and "What does "*CAP*" stand for?' (The Common Agricultural Policy is a set of mechanisms mainly designed to regulate farm prices, especially for production of cereals, beef, lamb, milk, wine and tobacco together with lighter regulation for fruit and vegetables.)

I would follow up my answers to these questions by emphasising that what really mattered was the effect of EU decisions on ordinary people, not how those decisions were taken, how many MEPs there were and so on. (After all, most people don't know how many MPs there are in Westminster – and why should they?)

I made speeches to all kinds of organisations and I was always interested to see and hear how other speakers approached their task. I was invited to a black-tie dinner of a professional organisation at the Adelphi Hotel in Liverpool. The speaker was billed as being the Chief Constable. I could not see him along the top table on the platform and made enquiries. It turned out that he had had an accident and had been replaced as speaker by a Liverpool comedian. The comedian was wearing a pink frilly shirt with his dinner jacket and had been puffing nervously on his cigarettes throughout the meal. He got up to speak. He began with a few ranging shots to see how well his voice carried to the back of the room. Then he tried a few slightly blue jokes. The more important guests were seated nearest to the platform, and they looked at each other to see whether or not they should laugh. One of them broke cover and chortled, so the others decided it was all right to laugh too and started to do so with gusto. The speech turned out to be a great success. Afterwards I talked with the speaker. He was drenched in sweat, a total bag of nerves, but content that he had given a performance which was enjoyed by all. He said he earned more from making speeches than from television appearances.

Few people are born great orators: even fewer are born joke tellers. From my experience, it is wise to be witty, yes, but if you can't tell jokes, don't try. I have seen many a company chairman trying to read a joke written for him.

Some will have practised the speech beforehand, perhaps in front of a mirror; some even engage a speech tutor! But at the top table in the banqueting hall, the lights may be low and the typed speech may be too small to read comfortably standing up without constantly putting one's glasses on and taking them off. Better to have a few trigger words written in large print on pieces of card as reminders. It is always useful to have a note of which function you are attending and which town or city you are in. There is no silence like that which follows your lyrical praise of the magnificent deeds of the Lower Twytterington Methodist Fellowship when in fact you are addressing the Belford St Martin Licensed Victuallers Association dinner!

In addition to the main Tory party within the Euro-constituency, I had excellent support from the European Union of Women (EUW). The EUW was an organisation to promote discussion of European affairs from a right-of-centre perspective. In Britain, it was associated with the Conservative Party but not officially part of it – at least not in 1979.

My local EUW members wanted to learn about the EU and debate how it should progress. I am sure that this was not entirely welcome in Central Office but no one ever said so! There was a freshness and openness about the EUW meetings which the Tory party's official discussion groups lacked.

EUW members sometimes went to meetings in London. The idea of holding meetings outside London on occasions was, of course, opposed by our metropolitan comrades. The London-based members could not even see that the start time of the meetings should be such that provincial members could arrive at the beginning without having to spend the previous night in a hotel, at their own expense.

The EUW had branches on the continent mostly under the umbrella of the Christian Democrat parties. Some of my members went to their meetings. I met a couple of our EUW members on their way from Crewe to a meeting in London. There was a young man in the vestibule of the train, by the doors. He started to punch another young man on the chest. One of the EUW ladies, a voluble Italian, berated the thug verbally but to no effect. She called to me. I got hold of the aggressor by his mop of curly hair and pulled him off. Afterwards I had to wash the grease of his hair off my hands. The incident did my reputation within the EUW branch no harm at all!

We had two EUW branches in my Euro-constituency. The word came down from Central Office that we could only have *one* but no explanation of why was given. We decided to keep two.

In the election, in June 1979, I received 93,589 votes, fifty-seven per cent of the votes cast. Labour were second with 47,276 votes, twenty-nine per cent, and the Liberals came third with 23,816 which was fourteen per cent. Some minor parties also contested this election.

So that is how I became an MEP.

Myra was much involved in local affairs. Here she is carrying out her role as Chairman of Wirral Health Authority

PART II

Parliament at Work

Strasbourg and Brussels

On 17 July 1979, I sat down on my own blue, numbered chair, with its desk, microphone, earphones and voting buttons, in the parliamentary chamber (the "hemicycle"), for the opening procedures of the newly elected European Parliament. I reflected on what the place represented. I had buttons to vote on parliamentary resolutions. How would this affect my country and my constituents? And how would the Parliament develop? How should I decide to use those buttons to vote for or to vote against a resolution being debated or to abstain?

That moment was what all my campaigning had been directed towards. From a slow and sometimes chaotic start in 1979, the directly elected Parliament grew into being a major part of the EU decision-making system – as it should be. I and my colleagues at that time played a part in this process, conscious that power is not given to a legislature unless that legislature wants it. I and my colleagues wanted it, so that the will of the people could be exercised.

There was no job description for MEPs. As I took my seat in the Parliament, I had no clear idea of *how* the Parliament as a whole or I myself would make progress towards achieving my objectives. People said it was only a talking shop; but that is what a parliament is supposed to be – a place where public issues are debated in public! But, as I discovered, it's not just about talk. MEPs' votes at the end of debates have come to play a major part in deciding EU policies and spending plans. Moreover, they have a major role in checking that the spending plans are properly carried out by the European Commission. They now have a major role in sharing power with the Council of Ministers.

When what became the European Union was founded, the search began for a location which would be convenient and suitable for the then six member states without being beholden to any one of them. The ancient and beautiful city of Strasbourg borders the river Rhine, a major "highway" for barge-born traffic. The Rhine, at this point in its long journey from Switzerland to the North Sea, forms the border between France and Germany. In 1979, Strasbourg

63

had already been the site of the Council of Europe[5] for several years. Its location was looked on as a symbol of reconciliation between France and Germany following centuries of conflict between them, the last within the lifetime of many people alive today. It was designated as the provisional seat of the European Parliament.

The fact that Strasbourg was, and is, also the headquarters of the Council of Europe causes endless confusion. The Parliament made use of the Council of Europe's premises throughout my period as an MEP as its provisional seat. Since my time it has moved to another building, built by the French government. It is important to be clear that the Council of Europe, guardian of the European Convention on Human Rights and the European Court of Human Rights, is not part of the constitutional structure of the European Union.[6] Many MEPs, including me, opposed the idea of Strasbourg being made definitively the seat of the European Parliament. However, in 1992 the EU Heads of State, under John Major's chairmanship, agreed that the city should be recognised formally as the seat of the Parliament, no longer the provisional seat. This decision was an error which continues to cost a small fortune by dragging MEPs, staff and equipment from Brussels, the effective nerve centre of the EU, all the way to Strasbourg. John Major could have stopped it.

Before 1979, there had been a European Parliament (or "Assembly") but it was not directly elected and was made up of MPs nominated from national parliaments. This met for five days each month, alternately in Strasbourg and Luxembourg, where some of the EU institutions are based.

In 1979, it was suggested that the new, elected European Parliament should also alternate its one-week-per-month sessions between Strasbourg and Luxembourg. The first and only plenary meeting of the directly-elected European Parliament held in Luxembourg was marred by all manner of organisational problems. Getting to Luxembourg was difficult to start with; there were very few flights from anywhere serving the city. Moreover the city had a severe shortage of hotels. There was only one hotel within walking distance of the European Parliament building. Getting to the Parliament building, situated on a plateau outside the city, making use of the limited fleet

---

[5] See Appendix.

[6] The story goes that there was talk in the early days of having a sort of Washington DC, a European federal territory, in Strasbourg. However, with the usual French insistence on having everything its own way, the site of the Parliament remains purely French territory.

of taxis and buses available, was difficult. There was nowhere in the building to have a coffee before the start of business in the morning and the UK newspapers did not arrive until the afternoon. There were no shops anywhere near the Parliament to buy the odd necessity. A trip to the loo from the parliamentary chamber meant going up three floors by lift! So Luxembourg was very soon rejected as a venue for meetings of the Parliament although meetings of the Council of Ministers continued to be held there. Strasbourg was much better organised.

In the Strasbourg hemicycle, MEPs vote either by a show of hands or (for very important matters where records showing how each MEP voted must be prepared), by pressing a button connected to an electronic system. The result of the vote is displayed almost instantly on large screens. The existence of this system permits there to be a very large number of votes on each piece of draft legislation, sometimes on every paragraph. Its use contrasts with House of Commons procedures whereby, when the wishes of the House cannot be ascertained by voice votes ("Ayes" or "Noes"), each MP walks through one or other division lobby to indicate which way he or she wishes to vote. The European Parliament system also contrasts with that of the United States Senate, under which, in the event that a voice vote which does not result in a clear decision, each Senator calls out his or her individual voting intention as the list of Senators is read out; this procedure takes perhaps fifteen minutes.

The British and American voting systems draw Members into the Chambers and afford valuable opportunities to network with people they would otherwise not have ready access to. In contrast, MEPs have ample opportunity to meet Commissioners and Ministers in the various cafés and bars within the building.

★ ★ ★

A problem to be solved was how to get to Strasbourg. For the plenary sessions at Strasbourg, I normally took the 06.30 flight from Manchester to Frankfurt and shared a car provided by Strasbourg City Council from there. The Labour MEPs with me were generally polite and friendly. However, this was not the case one day while waiting at Manchester Airport when one of them declared that he was not interested in supporting anything which did not advance the cause of socialism – even if a definite British interest was at stake in the matter under discussion!

The route via Frankfurt was the only means of getting to Strasbourg before the start of business without leaving home the previous day. There was a special plane laid on by Air France, charging normal airline fares, on the Monday of each Strasbourg session, and returning on the Friday, but it left Heathrow before the first connection from Manchester arrived there. I was quite happy to let the French pay for the car to Strasbourg from Frankfurt as a price for obliging us to go to this inconvenient location.

Jerry March wrote a piece in the *Chester Evening Leader* on 25 January 1984 describing a trip to a plenary session in Strasbourg on which he accompanied me:

"A fast car zooms up a German autobahn speeding Andrew Pearce off to the biggest show on earth. Mr Pearce has been up since five o'clock this morning. He flew from Manchester to Frankfurt and is now being taken on a two-hour journey to the European Parliament over the border in Strasbourg. Two Labour MEPs are with us in the car. When Andrew Pearce gets to Strasbourg he will have a quick lunch and attend a meeting with fellow Tories at half past three in the afternoon. In the meantime Mr Pearce will have to look at a constant flow of paper, letters and other material. It's a gruelling schedule, living out of an airline bag. 'It's sometimes hard but you get used to it. I don't like missing meals; it upsets my system,' he said. Andrew Pearce spends 453 hours travelling per year on his normal duties. 'I like travel but I'm sick of this kind of travel,' he admitted. 'The job is so interesting. It's not a question of watching something happening. It's a question of trying to make something happen.'

"We arrive at the Palais de l'Europe in Strasbourg. Despite its romantic sounding name, it is a concrete and glass monstrosity. The Chamber itself is like a giant bingo hall. Flashing signs at the front show how the votes have gone."

For Strasburg sessions, I sometimes stayed in hotels in the city but more often made use of inns across the Rhine in Germany. My favourite was an inn whose legally-imposed closing day each week was Monday, the day of the week when I would normally arrive. I would therefore go to a nearby farm, ring the bell, explain myself to the innkeeper's wife, who appeared at an upstairs window, and catch the keys for the front door and for my room which she would throw down to me. On a Tuesday evening, a local men's choir would come for a sing-song, all dressed in traditional green jackets and trousers with decorative braiding and badges. Some fifteen men would sit at one long table, order their beers together and burst into vigorous song from time to time. The proceedings were usually drawing to an end by the time I got there about ten o'clock at night and clearly a good evening had been had by one and all.

Breakfast was a substantial offering of bread, cheese, cold meats and coffee. The newspaper, wrapped round a short pole, would be handed around. 'Have a look at today's news,' one of the other guests would say to me. The newspaper was printed in the nearby small town of Kehl and contained virtually no news of Frankfurt, Bonn or Berlin, let alone Strasbourg, just a couple of miles away across the Rhine – or of "Europe". (I noticed that the locals would sometimes talk of 'going to Europe' when they went across the bridge to Strasbourg and beyond.)

A small inconvenience (pardon the pun!) in this pub was that there was a sloping roof above the toilet in my room. I could not therefore perform one of life's essential functions standing up straight. Nature did not design the male body to perform this function bending down. (Do I detect the hand of a female architect or a feminist here?) Perhaps the architect had in mind regulations which apply in certain German apartment blocks obliging tenants to perform all natural functions sitting down during the night hours so as not to disturb the neighbours through the thin walls.

★ ★ ★

The business at Strasbourg consisted mainly of plenary sessions in the hemicycle — debates and Question Times. I spoke as often as possible at Strasbourg, but being only one of, eventually, more than 600 MEPs, it was not very often. Not being one of the leaders of the Conservative group, I was not often called upon to make landmark speeches in the grand debates which sometimes drew many members into the hemicycle. This is not something which I particularly regret since the Parliament's most important work was often done in committee and some of the most important plenary votes were on details of the committees' reports. All speeches in the hemicycle were subject to strict time limits and even the leaders of the major political Groups such as the European People's Party (EPP), the Socialists and our own group were usually permitted no more than ten or twelve minutes. Some of the speeches by party leaders were boring surveys of the wider political scene and constitutional principles – no doubt valuable intellectually but useless as a basis for coverage in the UK media.

Life in the Parliament was not all friendship and European spirit. Clashes could be sharp, not least between British Labour MEPs, such as Barbara Castle and Alex Falconer, and British Conservative MEPs. I exchanged sharp words

67

with Alex on several occasions. In a Strasbourg debate in 1986 on a report on road safety, I noted that the British Labour Group had abstained in committee. I began my comments with a jibe: 'I notice that Mr Falconer, who I think is not favouring us with his presence at the moment...' and continued with a taunt that he supported 'a number of amendments which mostly seem to seek to increase public expenditure and protect the trade unions.'

In a debate, also in 1986, on protection of children, I gave an explanation of vote. I said: 'In view of what Mr Falconer said earlier, it is nice to see the lady and gentlemen of the Socialist Group scuttling in halfway through the vote. It is a pity they do not seem to view the protection...' The President interrupted me at this point to say: "An explanation of vote, Mr Pearce, not a comment on the proceedings please.' There were "mixed reactions" from the House. 'Mr President,' I continued, 'I was just coming to that before you interrupted me. The point that matters, I think, is the point that the *rapporteur* referred to. I regret that this report does not say more about the desirability of mothers staying at home with their children... The most natural way of bringing up children is to have a mother at home. I am glad to see I have such support from those who have scuttled in halfway through the vote.'

In another debate in 1986, Alex Falconer said: 'Is it not a disgrace that when Mr Stewart is speaking on behalf of the pensioners of Britain, there is not one Conservative Member from the United Kingdom in the Chamber?" The President responded: "I am afraid there *are* some Conservative Members present – three in fact: Mr Price, Mr Pearce and Mrs Daly!'

I found that the best effect, both upon Members and in attracting the attention of the media, was to ask for the floor during Question Time or to exploit a strange procedure called "Explanations of Vote". This was supposed to enable Members to give an explanation of their voting behaviour when it appeared not to be consistent with what they had previously said in debate. Several MEPs exploited this procedure to the maximum in order to have the chance to make a point in the hemicycle. These "Explanations of Vote" were given after the votes on the amendments but before the final vote on the resolution as a whole, so the Hemicycle was usually pretty full and the media people were listening also, while waiting for the result of the final vote on the measure under discussion.

Plenary week could be tiring. A catnap in some quiet corner of the building now and then, when nothing in particular needed to be attended to, helped to maintain one's stamina. Caution was required, however; a television crew filmed a dozing MEP in the lobby outside the Hemicycle during the lunch break and broadcast the film giving the impression that the Member was asleep inside the Hemicycle while a debate was taking place.

The highlight of many plenary weeks was the appearance of the Head of Government of whichever country had the presidency of the Council of Ministers, which rotated every six months. The visit of Mrs Thatcher in 1986 was one such highlight. Among her ringing words were:

'We have set a target date of 1992 for realising one of the Community's original goals: the creation of a genuine Common Market without barriers to trade between its members.

'We have made a determined effort to see that the Community counts for more in foreign policy and in the strengthening of the open world trading system.

'We must also adapt old policies to suit the changing times, so that they are not an unnecessary drain on Europe's vitality or its resources. This means above all action to deal with agricultural surpluses and to put agriculture on a more stable footing for the future.'

Much of what Mrs Thatcher asked for has been achieved. But not all of it.

★ ★ ★

Question Time was introduced into the European Parliament procedures at the suggestion of the British and proved to be one of the Parliament's most useful activities. Questions to the European Commission or to the Council of Ministers were submitted in writing with an indication as to whether an oral or a written answer was expected. There were usually too many questions for oral answers for the time allotted. When this occurred, answers to some of the questions were handed to the Member on paper when Question Time ended. After an oral answer was given, the Member who asked the question could ask a supplementary question, as could other members who then caught the eye of the President.

Questions could be asked in order to obtain information or to draw attention to particular matters. They had to be carefully targeted and concise if they were to produce the desired information or reaction. A vague question such as 'Is the Commission satisfied that its policy on such and such is being correctly implemented?' would only receive a vague answer. A question which asked for specific facts would do better, provided that it did not demand an unreasonable amount of detail.

Some Commissioners were concise, some verbose. I asked Commissioner Varfis during Question Time in September 1986 to give me a brief answer, a "Yes" or "No", on a certain matter relating to EU assistance to communities suffering from their location on islands and hence cut off from facilities on the mainland. The Commissioner took 128 words to reply. The Vice-President of the Parliament in the chair at the time commented, "I am glad you did not ask for a *full* answer, Mr Pearce."

I asked questions about all sorts of issues relevant to my constituency or what I perceived to be the national interest. Some of them were intended more to bring a point to public notice rather than to elicit facts. When the objective was to elicit facts, the Commission did not always provide them, though generally it did so, often in a remarkably helpful way. Whatever the answer, a question in the Parliament brought a matter to public notice and obliged officials in national governments as well as in the Commission to consider what their public position was as regards the matters raised. The Council of Ministers' representative, a Minister of whichever country currently held the six-monthly Presidency of the Council of Ministers, was on the other hand, rarely very forthcoming.

In 1985, I asked questions about the 845,000 tonnes of surplus butter in store – the so-called "butter mountain" caused by excessive production subsidies. A large quantity of such butter was stocked in the UK but the Ministry of Agriculture Fisheries and Food (MAFF), the responsible ministry at the time, kept the locations secret. (Some of it was near Whitchurch in Shropshire, just outside my constituency.) "Pearce fury on subsidies" was how the *Wirral News* ran the story on the 23 March. Fury, being a nice short word, is much favoured by journalists, but on this occasion at least, I don't think it was over the top.

In September 1985, I asked the Commission about speed limits on German motorways and whether it knew when the Germans would introduce them. (Drive down any German motorway at 120 kilometres per hour, nearly 75 miles per hour, and the Mercedes and BMWs just come tearing past you, one after the other.) There were speed limits on the motorways of every other EU country but not generally in Germany. Yet the Germans were among the first to complain about the pollution caused by car exhaust fumes. They were foremost in demanding that catalytic converters be fitted to cars. (Coincidentally, it was a German company that led the manufacture of such equipment.) Yet there is no doubt that high engine speed when driving fast on the autobahn causes heavy pollution, so the greater the speed, the more the pollution. But the Commission did not want to get involved. Its answer referred to experiments in Germany on the effect of speed on the level of emissions from cars. 'The results of this German experience will no doubt constitute a valuable input to this complex matter,' was the Commission's reply. It seemed that to suggest that speed limits imposed on German motorways was bound to be seen as an attack on German motoring virility.

★ ★ ★

The fourth week of the month was reserved for Group meetings, that is to say Party meetings. From 1979, the Conservative Group, being mainly British, usually met in London but sometimes in Copenhagen, at the behest of the small number of Danes in the Group. After Spain came into the EU and the *Alianza Popular*[7] party joined the Group (and the name of the Group was changed to European Democratic Group) our Group meetings were sometimes held in Madrid. Occasionally the Group met in Brussels to facilitate joint policy discussions with the European People's Party, the home of the Christian Democrats. The European Democratic Group merged with the European People's party after I had ceased to be an MEP. David Cameron later broke that link, leaving British Conservatives from 2011 in a Group with strongly right wing MEPs from Poland and the Czech Republic. It is argued that Cameron's act did considerable damage to UK relations with political leaders in Germany and France during the period of controversy about the euro, without gaining anything much in return.

Many visiting groups of ordinary citizens are baffled and even shocked by the number of empty seats in the hemicycle, and the fact that some of the MEPs who are there appear to be doing nothing.[8] Only the Commissioner present seems to be taking notice and commenting on what was said. Visitors often think that members should sit in the hemicycle and vote in the light of the arguments heard. No parliament in any modern democracy decides issues on

---

[7] The Alianza Popular was known in brief as the "AP". Early drafts of official documents were also known in French as "AP" (avant-projet). Moreover, the African, Caribbean and Pacific – European Union Joint Parliamentary Assembly was known by its French initials as the "AP", (assemblée paritaire) – see later. To compound the confusion, the letters 'AP' were also, of course, my own initials.

[8] The same is said about the House of Commons.

the basis of debates in the chamber alone. A vast process of consultation and lobbying goes on in the background. This hopefully ensures that every aspect of the problems under review is brought into play. The complexity of modern life and the impact on citizens and businesses of decisions taken is serious and far-reaching, so the situation could not be otherwise.

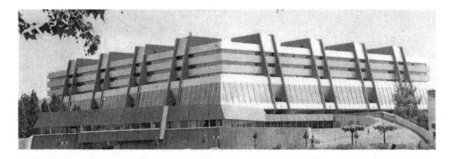

The building in Strasbourg in which the European Parliament met in my time: exterior and interior views

One thing after another

The European Parliament had twenty or so committees. This was where the real work was done. All proposals for new EU laws were debated by one or more of these. I myself dealt in the plenary or in committees with a wide variety of topics, some directly concerning my constituency, some not. Each committee had four or five staff to assist Members and in particular to draft reports, according to the wishes of the Member appointed by the committee as *rapporteur*. Some MEPs asked the committee staff to draft reports for them without getting too involved themselves. I saw one French MEP being handed a report drafted in his name on his way into the committee where he was to present it; he had not seen it before. Key sentences were indicated in red to help him present it. I myself determined that I would decide the contents and style of reports bearing my name, using staff only to research relevant facts and to tidy up the final draft.

The committee meetings were held in Brussels during two weeks each month. Each committee meeting lasted two, three or four days. Committee meetings started after lunch on the first day and finished before lunch on the last day, which kept down the number of days members spent away from home. MEPs who lived in London, including several whose constituencies were miles away from the capital, could do a half-day's professional or commercial work unrelated to the EU in London after a morning of committee work in Brussels, taking advantage of Belgian time being an hour ahead of British time. Having to travel back to Merseyside, I myself could not do this.

Much of the business in my time arose from the creation of legally enforceable manufacturing and trading standards throughout the EU, the 'single market'. This single market was as much an advantage for Britain as for any other EU country. Progress on this was a major triumph for Mrs Thatcher and for Britain. It did more to advance the concept of the common market as set out in the Treaty of Rome[9] than almost any other single measure. Those who think that Mrs Thatcher was strongly opposed to the EU should remember this. Much of value for Britain was achieved but, as British Ministers repeatedly said, much

[9] See Appendix.

Questions in the European Parliament

was left to be done in creating a single market in financial services. It is ironical that in 2012, when new EU wide banking rules were proposed, Britain was amongst those objecting to them.

On numerous occasions, in the plenary and in committee, I argued in strong support of one of Mrs Thatcher's most important actions in the EU – the creation of a real single European market. This was probably the most important single step in building up the effectiveness of the EU, and it was British pressure which brought it about. The barriers to trade between EU countries were no longer a matter of customs duties; those had gone. What impeded trade was the multiplicity of different technical standards regulating the design and characteristics of goods.

In speeches in the constituency I liked to quote two examples of how differing national regulations were counter-productive. One was about toothpaste. When Britain joined, there were nine countries in the EU – and nine separate sets of regulations about how toothpaste could be produced and

74

sold. Why should the standards for toothpaste for French, German or British mouths be different?

Another example was lawn mowers. At that time, the only motor mowers which conformed to the national regulations in all the EU countries were made in the United States, the firm which made them thereby having considerable advantages in the market place over the fragmented European producers.

While many of the differing national regulations were designed according to national officials' interpretations of what was in the public interest, others were simply devices for keeping out imports.

Mrs Thatcher appointed Lord Arthur Cockfield as a European Commissioner and supported him in proposing nearly two hundred pieces of legislation to harmonise a wide range of technical standards. In the vast majority of cases, a single standard could easily be made to apply in all EU countries.

Although cutting the cost of coping with a multiplicity of different sets of rules was bound to be good for all concerned it was hard to persuade the voters of this. Many people in Britain spoke as though all the other EU countries should simply adopt British practices. This would have been ideal but for the fact that the French thought everyone else should simply adopt *their* way of doing things, the Germans *their* way, the Dutch *theirs* and so on. Lord Cockfield's harmonisation of technical standards was a great step forward but it only applied to goods. Work on harmonising rules about commerce and banking, of particular interest to the UK, has taken longer.

When seeking to open up continental markets for British goods, we were sometimes criticised because of the British ban then in force on imports of milk from France, Holland, Denmark and Ireland, allegedly to protect UK consumers from inferior hygiene standards abroad, but in fact to protect British farmers.

Much of this work on harmonisation of standards was done in the Environment, Public Health and Consumer Protection Committee, ably chaired for many years by Scottish Labour MEP, Ken Collins. I was a member of this committee for several years.

In this committee, I found myself seated next to a French MEP, Jean-Thomas Nordmann. There was much discussion about a Commission proposal to end the long-standing ban on British chocolate being sold in continental countries on the grounds that it contained vegetable fat other than cocoa butter. This ban was unfair because continental chocolate producers were allowed to sell their products in Britain. British chocolate producers preferred to take out some of the cocoa butter, which could be sold at a better price for the manufacture of cosmetics, and substitute for it the oil of shea nuts. Both cocoa beans and shea nuts are found in West Africa so there was not much to choose between the two in terms of loss of exports from developing countries.

Mr Nordmann supported the interests of a French chocolate manufacturer, which was opposed to British chocolate being sold in France. It was MEPs, mainly French ones, not the Commission, which came up with the nonsense that the British product should be called "vegolate" rather than chocolate. British MEPs heard little from the British chocolate producers but we did hear from the makers of Mars bars, an American firm. Mars brought a supply of Mars bars to the Parliament and challenged members of the committee to tell the difference between Mars made for the British market and Mars made for continental customers, with different vegetable oils. Nobody could tell the difference.

The press billed this episode as the valiant British beating off the dreaded harmonisation of standards which would destroy vital British interests. In fact, the Commission's proposal was precisely in line with the British interest and Fleet Street's cries to beat it back did our own industry no favours. It was many years before a proposal which finally allowed British chocolate to be sold on the continent went through. I mocked Mr Nordmann by asking that if we could not use the word chocolate for the British product, would expressions like *crème de menthe* and *crème de la crème* also be banned because they were not cream in the literal sense? In the plenary debate in December 1985, I said: 'Into this prickly debate steps Mr Nordmann who says he supports free trade. However, the reality is the opposite. What he wants is a protected market for certain French companies that seem to have some difficulty in selling their product. We in Britain, Denmark and Ireland have good chocolate. We market it successfully. We have an excellent system of brand names and quite honestly the public likes our chocolate more than they like Mr Nordmann's chocolate.'

On another point, an Italian MEP proposed in a committee report that there should be a place where botanical species would be safeguarded. In a debate on the preservation of botanical species, I pointed out that the Royal Botanical Gardens at Kew in London had been engaged in this kind of work for 200 years and suggested that EU funding be provided to assist this work on a European scale. I went to Kew and spoke with a senior official there. He knew nothing of the EU. I suggested he enquire about applying to Brussels for funds. I heard no more but am pleased to note that Kew later began to benefit from EU finance in projects such as HOTSPOTS, HOTMED and the Darwin Initiative.

Moods

A matter of considerable interest was the measure to limit the activities of time-share salesmen, best known for promoting part-ownership of villas in Spain. The new law laid down various rules including a cooling-off period during which a deal could be cancelled. The law applies in all EU countries and, a point to be noted by the Euro-sceptics, could not have been made to apply in Spain by the British Parliament on its own.

On the Regional Policy committee, of which I was a member for a time, my main concern was making sure that my area received its entitlement of EU funding (more if possible!). I deal with this later in the book.

For all of the ten years I was in the Parliament, I was a member of the Development and Co-operation Committee which was responsible for policy on food aid and for capital investment and training projects in the Third World. (More about this later.)

I was posted to the Committee on Women's Rights. This was a stomping ground for feminists. While I never had any doubts about the rights of women to equality under the law and within the economy, I found some of the affirmative action proposed in the committee to be beyond all sense. My main role on the committee on behalf of our Group was to combat the more nonsensical suggestions brought forward.

In 1989, I was *rapporteur* (editor of a report representing the committee's

With the Mayor of Reutlingen (on the right)

view) for a report on spouses in agriculture and family businesses. There was a sound purpose behind this because in certain EU countries, a farmer's wife – or any other spouse of someone in business – although working in the business and being an essential part of it, was counted as being "non-working" from the point of view of pensions, sickness insurance and marital separation. This was totally unfair. The report put forward the case for recognising that such women worked in the business every bit as much as their spouses.

I wanted to test the opinions of ordinary country women on this matter. While it is useful to obtain briefings from politicians, civil servants and the leaders of trade associations, I consider it essential to obtain a worm's eye view of the situation, information from the coal face. I turned to Reutlingen in Baden-Wurttemberg in Germany. This town was twinned with Ellesmere Port & Neston in my constituency. It is in one of Germany's most prosperous regions. I asked Dr. Manfred Öchsle, the Oberbürgermeister (the elected executive mayor) if I could borrow a room in his Town Hall for a meeting with representative ladies and whether he would invite suitable ladies to be invited. He welcomed the idea warmly. The meeting was most successful, even down to the coffee and sticky cakes provided by our host. No doubt Dr.Öchsle was pleased with the photos of the event in his local paper.

One of the dafter ideas to come from socialist members of the Women's Rights committee was a proposal that pensioners should be given sex lessons. My comment as quoted in the *Daily Telegraph* in September 1985 was: 'A little love in the twilight years is no bad thing for the single pensioner, but sex lessons on the taxpayer for people of any age is ridiculous and insulting.' The proposal was thrown out.

Sometimes in debates on these matters, things got bogged down in committee because the European Commission officials involved simply did not understand how their proposals would affect all of the EU countries. An example came in the course of applying general EU competition (anti-trust) provisions regulating premises serving alcohol (for instance British pubs). The law is complicated and gives rise to expensive legal cases. Its application makes a huge difference to what we all pay for the goods and services we buy and the profitability of the companies which produce them. Put in the most general way, a person selling something cannot impose conditions on the buyer about what he, the buyer, does with the goods he is purchasing. In the 1970s, many pubs in England and Wales were run by tenants who leased the premises from brewery companies but then ran their own businesses in them. Many of the brewers who owned the pubs were coalescing into larger groups. They were beginning to undertake the sale of wines and spirits, and the hire of space-invader gaming machines and "fruit" machines. They sought to prevent their tenants obtaining these goods and services from anyone other than themselves, the owners of the pubs, by the so-called "brewer's tie". It was claimed that this practice increased the prices which customers had to pay.

The Commissioner in charge of this proposed legislation, Frans Andriessen, was Dutch. He had seemed perverse in his opposition to maintaining the "tie" at least for draught beer, if not for bottled beer and the other products. I cornered him early one morning in his office in Strasbourg and discussed the matter with him. In many countries pubs were either run as businesses entirely independent of the brewers or were owned and managed by them. I realised that the "tie" tenancy system did not exist in most countries, and that Frans Andriessen had not been properly briefed about this. I told him what I knew about the British pub sector. In the end the "tie" was relaxed except for draught beer. Following this and subsequent UK measures to combat monopolistic tendencies, pubs now offer their customers a much wider choice of drinks.

One can ask how it can come about that a Commissioner could be inadequately briefed on the background to legislation. It is up to European Commission staff to give correct briefings. It is also up to MEPs to bring their knowledge to bear during discussion of proposed legislation in the European Parliament's committees. In my time, the advice given by MEPs would have been better if British businesses had taken more effort to inform Commission staff and MEPs of their needs.

One aspect of EU policy had a particular effect on management of the beach at West Kirby, in my constituency and close to our house. The beach was a broad stretch of sand, fringed with sand dunes on one side of the Dee estuary and with a panorama of the Welsh hills of the other. The sand banks in the estuary are a major stopping-off point for migrating birds and the edge of the dunes a habitat for natterjack toads. From nearby Hilbre Island, once inhabited by monks, seals can be seen moving with the tide or resting on sandbanks when the tide is out.

The beach here had long suffered from silting which encouraged the growth of spartina grass. The spartina grass, in turn, encouraged more silting. The Nature Conservancy, a public authority located far from Merseyside, decreed that the grass should be allowed to grow. Silting, it said, was a natural process and should be unfettered. The fact that the grass encroached on to the beach, used by swimmers, sun-bathers and playing children, apparently did not concern them. Local people said that their opinions had not been sought. In

November 1988, I joined a forty-strong band of locals to dig out the grass. The November day was so misty that one half of the digging party could not see the other half. We dug as hard as we could! The "battle of the beach" was how the *Liverpool Echo* described the occasion.

There were EU guidelines for the cleanliness of beaches, including that at West Kirby. The EU Blue Flag scheme indicated the state of cleanliness for the public. The British government had a strategy in the 1980s to prevent the unacceptable quality of many of Britain's bathing beaches being too evident. The poor quality of our beaches was mainly due to effluent pipes not stretching out far enough into the sea. To determine which beaches should be described as suitable for bathing, the government organised a survey of the number of people bathing per mile of beach. Unbelievably, neither Blackpool beach nor Brighton beach were classified for these purposes as bathing beaches, the survey being carried out in such a way that the truth was hidden. Their inadequate standards of cleanliness therefore escaped the publicity which would have ensued if the truth had been revealed.

As regards West Kirby beach, a different means to conceal the poor standard of beach hygiene was used by Whitehall. This beach was to be excluded altogether from the survey of English beaches on the grounds that the authority responsible for the *water* was the Welsh Water and Drainage Authority rather than the authority for North West England which, at this location, was only responsible for the beaches. This sleight of hand did not prevent protests being made by the public about the condition of the beach and little by little improvements were made.

Another topic of debate in Strasbourg was rice. For many years, Italian producers of the kind of rice used for risotto had succeeded in keeping out imports which would have been offered at lower prices than their own product. Over the years, the consumption of rice in Europe had vastly increased but the barriers in place to protect Italian rice production continued in force and these tariffs applied to types of rice which could not be used for making risotto. I attended a tasting in the Parliament building where different kinds of rice were offered to us. There was plain American-style rice, "pudding rice" for English rice puddings, fragrant basmati rice to go with curries and the short-grained rice used for risotto, such as Camaroli or Vialone Nano. The differences between the various types in terms of shape, taste and stickiness were very obvious. I asked Commissioner Sutherland in a Parliamentary Question if he had spotted the difference between rice pudding in the English style and rice used in curry in the Indian style. Had he encountered the use of Community (Italian) rice for rice pudding, which would make it feel like eating ball bearings in milk, and had he tried the use of pudding rice for Indian-style curry, which would taste like clotted wallpaper? Had this finally got through to the Commission and would it in future stop taxing imports of types of rice which cannot be produced in the Community? The Commissioner replied: 'I have some difficulty in answering for the Commission as a college on the issues which have been raised, but speaking for myself, I have established that the two types of rice – that used for curry and that used for rice puddings – are different. I do not know whether that answers the question. Certainly, as far as the Commission is concerned, we are actively considering research into both types of rice in order to establish which has the better market in the north of Europe.'

A political issue of interest to many MEPs, on a different scale, concerned stories about the controversial activities of the then President of Austria, Kurt Waldheim, during World War II when he was a German Army intelligence officer. On 3 March 1988, I asked the Parliament's President why my attempt to elicit the views of the European Council on this had been deemed inadmissible. On the face of it, I got nowhere with this but it broke the unhealthy convention that MEPs would not generally interfere in other Member States' activities even if such activities had a wider impact.

Another political issue revolved around Sir Joshua Hassan, Prime Minister of Gibraltar, who paid a visit to the European Parliament. I had heard that he had not been given the full diplomatic treatment normally accorded to a person of his standing – no doubt due to Spanish pressure. Apart from Question Time directed to Commissioners and Ministers, a question could be asked of the Parliament's own President. On 17 September 1987, I made use of this facility to ask: 'What facilities had been granted to the democratically elected Chief Minister of Gibraltar? As you know, it is normal in this Parliament for people of that status to be received officially, and I should like your assurance that these (courtesies) were in fact accorded to Sir Joshua.' The Parliament's President replied that this had only been a private visit. At least I had got this out into the open and deterred such behaviour towards Gibraltar becoming a precedent.

A matter wholly within the responsibilities of the British government, not the EU, was television. Yet this was something which would evidently come to have influences across borders. I have long thought that one of the forces encouraging violence in our society is television. Many television producers will broadcast anything they can get away with if it increases viewer numbers. Perhaps, in former times, idealism and public service were the guiding principles of the press, but nowadays it is too often just ratings – and, of course, bigger salaries for television and radio "personalities", presenters, chat show hosts, disc jockeys etc as a result. I raised the point in Strasbourg in September 1985. I said: 'For many of our young people born in the period in which it has been all around us, television is the biggest single influence in their lives. It is more real than reality itself. Imagine people living in a high-rise building: television shows them what they think real life is like.' I did not imagine that any useful action would come out of Europe on this but it got some publicity at home for the issue.

Sometimes humour helped to draw attention to a matter or to build a bridge with colleagues. In 1987 there was a resolution about the unique raised bogs of Ireland which were, and still are, threatened by the use of peat ("turf" to the Irish) for domestic fuel or for generating electricity. Bogs cover one sixth of the surface of Ireland. I could understand the concept of "blanket" bogs, deposits of partly-rotted plants, but "raised" bogs which apparently grow upwards from the hollows in which they were formed baffled me, so I steered clear of such technicalities. I gave an explanation of vote as follows:

'I rise to support the preservation of the Irish bogs. For your convenience, Mr President, I shall be brief. To every visitor to Ireland I say, go to the bogs, relieve the tensions of life, shut out the modern world and closet yourself in the special world of an Irish bog with birdsong and the fragrance of blanket bog vegetation all around and water gurgling beneath your feet. On my last visit to Ireland, after a busy week, I had time to go to the bogs, and there I watched a man who was cutting turf, flushed after his exertions, evidently nursing some deep private sadness. There in the words of one of the poets – I don't know whether it was W.B. Yeats – there he sat broken-hearted in the bogs. It brought home to me all the greatness, the sadness, the beauty, the timelessness of the bogs of Ireland – a moving experience indeed. I hope this may be preserved for ever. I shall support the motion, Mr President.'

The official record said there was laughter and applause. Paddy Lalor, an Irish MEP, commented: 'I was listening to Mr Pearce. He has this beautiful picture of all Irishmen sitting on the bog, drowsing and browsing.'

An Irish MEP, Tom Raftery, spoke about inculcating European trainees with the European spirit. Most British people viewed this as interfering nonsense. I tried to deflect the question by asking the Commission whether the "European spirit" might be esoteric and philosophical or do with ouzo, schnapps and poteen. I suggested that trainees should be more concerned with achieving practical results in building a genuine common market such as that proposed by the Kangaroo group, a business lobby. But I congratulated Mr Raftery on his motion, commenting on the fact that he bred kangaroos at his farm in Ireland, surely demonstrating a world spirit rather than a purely European one.

Anti-Europeans liked to mock the volume of EU laws sometimes citing the brevity of the Ten Commandments in comparison with some of the obscure and highly detailed EU Directives. It all depends what you compare with what. For example, as a template by which Christians should live, the Bible contains not just the Ten Commandments but a total of about 700,000 words.

At the end of 1988, the European Parliament's Research Service provided me with figures derived from the House of Commons Library, the EU Celex legal catalogue and Halsbury's Statutes of England. These showed that in 1987 and 1988, taken together, British legislation originating in the EU amounted to one Act of Parliament, 163 British Statutory Instruments based on EU measures and 2,790 EU regulations, making a total of 2,955 UK legislative documents derived from EU measures. In comparison, the total of purely British measures in the same period of time was 3,402 – 103 Acts of Parliament and 3,299 Statutory Instruments. EU measures therefore accounted for about forty-five per cent of the total legislative measure passing through Westminster.

Such comparisons, of course, give a far from comprehensive or balanced picture of the situation. British legislation covers many matters which Brussels does not touch. But the notion that the EU produces a blizzard of new laws compared with Westminster's output simply does not stand up. Nevertheless, the number of EU measures introduced reinforces how important it was and is for industry and commerce to pay proper attention to what is in the pipeline in Brussels and Strasbourg early enough in the legislative process to influence the outcome.[10]

I was not a member of the Parliament's Agriculture Committee but I kept myself aware of its work. The National Farmers Union (NFU) was certainly effective but I wondered if it was always wise in the approach it took. It was obsessed with subsidies for the bulk production of milk, meat, grain and so on. Only much more recently have farmers realised that if they produce what customers want to buy, guarantee the quality and brand it effectively, as many continental farmers realised long ago, they get better prices. In the twenty first century we see all manner of high-grade dairy and meat products proudly bearing the Union flag. Perhaps this is the result of the mass-audience cookery programmes which we now see on television and the emphasis in them on quality and provenance.

[10] See Appendix.

The NFU was one of the best sectoral lobby organisations in the British economy. Although it was subsequently reorganised on a regional basis, when I became an MEP in 1979 it operated on a county basis. The farmers were natural Conservative voters and they made their parliamentary representatives work for their money. I attended meetings of the county committee and *ad hoc* meetings to discuss particular issues.

Dairy farming was the predominant type of agriculture in my area. Cheshire has some of the most productive dairy country in Britain. Cheshire cheese was as famous in London centuries ago as it is today. Cheese made in many places is sold as Cheshire cheese. (It is far too late to apply for 'appellation controlée' status (controlled designation of origin).) The best Cheshire is that labelled "Farmhouse", which goes some way to protect the quality of some of the product. I tried to help one of the remaining producers of Farmhouse Cheshire. This producer could not obtain enough milk in certain months of the year because the milk distributors found it more profitable to send milk for processing into butter, much of which ended up in the butter mountains. There were many complaints about imports of New Zealand butter. The milk production quotas imposed on British farmers were lower than they would have otherwise been as a result of the quota for New Zealand imports. Maintenance of imports of New Zealand butter had been a major UK insistence when our country was negotiating to join the EU.

I had vigorously joined my colleagues in opposing the production of surplus milk and the consequent building up of the butter mountains. However much this excess production benefited the farmers, it was indefensible waste and highly unpopular with the rest of the population. Quotas on the production of milk were imposed by Brussels in 1984 on dairy producers in all EU countries in order to get rid of these infamous surpluses. Some of my farmers screamed blue murder when quotas on milk production were to be introduced. They complained that the government had recently been encouraging them to produce more, which had been true during World War II and in the years following it. Now they had to produce less. They had in fact been warned of this but, as an industry, chose not to take much notice of the warnings. Improvement of the marketing of their products seemed to be a low priority for them. The one way forward was to step up the marketing of their products so as to meet the demands of consumers and thereby achieve higher prices. Here I did not feel that the National Farmers Union and the Milk Marketing Board were as helpful as they might have been. Their minds were on bulk supply and national contracts. I wanted farmers to be more concerned about what customers wanted to buy, to respond to market conditions, to be concerned about what happened to their milk when it left the farm.

In a discussion with a Milk Marketing Board official, I asked why it was so difficult (at that time) to find a drink made of strawberry, raspberry or chocolate-flavoured milk in Britain. I had heard that in Australia such products competed well with cola drinks. The official expressed no interest and went back to his map showing the bulk movement of milk from one part of England to another, rather like Eisenhower directing his troops after the Normandy landings. Assessing what consumers might want did not seem to be on his agenda. However, flavoured milk has now become widely available in Britain, mainly due to the actions of manufacturers of chocolate and confectionery products.

I am pleased to say that the butter mountains were in due course greatly reduced. The quotas are due to finally disappear in 2015.

Another bone of contention with the farmers was the production of lamb, not originally covered by any EU scheme. When the EU scheme for what they call "sheep meat" ("viande ovine" in French) was brought in, Britain opted for a different system from other EU countries, one which offered make-up payments when the market price was below a certain level but clawed them back if the meat was exported. This of course damaged the export trade and lowered the price which farmers received. As the *Ellesmere Port Pioneer* put it on 17 September 1981, "It was difficult to complain because, basically, Britain had got what its negotiators wanted". The system was later changed, giving farmers much higher incomes for lamb production but increasing prices of the product in British shops.

One farmer (I'll call him Ralph) had been producing Jerusalem artichokes – the round artichokes rather like potatoes that are used for soup, not the vegetables like large, green flowers. When he complained that nobody wanted to buy them and that "the EU should do something about it," I suggested he should grow something else. I mentioned green peppers, for example, which, thanks to new types of seed, could now be grown in more northerly climes than previously. 'I don't want to grow green peppers,' he said. 'I want to grow Jerusalem artichokes.' Ralph was very determined. He would phone my office quite often with his complaint, usually in the middle of the afternoon but sometimes late at night, from a phone box outside his local pub, sometimes asking me to pay for the call. On one occasion he drove up to the home of the local MP at about midnight, got out, headlights shining into the house, slammed the car door and demanded

1O DOWNING STREET

LONDON SW1A 2AA

THE PRIME MINISTER   5th June, 1989

Dear Andrew,

Thank you for your letter of 26th May.

I am most concerned to learn that you have found that some of
our supporters believe that we should not have entered the
Community and do not intend to vote on June 15th. I have always
made it absolutely clear in all of my speeches that we are
fully committed to our membership of the Community and that it
is essential that we should win the elections for the European
Parliament. I enclose a copy of my latest speech to the
Conservative Women's Conference, from which you may like to
quote. It makes clear that the choice before us is <u>either</u> a
Socialist <u>or</u> a Conservative European Parliament. So every one
of <u>our</u> voters is vital to <u>our</u> future.

With best wishes

Yours ever

Margaret

Andrew Pearce Esq

Word from the top

to see the poor politician! On another occasion, he went to Blackpool during the annual Conservative conference and, despite the security, found his way to the bedroom of one of the British Conservative MEPs.

A company in my constituency which packed nuts for the pub and supermarket trade was under threat from new competition in Italy. The company had been importing nuts from Turkey. An Italian firm had been given an EU grant, not only to grow hazelnuts but also to pack them. On 19 May 1988, I asked a question which in effect demanded that the nut-processing industries of northern Europe, particularly those in areas of high unemployment like Merseyside, should not be penalised by EU grants being given for the processing and packing of nuts in southern Europe where new crops of nuts were being grown. I had come across the information on which this question was based in the course of committee discussions. Neither Whitehall nor the firm's own trade association had spotted it.

Although health care was outside the scope of the EU, it was not uncommon to compare national health systems between countries. In the early 1980s, before improved NHS accounting procedures were put in place, I talked with two medical consultants about continental health systems. In many countries, the system is that everyone has to have medical insurance and then the insurance companies pay out the greater part, but not the total, of any costs arising from illness or injury. Such a system means that the patient has an interest in the size of the bill and the doctor too has an interest in justifying the cost of treatment both to the patient and to the insurance companies. The two consultants with whom I spoke were not impressed. 'Of course, you cannot set a price for treatment. Every case is different. It all depends on circumstances,' they said. 'No accounting system for an insurance scheme would ever work. Far too complicated and you would never get the right figure.' I explained that in continental countries where insurance-based health care operated, there were far fewer complaints about the service provided than there were about our own NHS. Courtesy prevented me commenting that British doctors are quite capable of carrying out the necessary accounting procedures when they see patients privately!

I obtained a personal view of paying privately for health care. I have a recurring eye problem and at intervals over the years had to have a test to monitor the problem; this involved using a machine. When I had the test carried out in Brussels, I would phone the doctor who answered on his mobile phone. I went to his surgery at the appointed time and pressed the doorbell. The doctor let me in by pressing a button in his surgery. I had the test. The doctor gave me some pills free of charge and then wrote out the bill which I paid in cash. The doctor gave me a receipt and I departed. I submitted the bill for partial reimbursement to the EU medical insurance people which provided cover for MEPs and European Commission staff. When I had the same test done in Britain, I went to the local private hospital to be greeted by a beautiful receptionist, flowers, newspapers and coffee. The test, the machine and the pills were the same as in Brussels. The consultant sent me the bill by post. I paid this by post, asking for a receipt to submit for reimbursement. At the end of it, the bill for the private British consultation was twice that of the Belgian bill – for examination by the same machine, receiving the same advice and being supplied the same type of pills. What I got for the higher UK charge was the beautiful receptionist, the flowers, the newspapers and the coffee!

Another topic which concerned me was drug abuse – a problem in several parts of my constituency. I worked on this with Sir Jack Stewart-Clark, a colleague MEP and draftsman of a European Parliament report on drugs. I invited parents from several EU countries to Strasbourg to launch EURAD (Europe Against Drugs) and worked with Parents Against Drug Abuse (PADA) in Birkenhead. I frequently raised the problem of the open sale of certain drugs in Amsterdam, which I called "the drugs capital of Europe". In my office I kept a menu from an Amsterdam café advertising various drugs. I wanted to show people how slack the rules were in the Netherlands. In my constituency a small

Lord Plumb. Enrico Vinci, Secretary General of the European Parliament in the background.

government-funded agency was set up to take particular actions to mitigate drug-taking. Its programme was to last two years. The official appointed to lead this, on a two-year employment contract, set out to do his best to fulfil the tasks laid down, and, very evidently, to do so in such a way that a further two-year contract would be provided for him when the present one was finished!

I did not have much to do with the world of high finance but I did have one small brush with "City" people in 1982. Word came to me from a confident source that the British government intended to remove the exemption from value-added tax of gold coins which were legal tender in the countries in which they were produced. (This was to prevent the VAT-free purchase of gold coins and their subsequent melting down by criminals into bullion at a time when the sale of bullion itself was liable to VAT). I called a meeting of half a dozen City of London people about it at the Institute of Directors' building in Pall Mall in London. I thought it would be useful for companies in this line of trade to be aware of proposed changes and either to make representations against it or to prepare themselves to deal with the new situation. The Bank of England very reluctantly sent somebody after repeated requests for them to do so. All those present pooh-poohed my warning. They were adamant that my warning was without foundation, with the clear implication that I, coming from far away Cheshire and Merseyside, couldn't possibly know about this sort of thing. The meeting got nowhere. Three weeks later value-added tax was imposed on those gold coins! I wrote to the people who had attended the meeting to remind them of my warning.

★ ★ ★

Much is said nowadays about how little politicians are thought to understand the world in which we live. The Industry and Parliament Trust is an organisation which arranges for MPs and MEPs to have several in-depth visits to a particular industrial or commercial company to learn how the real world operates. I was invited to make use of its services and made very interesting visits to several installations owned by Blue Circle Cement. One of its cement plants was on the site where the Blue Water shopping complex was later built in Kent. The company also owned a quarry in the Derbyshire Dales. There were plenty of people who complained about having such an industry in such a beautiful area, despite the great efforts made by the company to mitigate noise and traffic. The complainers did not include nearby residents who depended on the quarry for their incomes and the revenues which the quarry brought to the area.

All that foreign-speak

In much of our work, the British MEPs had to combat the constant desire of the French to dominate the EU. Perhaps this was a throwback to the heady days of King Louis XIV (1638-1715) when France really was top-dog nation in Western Europe. After World War II, Germany was content to let France dominate the EU politically; in return Germany wished to exercise economic domination. This did not suit Britain! The French saw no conflict between being strongly pro-France and strongly pro-EU. They integrated many of their policy objectives at the national and European levels. They were frequently better prepared than the UK to take initiatives in the EU. The UK often seemed to be merely reactive or passive. We should have been – and to a considerable extent were – the biggest gainers from creating a real common market. The general desire of the French to dominate particularly concerned the use of their language.

I took many opportunities to oppose the supposition that France and the French language were privileged in the EU. It was originally the custom that all the notices in the committee rooms indicating where people should sit, such as *Conseil* (Council), *Démocrates européens* and *Secrétaire*, were always in French. Having protested in vain for some time about this, I went round to one of the committee rooms one day and tore up all the notices in French. I also protested about the naming of the European Commission's London office *Jean Monnet House*, after one of the EU's founding fathers. In a statement reported in the *Liverpool Daily Post* in 1988 I said it should have been called 'Margaret Thatcher House' as she had done as much as anyone to create a sensible, freedom-loving Europe. I added that the Commission's office in Paris might be renamed *'Maison Maggie'*. None of these actions in themselves had much effect, but, as is the way of politics, actions follow the direction of opinion. What I and other British MEPs tried to do was to shift what was regarded as the natural viewpoint inside the European Parliament.

As the years have gone by and more countries have joined the EU, English has been firmly recognised as the main language of communication, while

91

respecting the rights of people for whom it is not their mother tongue.[11] The dominance of English has come about without any formal decision that it should be the pre-eminent EU language. It would be very good for the British if everyone spoke English but it would be as unacceptable to suggest that only English be used in EU debates and documentation, as to suggest they should all be in French or German only.

When I became an MEP, Members attending plenary debates in Strasbourg were provided with full interpretation amongst the languages then used. These were Danish, German, Italian, Dutch, French and English, to which Greek, Spanish and Portuguese were added as the countries using these languages joined the EU. For plenary meetings, interpreters sat in booths behind the Members, listening to what each MEP was saying into the microphone on his desk. Each interpreter rendered the speech into one of the other languages so that every MEP could follow the proceedings in his or her own language through ear phones. As the number of languages in use increased, it became necessary for speeches in the less-used languages to be interpreted into one of the "bridge" languages, usually English or French, and then re-interpreted into each of the other languages. Naturally, some of the meaning and style became lost and the rhetoric blunted by this process. Several Greek MEPs who had an excellent command of English would switch to English when vital points were being made so as to be sure that their meaning came across properly.

Official EU publications had colour-coded stripes or spines for ease of identification – purple for English, blue for French, yellow for German etc. When Ireland joined the EU in 1979, the same year as Britain, Irish was nominated as an "official" language. I was told that the translation of the Treaty of Rome into Irish, colour-coded black, was such a burden on the Irish linguistic community that Ireland has been content with English since then. That said, the first words spoken in the European Parliament by Jack Lynch, the then President of the European Council of Ministers, were in Irish Gaelic, about which Ian Paisley lodged strong protests. Myra, my wife, having been obliged to study Irish at school like all Irish children, once told me that the Irish language has no clear equivalent for "Yes" and "No". This may be the cause of much uncertainty as to Irish intentions!

[11] On a visit to Brussels in 2009, I attended a meeting of representatives of chambers of commerce from all over the EU. Although interpretation was available, of some three hundred delegates I could only see four who were using it. Almost everyone spoke and listened in English.

When Austria was negotiating to become a member of the EU, there was talk of demands from Austria for providing interpretation and translation between *German* German and *Austrian* German, which had a number of its own distinctive words. Austrians (and Bavarians) greet each other with *Grüß Gott* – May God greet you – instead of *Guten Morgen* or *Guten Tag* used in most of Germany for Good Morning or Good Day. Fortunately, sense prevailed and there is just one system for interpretation to and from German.

Languages can do much to divide nations. Having some knowledge of the local language, even just a few words, is useful for the traveller, notwithstanding the increasing use of English throughout the world. Being able to speak the local language is also a courtesy to local people – and much better than shouting, which some Brits still resort to.

When using English, it is best to speak clearly and slowly and avoid linguistic clutter. Phrases like *"sort of"*, *"what do you call it"*, *"more or less"*, *"might as well"* and *"if you don't mind me saying so"* all add little to the meaning conveyed and confuse people who have poor command of English. Some British regional accents like Glaswegian, Geordie or Scouse can be difficult for foreigners. However, I noticed that the greatest problems seemed to be with Cockney and old-fashioned Oxford English, I think because these two accents involve altering the normal vowels into diphthongs. Also, Scots, Merseysiders and Tynesiders know they have accents and often tone them down when speaking with foreigners, but too many people with Cockney or Estuary English accents believe that they speak standard English, when this is in reality far from the case.

One can be beguiled into thinking that one knows the meaning of a foreign word when in fact it means something quite different. In French, *toilette* means toilet or loo but can also mean dress, appearance or make-up (as in toilet bag). I was told of a Belgian Prime Minister who, not understanding the full subtlety of this difference, arrived in Washington and complimented the smartly-attired American President's wife on her "toilet"!

In Germany, Belgium and the Netherlands, staff in restaurants use the equivalent of 'please' when they bring something to you – *"bitte"* or *"s'il vous plait"* or *"alstublieft"*. But in France they use the English equivalent of *"there you are"* – *"violà"*. If you say *"Danke"* meaning *"thank you"* in Germany when a waiter approaches with the menu, he goes away again, thinking that you don't want it. Until I got the hang of this, I found it quite embarrassing to be offered a menu three or four times through failing to understand that my response meant '*no thanks*' to them, causing them to go away.

The use of *"thee"* and *"thou"* has more or less died out in England but on the continent it is very important to get the use of the equivalent words right. In Belgium, where I learned to shake hands with each of my Belgian office colleagues at the beginning of every day, it would be many months before it was suggested to me by my colleagues that we could call each other the more familiar *"tu"* instead of the more formal *"vous"*. There is even a French verb for this: *"tutoyer"* meaning to accept the mutual use of *"tu"* with a particular person. The singular form '*tu*' is usually used when talking to children.

Differences within one language can present problems to native speakers. One of the Heads of Unit for whom I worked in the European Commission was an Italian Baron; he was a scion of a famous family and had spent all his working life in the Commission. He had some bitter fights with one of the Commission's team of translators. "This isn't good Italian," stormed my Head of Unit. 'I can't understand it!' The translator responded by saying, 'If you write it like *you* want to, in the grammatical style of the 1940s, nobody in Italy today will understand it.'

There is a linguistic problem in parts of Spain. Barcelona is the capital of the region of Catalonia, which has its own language, and it is common to see multilingual notices outside restaurants bearing menus seeking to attract tourists. However, the Spanish version has often been scratched out by some linguistic zealot, leaving the Catalan, German and English versions intact.

I have heard it said many times that the French refuse to speak English. Whatever may have been the case in the past, it is seldom the case now. I myself have never met a difficulty of this kind. In any case, why should one not try to use the language of the country one is in (an argument which no doubt appeals to the people of North Wales!). Indeed, many young French men and women are so keen today to speak English that it is difficult to get them to speak French, even if their English is not very good. At one time the French government discouraged the use of languages other than standard French in those parts of their country which had local languages, such as Alsace, Brittany and southern France. I was surprised to find recently that the school in south west France where my daughter and her children live, now teaches Occitan to the children. When my daughter and her husband were negotiating through a solicitor to buy a house from an old lady, they took along a French/English dictionary. The old lady carried a French/Occitan dictionary with the same intent.

A Parliament of characters

A total of 410 MEPs were elected in 1979; 434 in 1984 and 518 in 1989, Greece, Spain and Portugal having joined the EU over this period. These MEPs belonged to a large number of political parties in their various countries. In the European Parliament they formed themselves into Groups, each of which had to contain Members from several EU countries. The Socialist Group was the biggest of the Groups and contained Members from all the EU countries, including the British Labour party Members. The European People's Party, consisting of mainly German and Italian Christian Democrats, was the second largest Group.

There was a Communist Group made up partly of Stalinist French Members and partly of Italians. The latter oddly agreed with the British Conservatives on many EU issues. (These Italian Communists were united in their dislike of the political power of the Roman Catholic Church). There was also the Liberal Group which was generally to the right of the British Conservatives and was very strong on individual human rights. Winnie Ewing of the Scottish Nationalists was a member of this Group. There were also various Independent Members including the Rev. Ian Paisley of the Northern Ireland Democratic and Unionist Party and some extraordinary Italian Radicals. Each Group had a staff of researchers and assistants, paid for by the European Parliament. The Groups aimed to determine their policy as a bloc and usually succeeded in doing so although differences between the national component parts of Groups sometimes made this impossible.

We British Conservatives were initially allied with a number of Danes and later with members of the Spanish Alianza Popular, forming the European Conservative Group, which later became the European Democratic Group (EDG). As regards the British MEPs, in 1979 there were four who were also currently Conservative Members of the House of Commons plus one former Conservative MP and a couple of Conservative Members of the House of Lords. The MPs did not maintain their dual mandates at the succeeding UK national elections. It was considered that the first leader of the EDG should be one of the MPs. Jim (later Sir James) Scott-Hopkins got the job. He held the Group together and survived a good deal of criticism from Downing Street over some of the pronouncements of some of the members of the Group. The other holders of dual mandates were Jim Spicer, Elaine Kellett-Bowman and Tom Normanton.

The EDG intended, like the other Groups, to determine how its Members should vote in the hemicycle. There could be votes on every paragraph of every parliamentary resolution and every European Commission proposal. In general, EDG members followed the agreed line. The Group's view was normally in line with the policies of the UK Conservative Party, then in government, but the Group did not always welcome being dictated to by the party at home. This upset the Tory leadership at home on not a few occasions. One bone of contention was over the vote for the leadership of the Group. Mrs Thatcher thought that she could decide on her own who the EDG's leader should be. She was forced to realise that while she could decide who the leader of the British Members of the EDG should be, she did not have the authority to decide who should be the leader of the Group as a whole including its Danish and Spanish members.

The Groups had several functions and powers. Senior positions in the Parliament such as that of the President and the Committee Chairmen were determined by the *d'Hondt* system. This is a method of dividing up the places to be filled proportionately to the number of MEPs in each Group, which could be called its quota. A simple division of places could result in the biggest Group not only receiving the most places but also the most sought-after places. The *d'Hondt* system provides for the largest Group to choose one position first, the next largest Group next and so on up to the limit of each Group's quota. This results not only in a proportionate allocation of places but permits each Group to share in the most sought-after places.

The Groups could and did produce policy statements. In 1981, Jim Scott-Hopkins asked me to chair a working party of Tory MEPs to prepare a policy booklet on agricultural policy. Alasdair Hutton, Kent Kirk (a Danish colleague), Robert Jackson, Sir Fred Warner, Christopher Prout (later Lord Kingsland), David Curry and Paul Howell were part of the team. The press asked why I had been asked to lead this rather than David Curry, the Group's spokesman on agriculture or Henry Plumb, the former President of the National Farmers' Union and later the President of the European Parliament. Perhaps my relative ignorance of farming matters and the fact that nobody could possibly accuse me of being an agent of the farmers was the reason.

In fact I myself and Stephen Hurst, the group's staff expert on farming, did most of the work with input notably from Robert Jackson. Stephen and I completed the draft in the Conservative Party office in Ormskirk in Lancashire, near my family home. I had the cover designed by an artist I knew in West Kirby, who produced exactly the right image I wanted to convey. The cover illustrated the theme of the booklet which was that farmers should produce the types and quality of food that the market wanted, not just food for its own sake. Nobody could or ever will change agricultural policy overnight but the scandal of food mountains has come to an end and there has been a vast improvement in the marketing of British farm produce.

Showing a local farmer a booklet on farm policy which I edited

Henry Plumb was no linguist but had great charm and persuasiveness. In October 1985, Henry asked me to initiate a more regular flow of material from the EU to the UK media about our colleagues' activities. The planning, timeliness, drafting and volume of material fed to the media by our Group were capable of improvement, as I believe I proved. There were three factors which limited success in showing the European Parliament in general, and the EDG in particular, in a good light.

The first was the determination of the media to rubbish the Parliament. Certain London newspapers live by mockery and scorn, whether justified by the facts or not. The fact that events in Brussels and Strasbourg interrupted the cosy life of political journalists, who otherwise didn't have to move far from their watering holes in Westminster, made matters worse.

The second factor was that a number of Westminster MPs were very willing to take every opportunity to knock the EU and the European Parliament. I think that some of this stemmed from resentment that, having got to the top of the ladder or close to it (in London), they found that many of the political decisions were not taken any more in London but in Brussels and Strasbourg.

I heard criticism of the salaries and expenses of MEPs. This was strange as British MEPs' salaries were pegged until 2009 so as to be to precisely the same as those of British MPs. The expenses which MEPs received were not dissimilar to those of MPs, albeit paid in different ways. For example, MEPs received cash allowances to pay for staff and office costs whereas comparable facilities were provided for MPs without the MPs handling the cash involved. A further point was that many MPs have other paid jobs, as lawyers, consultants, company directors etc. It was difficult for MEPs, especially provincial ones, to have outside jobs because of the time occupied by Parliament meetings on the continent and the travel involved getting there.

The last factor was most intractable, but something within our own Group's responsibility; this was a reluctance by some of my colleagues to go for the jugular, to fire from the hip. In my view, the media is a key way of influencing governments and voters. To use the media effectively means you must know the facts, understand how the media and the voters will view matters and be willing to give opinions rapidly and clearly. This approach brings the risk of getting things wrong or of ruffling feathers by mistake. But a bland press release, issued a day or two after an event reached the attention of the journalists, however "well-honed", is a complete waste of time. The leadership of our Group was not always interested enough or determined enough to win points through the media.

Some of my colleague MEPs of other parties had been or still were Members of the House of Commons. These included Barbara Castle, John Tomlinson, Ian Paisley, John Hume and John D. Taylor. Other MEPs went on to careers in Westminster after service in the European Parliament. These included Labour's Geoff Hoon, Joyce Quinn and Richard Caborn, and the Tories' Eric Forth, David Harris, Robert Jackson, Gloria Hooper (later Baroness Hooper) and David Curry, all of whom attained ministerial office. John Marshall became an MP; Christopher Prout (who later became leader of the EDG) entered the House of Lords as Lord Kingsland, and John Tomlinson (Labour) as Lord Tomlinson. In contrast to most of their English, Scottish and Welsh colleagues at the time when they became MEPs, the three Northern Ireland MEPs (Ian Paisley, John D Taylor and John Hume) were already well-known, established politicians.

The EDG was not short of characters. Dame Elaine Kellett-Bowman was one of them. She had a heart of gold and a voice which became shrill when she was aroused. She had a determination that the rules should be followed. It was the practice that small meeting rooms in the Parliament building were allocated to Members for meetings for various purposes for one-hour periods. Usually a little tolerance was allowed when a meeting of one group of people was to be followed immediately by a meeting of another group. As far as Elaine was concerned, when it was time for her meeting to start, she came into the room and took a place at the table even if the previous meeting was still going on. If the previous group showed no sign of leaving, she would get out the previous week's edition of the *Lancaster Guardian* and a large pair of scissors and do her press cuttings.

In certain continental cities, the tourist guidebooks list not only respectable night clubs but also red-light establishments. Booklets containing such information were available at the City of Strasbourg's information desk in the European Parliament's building. Dame Elaine was so affronted by the references to red-light districts and what they represented that she commanded that all the copies be sent to her office. She then systematically tore the offending pages out of each and returned the purged booklets to the information desk for distribution.

Sir Jim Scott-Hopkins, our Group leader, had, at an earlier date, been on an information visit with colleagues to Angola. The convoy of vehicles in which the MEPs were travelling came into conflict with a rhinoceros, which overturned one of them. The rhino then moved off and the party scrambled out of the vehicles. Jim decided to answer a call of nature behind a tree. The rhino first went away and then came back towards the group causing Jim to "run for his life". "Run" should be taken in the figurative sense. The life-style of MEPs of mature years is not consistent with maintaining a highly athletic physical condition. It would therefore be more accurate to say that the intrepid Member "moved with all possible speed" to avoid the rhino. He duly reached safety. 'Damn near thing', he said afterwards, 'almost caught myself in my zip!'

Sir Tom Normanton came from a Manchester textile family. He arranged for his firm to manufacture ties bearing the European Parliament's badge. I wore one of them when Her Majesty the Queen and the Duke of Edinburgh came to Ellesmere Port. The Duke asked me what it was. I explained the badge, which consisted of "EP" above "PE". The Duke commented that it was good to see the English version of the initials above the French version. The royal couple's next stop was in Tom's constituency. Tom was there, tie thrust forward as prominently as possible. 'May I explain this tie, your Royal Highness?' said Tom. 'Oh, I know all about that,' said the Duke. 'Just seen one down the road in Ellesmere Port.' Collapse of morale by Sir Tom!

At the opening session of the Parliament, Tom tried a House of Commons tactic to wrong-foot the President of the Commission, Roy Jenkins. "What are your engagements for today?' he asked. This was in order to give him a chance to ask a supplementary question on any subject he liked, for which the Commissioner could have made no preparation. The Commissioner duly responded. It might have looked slick in the House of Commons but it went down like a lead balloon in Strasbourg. The European Parliament was not the House of Commons – and nor did it want to be!

When the elected European Parliament held its first session in 1979, the rules decreed that the oldest member should preside over the election of its president. Needless to say, the French were well prepared. The oldest member was French – Louise Weiss – so she had the honour of speaking the first words in the elected Parliament. (Her name was perpetuated in the title of a new Parliament building constructed in Strasburg a few years later.) The French were also ready for the election of the first President of the elected Parliament. They put forward the strongest candidate for the job, Simone Veil, who was duly elected. Mme Veil was a former French Health Minister and a Jewish survivor of the Auschwitz death camp. When she became President she neither spoke nor understood English. In her first long summer vacation, she took a language course in the USA and came back speaking English with a strong American accent.

Sir James Spicer nearly always wore a Parachute Regiment tie. He was of the "Come on chaps; let's rally to the colours" school. One of his later jobs for the party was trying to drum up votes for the Conservatives among the British living in retirement in Spain after expatriate Brits had been given limited voting rights in European elections. I was one of several MEPs who visited one of the British enclaves on the Costas to tout for votes.

Barbara Castle (Baroness Castle, to use her title, though she herself seemed to avoid using it on the continent) was the most well-known of the British MEPs and sat with the leadership of the European Socialist Group. The British press always viewed her as a star performer because of what she had been rather than for what she did in the European Parliament. Though past her best days, Barbara had an extraordinary skill in hitting the nail on the head and selecting the most telling moment to do so.

With (L to R) MEPs Ken Collins, Barbara Castle and Janey Buchan in the corridors of the European Parliament in Strasbourg

Bob Battersby was the Tory spokesman on fishing matters and spoke about it frequently – and at length. He was a Yorkshireman and had been sales director of a major engineering firm. While serving with MI6 at the end of the Second World War during the successful British efforts to prevent a Communist takeover of Greece, he became a proficient Greek speaker, but with a Yorkshire accent! He could speak nearly a dozen languages.

Sir Peter Vanneck was a former Lord Mayor of London. He and I went to a ceremony to commemorate the victims of a Nazi concentration camp at Natzweiler-Struthof in a forest near Strasbourg. We wanted to counter the impression that a number of Socialist MEPs were spreading that members of their party had been alone in crushing fascism. We travelled in Peter's sports car, in which he drove down to Strasbourg for the plenary sessions. On the way back, we were caught in a police radar speed trap. Peter, who spoke very little French, pulled out his European Parliament identity card. I explained to the police inspector that this gave him exemption from prosecution. The officer radioed his superiors who confirmed that this was the case. Peter did not understand the inspector's words but the reprimand was quite clear. The officer saluted. Peter took out a small pouch of snuff, sniffed a pinch luxuriously and then with great dignity looked the officer in the eye, started the engine and drove the car off at speed. Peter gave the appearance of taking the job of being an MEP fairly lightly, perhaps because he did not indulge in some of the Euro-waffle that some of our colleagues perpetrated, but he was a shrewd operator who would sometimes bring common sense to bear where others failed to do so.

Madron Seligman, a lifelong friend of Sir Edward Heath, led various campaigns in the European Parliament against cruelty to animals. I worked with him in trying to get bullfighting banned in Spain. He himself campaigned against the use of tiger cubs for tourists to hold while pictures were being taken by professional photographers on beaches in Spain. The tiger cubs were drugged to make them docile and sometimes had had their teeth extracted so that people could stroke them without fear of being bitten. Madron was a great wit and played the piano at the Tory MEPs' Christmas party for Flanders-and-Swan type songs with Adam Ferguson.

Ken Collins, a Scottish Labour Member, was a long-time member of the Committee on Environment, Public Health and Consumer Protection. The considerable expertise he developed on these topics proved the value of allowing politicians to stay in the same area of politics long enough to really master the subject.

One of the oddities of life at Strasbourg was that John Hume, John D. Taylor and Ian Paisley, all MEPs as well as Westminster MPs, were quite civil to each other in private and co-operated on bread-and-butter issues affecting

Northern Ireland. John Hume and some of the Parliamentary staff of Irish nationality used to have dinner regularly in a particular restaurant. This was known to us, for some reason, as the Bang o' Bells. Customers did not have to bang a bell to gain entry but they did have to press a bell push. John's friends and John himself usually sang Irish folksongs, sometimes in Gaelic, after the meal. I was invited to join them several times and was often the only English person at their table.

Ian Paisley could be witty – in a strange way. The seats in the hemicycle allocated to his Group were on the back row, underneath the public gallery. Unfamiliar with needing a microphone to magnify his booming voice at home, at first he did not realise that if he did not switch his microphone on, the interpreters could not hear his words and relay them in the other languages. On one occasion, finding that the lights under the gallery had not been switched on, he called out to the president in a loud and declamatory voice, 'Would you please shed some light on our darkness.' Enough of the Members knew their biblical references sufficiently well for his point to be understood. One day, I had made some remarks in the hemicycle which were taken to be fairly humorous. Ian came up beaming all over his face, punched me jovially on the shoulder, and said, 'That was a great bit of crack!' I reeled back under this sudden gesture of affection. As I regained my balance he came back, beaming even more broadly and gave me another blow on the shoulder as he repeated the remark.

In countries which have proportional voting systems, each party tries to have some of everything on its list: candidates young and old, more right-wing and more-left wing, northern and southern, fervent about this and loquacious about that. The Dutch Socialists had MEPs specialising in Third World aid, consumer protection, social affairs and so on. Hemmo Muntingh was their specialist on protection of wildlife. He did much work on protecting whales, tigers and so on but took little interest in debates on consumer affairs, which were part of the remit of the same committee as environmental matters.

George Marché, leader of the French Communist party, was top of his party's European voting list but I never heard of him setting foot inside the European Parliament once elected. Jean-Marie Le Pen carried the flag of the French extreme right in the Parliament. He was usually accompanied by a huge ex-boxer with a cauliflower ear. Rumour had it that this man carried a pistol.

An extraordinary Italian Christian Democrat was Giovanni Bersani, who, according to legend, played a part in the resistance to Communist insurgents in Bologna at the end of the Second World War. He was President of the ACP – European Union Joint Parliamentary Assembly (of which more later). Bersani was immensely long-winded, a hopeless chairman in any situation requiring firmness, but a great conciliator and a charming companion. He had apparently been everywhere in the developing world. His passport, through overuse, was a collection of separate pages in random order.

I heard of an incident when Bersani had to give a lengthy speech in some distant place. He had to use a prepared text which had already been issued to the media and to make use of a screen for showing pictures illustrating his theme. He was therefore aghast when he discovered on entering the conference hall that he had left his essential reading glasses on the plane. The only person on the conference platform who had the same type of lenses as his was the conference chairman – an elegant African lady with a broad nose; she had bright red butterfly-style spectacles. Undeterred, Bersani persuaded the lady to lend him her glasses to read his speech. He had great difficulty keeping them from slipping down his own relatively slender nose while holding his speech notes, the microphone and a baton for pointing to the screen.

I saw him several years after we had both left the European Parliament. We were on a moving walkway, a *travelator*, in Zurich airport, but going in opposite directions. When I came within his focus (he had very poor sight and thick spectacles) his eyes filled with emotion. We spoke for a few seconds as we passed on our respective walkways. Then, perforce, we went in our respective directions, never to meet again.

Bruno Ferrero was a charming Italian Communist, who often voted the same way as the British Conservatives. (This is a comment on the Communists' lack of truly socialist inspiration, not a suggestion that the Tories had gone left!) I had a long car journey with him in South Africa. Sharing a car for many miles is one of the best ways of getting to know someone. He wanted to know how I, as a British Conservative, got on with the Afrikaners.

'Not at all well,' I told him. 'I am totally opposed to the apartheid system which most of them support.'

'But surely, as they are of British origin, you must think the same way as they do,' he said. I explained carefully that the Afrikaaners were of predominantly Dutch and French, not British, origin. He was amazed.

'Surely their language, Afrikaans, is derived from English?' he said. I explained the error of his thought. He was the Communist Group's spokesman on South Africa!

A Danish member of the EDG was Klaus Toksvig, a well-known TV personality in Denmark. His daughter, Sandi, now a writer, broadcaster and a comedy star on the BBC, visited us sometimes in Brussels. Klaus had a house in Surrey.

Otto von Habsburg was a descendant of the former imperial house of the Austro-Hungarian Empire and would have become emperor had the dynasty survived. The story was told that one day when he was sitting in the hemicycle, the MEP next to him arrived late. 'I'm afraid I was watching the Austria/Hungary football match on television,' he said. 'Oh?' said Otto. 'Austria-Hungary? Who were they playing against?'

One of the German MEPs had been in trouble in her country on charges relating to terrorism. I spoke to her at length during a barbecue on a visit to Africa. She had never spoken to a British Conservative before and initially viewed me as an incarnation of the devil. But she warmed to me as I tried to demonstrate that we had honourable and worthy aims, and that if we were sometimes aggressive in the European Parliament, it was to expose the inefficiency and immorality that the then fashionable socialism often entrained.

Olivier D'Ormesson, a French Liberal, was a close ally of the British Conservatives – except on farming matters. He told me his family had owned some of the land on which Charles de Gaulle Airport was built. He himself, as was the case with several of the French members, had been a local councillor, the mayor of a small town and the holder of various national offices. He was the soul of courtesy and a natural ally of the more upper-class Tories. He spoke English well and willingly but always called me "Purse".

Emma Bonino was an Italian Radical who later became a European Commissioner. She often worked with Marco Pannella, another Italian Radical, who could bring a debate in the European Parliament almost to a halt by raising points of order, mostly not judged valid but all containing enough sense to require an answer. His vote and those of other Radicals could sometimes swing the outcome of vote in the hemicycle. Pannella and Bonino gave the rest of us an insight into Italian politics. Their main driving force seemed to be opposition to the power held by, and sometimes abused by, the Roman Catholic Church in Italy and suspicions about its relationship with the Mafia. On one occasion they organised a meeting with an Italian national MP, Ilona Staller, a Hungarian-born Italian porn-star and campaigner on many radical issues. Known as *La Cicciolina*, meaning *Cuddles*, she was formerly a porn star whose trademark attire, I was told, was a low-cut dress exposing one breast. This meeting took place in her hotel bedroom with, I hasten to add, the star fully clothed and with about thirty journalists also present. *La Cicciolina* would switch on a beaming smile and flutter her eyelashes when the cameras were on her and switch back to grim seriousness the moment they moved away.

T. J. Maher, generally known as "TeeJay", was an elderly Irish MEP who spent every waking hour defending the interests of Irish farmers. One day when the next Euro-election was in sight, I saw him munching a ham sandwich in a rather smooth little bar-cum-restaurant behind a block of flats near the European Parliament in Brussels. 'No, I'm not standing again,' he said. 'I've done ten years. I've got this little farm in Donegal. I want to get some mud on my boots again.'

A German MEP, Frau Bloch Undine-Uta von Blottnitz, lectured the world on the need to "go green". I understood that she lived in a castle. She was always absent from the Parliament on a certain day of the year because, so it was said, she had to be at home for some kind of rural festival which her tenants attended.

Another German MEP, Dieter Rogalla, had a passion for getting rid of frontier formalities when crossing from one EU country to another. In the summer he would ride his bicycle around Europe, challenging the legality of customs and passport controls as being contrary to the Treaty of Rome. He appeared one day in the hemicycle waving posters calling for frontier procedures to be banned. There has been a great deal of progress in easing the crossing of frontiers more recently through the Schengen Agreement of 1985 which abolished frontier controls between most EU countries. The UK however maintained its border controls except for the border between the Irish Republic and Northern Ireland – across which, one might have thought, most of the terrorists seeking to attack targets within the UK at that time would have come!

Pierre Pflimlin, a native of Alsace, was one of several former Prime Ministers who became MEPs. His name is similar to the German word *Pflaumlein*, meaning a "little plum". Not to confused with our own Henry Plumb! M. Pflimlin was also the Mayor of Strasbourg. He always seemed a little perplexed at the sometimes vigorous parliamentary behaviour of the British MEPs. Such behaviour was loosely based on House of Commons standards.

Vigour was sometimes necessary to combat French assumptions, often limply supported by German MEPs, that *their* way was always the right way. The French were often much better prepared in their tactics and better supported by their national authorities than British MEPs.

Another former Prime Minister who became an MEP was Willy Brandt. (He had been born Herbert Ernst Karl Frahm but changed his name after escaping to Norway in 1934 to avoid the Nazis.) He later became Mayor of West Berlin and then Chancellor of West Germany from 1969 to 1974.

With MEP Seàn Flanagan

Michel Poniatowski, a large man, in all senses, whose family had princely origins in Poland and had been Minister of the Interior in France. Just before a profoundly boring OECD meeting in Paris one day, I found him reading in a French newspaper some alleged scandal about his personal life. Conscious of how the British press lambasts any politician caught *in flagrante*, I asked him whether he was concerned about this negative publicity. He just laughed. A British politician would have been deeply worried.

"Ponia", as he was always known, had been put out to grass in the European Parliament by his French right-wing colleagues. He was made Chairman of the Parliament's Committee on Development and Cooperation, responsible for overseeing relations with the Third World, especially Africa. The French viewed their links with their former colonies in Africa as of considerable importance as markets for French imports and exports. In an effort to curb the loquacity of some of the speakers on his committee, Ponia bought a large egg timer about 25 centimetres tall and containing bright blue sand. At this time, while speeches in the plenary sessions of the Parliament were strictly limited – two, five or ten minute limits being commonplace – in committee there was normally no such limit. The greatest windbags were not in fact the MEPs but invited experts of one sort or another, who once they got going, just couldn't stop. The egg timer would give them about four minutes' warning and then it would then be turned over for another four minutes. Then the speaker would be invited to finish. It seemed a good idea.

The day Ponia first brought in his new toy he showed it to me at the end of the meeting. The meeting room had glass-fronted interpreters' booths. I know now, but did not know then, that the glass fronts were sloping, projecting into the room more at the top than at the bottom in order to prevent reflections impeding the interpreters' view of the speakers. Ponia held up the egg timer for me to examine. I took it and lifted it higher to be able to see it better. It hit the sloping window of the interpreters' booth and smashed into smithereens; the bright blue sand went everywhere.

'You have smashed time,' Ponia said to me. Somehow this incident got into the main Belgian newspaper. On 28 November 1983 under the headline "Chronocide", *Le Soir* commented that Ponia was a distant descendant of a Napoleonic Marshal and that the battle of the egg timer might be viewed in Brussels as a renewal of Anglo-French hostilities! I told Ponia that I would search for a new egg timer, a British one, filled with red sand because it was the left-wingers who talked too much. *Le Soir* advised Ponia to find an egg timer with grey sand in order to be impartial and because that was the colour of most of the speeches by members of the committee. I couldn't find a large egg timer but Ponia eventually produced a replacement.

Our Westminster "allies"

My personal objectives, the people in my constituency and my colleague MEPs all guided what I myself did and said and how I sought to influence the collective policy of my Group. There were also other pressures and influences including the Conservative party leadership back in London, the Tories being in government for the whole of my time in the European Parliament. MEPs also had to be in touch with local MPs and County and Borough Councillors.

The Tory MEPs were invited to No 10 Downing Street once each year for a pep talk; the format varied. One year, we were seated in rows prior to Mrs Thatcher's entry, with strict instructions about who should speak and who should not. On another occasion, we all stood about the room having drinks with the PM and various Ministers. When the time came for her "few words", Mrs T stamped on the floor to call for silence; this was achieved with some difficulty as the decibel level of the general conversation was quite high. There seemed to be no other way of calling for silence other than shouting or stamping the foot.

'Those of you who can find a chair to sit on, please sit down,' said the PM. Although I was standing next to an empty chair, I demurred because Lynda Chalker, a Minister, was standing next to it. I thought she would sit down on it but she did not. Mrs Thatcher glanced round in my direction. "Sit!" she said, in a voice reminiscent of a popular dog-training programme on television. I sat.

We Tory MEPs were members of the same party as the Tory members of the House of Commons. We had been elected thanks to the efforts of the same party machines in the constituencies that campaigned for Conservative MPs and local councillors. But you might not have thought so from the way we Tory MEPs, as a bloc, were treated by the party in London. We did not dispute that the Conservative leadership in London set the party line which we should follow; after all we were Conservatives too, with mostly the same hopes for our country as our colleagues in Westminster. Yet while as individuals most MPs were courteous and friendly towards us, they sometimes behaved as though we were supporters of an alien power. Most of us thought that on certain occasions the policy of our government on EU matters would have been better if Ministers had taken the trouble to listen to the advice and opinions which MEPs were willing and able to give. I had the impression that our Labour colleagues met similar attitudes with their Westminster opposite numbers.

For most of my ten years in the European Parliament, MEPs had little more access to the lobbies of the House of Commons than that accorded to tourists. It was said that the building was already too crowded and that there was no room for us. Yet more than 2,000 people – press, lobbyists, assistants, officials etc – had passes allowing them into the building, as well as the MPs themselves. On one occasion, I had two appointments in the House of Commons in two different parts of the building, with an hour between appointments. I was not allowed to stay in the building between the two meetings. I had to go outside for an hour after the first meeting and then undergo the security procedures all over again when it was time for my next meeting. Another MEP was called to give evidence before a parliamentary committee. He arrived at the appropriate time outside the building and was told that he would have to join the queue for security searches behind a line of Japanese tourists. When he got to the committee, he was criticised for being late.

These sorts of encounters did nothing to enhance or improve relations between MPs and MEPs. Not surprisingly, MEPs soon got tired of trying to cooperate with their opposite numbers in the House of Commons and many ceased maintaining such contacts. While the *amour propre* of many MPs was no doubt assuaged by the Commons' policy of treating MEPs as people to be kept out, I believe that this attitude damaged the interests of the Conservative party and, more importantly, the national interest. I understand that since my time, MEPs have been granted better access but the initial refusal by the Commons authorities to make it possible for MEPs to have informal contact with MPs, prevented the two groups of politicians within each party acting as members of the same team. I do not believe that this damage was been healed, even more than twenty years later.

The British MEPs fared better with the House of Lords than with the Commons. While the House of Lords has greatly increased in prominence and grown in respect in recent years, it was then viewed as a place of much less influence. Perhaps an elderly police constable marshalling the queue of tourists waiting to get into the public gallery of the Commons had it right. He had been saying a few words to an American tourist about how the House of Commons operated.

'What about the House of Lords?' asked the American.

The constable looked somewhat wrong-footed by this and paused. Then he pronounced: 'I don't really know. I don't think they do very much at all.'

The House of Lords soon realised that contact with MEPs would be useful but did not feel able to offer privileges to MEPs too far ahead of the Commons, which offered nothing. It was arranged some months after MEPs were first elected that they would be allowed to enter the Palace of Westminster through either of two of the Lords' entrances and proceed via a specified route to the Central Lobby, which serves as a meeting place for Members of both Houses. This concession was useful for MEPs because it bypassed the queues of tourists but they were still hampered by petty rules. For example, they were not permitted to hang their coats up except on particular pegs, and there were only two places where they were allowed to sit and wait – the Central Lobby, where one could only sit while waiting for an appointment, or the Lords' bar. This latter establishment was frequented by various people, including policemen and ushers, but not by Lords. In summer, the Lords' bar had access through some French windows to the riverside terrace but this was out of bounds for MEPs.[12]

In the medieval fashion of beating the bounds, I exercised my right of access to the Palace of Westminster on every possible occasion. Each time, a different policeman was on duty and each time a telephone call would have to be made to higher authority because the officer was unaware of our special right of access.

The divergence of the paths of the two types of parliamentarians was enhanced by the manner in which the Commons vetted European legislation. The House of Commons discussed European legislation, if at all, after it had been enacted. MPs could then complain that EU legislation was foisted on them. Since the British press generally did not publish information about the European Parliament's debates during the EU legislative process, MPs could feel free to savage what had been already decided but without fear of counterattack. The Lords, on the other hand, examined many draft EU laws as they went through the system.

---

[12] Diana Elles (Baroness Elles), who was already a Member of the House of Lords when she was elected an MEP, played a major part in attaining these modest but important concessions for MEPs. (She died in 2009). In January 1989, the House of Commons debated the question of access to the House by MEPs. John Wakeham, for the government, supported an amendment which would merely allow MEPs access to that part of the House to which members of the public already had access, except that they would be able to enter the building without the security checks imposed on tourists. Such is progress!

I was myself invited to appear before a Lords' committee to give a detailed explanation of an EU procedure which exempted imports from certain countries from normal customs duty, which I have mentioned earlier. Their Lordships were a little doddery of foot and watery of eye, but razor-sharp of mind and very well-informed – but to what avail? I asked a House of Lords clerk what happened to the reports of such meetings about European legislation in the pipeline. It appeared that they were formally approved by the House of Lords and then published. I can vouch for the fact that they are among the most highly valued parliamentary reports circulating in Brussels. The reports are then sent to Ministers in Whitehall and then filed away. Even if ignored by Whitehall, they sometimes surfaced in the press, offering intelligent analysis of Brussels' actions in contrast to the jingoistic columns which often passed for journalism.

The antipathy of several Tory MPs towards MEPs was compounded by the problem of access to Ministers. It was only infrequently that I asked for a personal meeting with a Minister but when I did, I got one without much difficulty. I'm not sure that backbench MPs had quite such easy access. Backbench MPs might use the time spent passing through the division lobbies to cast their votes as a means of buttonholing Ministers.

Our political Group in the European Parliament (EDG) made regular visits to London for various meetings. These usually happened monthly and should have been opportunities to make contact with MP colleagues. Sometimes we had special meetings in the European Parliament's London office close to the House of Commons, in order to meet outside organisations such as the Confederation of British Industry (CBI) or the National Farmers Union (NFU). Tory MPs known to be interested in the topics to be discussed would be invited to join us; very few did.

One of the regular critics of the EU was Anthony Beaumont-Dark, MP for Birmingham Selly Oak, once described in the *Guardian* as "king of the *rent-a-quote*". It was he who set up a high-cholesterol gastronomic "Currie Club" in opposition to Edwina Currie, then a Health Minister, who was advocating better diets. (Edwina got her own back when Beaumont–Dark was bitten by a Rottweiler. She sent the dog a get-well card!) In 1989 he launched a furious attack against the cost of a meeting of the ACP-EU Council of Ministers (see later) held in Barbados. I pointed out that twenty five Westminster MPs were about to go to a Commonwealth Parliamentary Association meeting on that island. I told the *Daily Post*: 'It is just pure envy and spite,' commenting that the

MP was upset because he was not going and that the party whips should tell him to shut up. Beaumont-Dark was "unavailable for comment" when the press contacted him after my statement. Referring to me, his secretary told the paper: "I don't know who this little man is. I have never heard of him. I'm sure Mr Beaumont-Dark will not be the slightest bit interested in what he has to say." I have never been to Barbados in my life, despite the *Daily Post* printing a picture of where I was allegedly staying. Anthony Beaumont-Dark died in 1996. The significance of his utterances is that they were ready fodder for the anti-EU press which abounded in Fleet Street, and that the Tory party leadership seemed never to rein him in. Politicians from other EU countries could not be blamed for thinking, as some of them did, that any initiative from the UK was of a wrecking nature and therefore to be opposed.

Within the Euro-constituency, I needed to keep in touch with the seven local Conservative MPs in order to keep in line with party policy and also with Frank Field, Labour MP for Birkenhead, on local issues of common interest. With the exception of one or two initial difficulties, I had excellent relations with and full support from the local Tory MPs and friendly co-operation with Frank. I did my best to reciprocate.[13]

David Hunt, now Baron Hunt of Wirral, a pro-European and a most effective and popular constituency MP for Wirral West, was unceasingly helpful. He used every opportunity to advise and assist me and let me share some of his limelight. As a constituency MP he was exemplary in answering letters. At constituency events he was a master of circulating around the room so that everybody present had a chance to talk to him. David became Secretary of State for Wales and was a very senior Member of the Cabinet. In 2008 he was given the task of shadowing Peter Mandelson in the House of Lords and in 2011 became Chairman of the Press Complaints Commission.

Lynda Chalker, later Baroness Chalker of Wallasey, was also extremely helpful. She was MP for Wallasey and as such had a much more difficult constituency to nurse than David. Her party workers sometimes took careful handling but gave support which was amazingly effective in view of their limited numbers. Lynda played a big part in the electoral campaigns of local

---

[13] I was completely spared the difficulties encountered by some of my Tory MEP colleagues who had to obtain the permission of their local MPs before going into their own Euro-constituencies. The fact that I lived in mine would have made such constraints impossible to follow. I would not, of course, have accepted such limitations.

Tory councillors. I did what I could to help with this. Lynda was Minister of State for Europe 1986-89 and Minister for Overseas Development 1989-97.

Peter Morrison, MP for Chester, although no fan of Europe, fully accepted me as a fellow-member of the party. Whereas David and Lynda would ask me to speak at functions after they had said their few words, Peter would do all the talking but always make reference to me in a supportive way.

With David Hunt, Mrs Thatcher and Lynda Chalker

Barry Porter, MP for Bebington & Ellesmere Port and then, after boundary changes, for Wirral South, was not a fan of Europe. Soon after I was elected, we crossed swords in the local press on the then fashionable bandwagon of visits abroad by MEPs. He was fiercely critical. I rebutted his criticisms equally strongly. He criticised the cost of running the European Parliament, which he said was £125m a year. I replied in the *Ellesmere Port Pioneer* of 2 April 1981 by quoting Sir Geoffrey Howe's written answer on 2 July 1980 to a parliamentary question. This said that the cost of the Westminster Parliament for 1980-81 was £51m and that Britain's share of running the European Parliament was under £30m. I pointed out that the cost of running Westminster does not have to include the use of several languages, as is the case in Strasbourg and Brussels. In April 1981, Barry stated that MEPs had no foreign affairs function (which was wrong both then and now) and that MEPs would never use their power to sack the European Commission. In fact, the Parliament forced the Commission to resign en bloc in 1999 over allegations of fraud. The Parliament cannot sack individual Commissioners; its power is to sack all or none.

Myra (left), me, Lynda Chalker (centre) and Henry Plumb

Alistair Goodlad was MP for the safe Tory seat of Eddisbury. I found it difficult to make the Tories there understand that while Alistair would be elected with even a half-hearted campaign, I needed every vote to counter-balance the Labour vote in Birkenhead and Ellesmere Port. At social events organised by his party workers, Alistair's presence was very low-key. This made it difficult for me to be forthright about my need for strong support there. Alistair later became British High Commissioner in Australia. He is now Baron Goodlad.

Mike Woodcock was MP for Ellesmere Port & Neston for just one parliament.

I was able to provide a small service one day for one of the Tory MPs in my area who was a Minister at the time. British Ministers are pursued around the country by government couriers bringing red boxes containing important papers for their urgent attention. This particular day the Minister was due to make a speech, the text of which was in the box. But the Minister could not find the key. An off-the-cuff speech was not acceptable; the exact text had to be read out because it was an official policy statement. My assistance was sought; more specifically, the use of the hammer and chisel in my garage was required. The metal-lined box was eventually sprung open and the speech retrieved. I was not told how the damage to the box was explained afterwards.

There were, and still are, a number of back-bench Tory MPs who seemed to hate the EU. I remember a conversation with Teddy Taylor, a Tory MP who often spoke strongly against the EU. Just before a meeting we attended at Westminster, we talked briefly looking through the windows of the committee room overlooking the Thames. His opposition to the EU was well-known, honest and not just a matter of jumping on a fashionable bandwagon, as was the case with a number of other MPs in the Thatcher era. Talking with him, I had the impression that he had never actually talked with an MEP before. I found that there was much we could agree on although our basic positions about whether or not we should be in the EU were incompatible. Perhaps other eurosceptic Tories just didn't understand the EU or perhaps they thought that it robbed them of some of their own power and glory.

I needed to keep in touch with Conservatives on the local Councils on matters of mutual interest, which included the use of grants from the European Regional and Social Funds. The local Conservative MPs and I met members of Wirral Borough Council from time to time. These meetings tended to be all tension and cigarette smoke. Similar meetings with Conservatives on Cheshire County Council usually took the form of a leisurely lunch at County Hall.

The history of Britain's membership of the EU would have been different if there had been a proper and amicable system of contacts between MEPs and MPs. I and several of my colleagues (notably Lady Elles) did what we could to create better relations but it takes two to tango. I myself thought that while it was right and proper for MEPs to show due deference to the "Mother of Parliaments", the relationship between the two bodies should consist of more than Westminster MPs criticising their Strasbourg colleagues for the sake of cheap publicity.

Handling the paperwork

The European Parliament provided an office for each MEP in the Strasbourg building. Each of these had one desk, two chairs and a small sofa, plus a toilet. The idea of the latter was that the building, which was owned by the French authorities, could be let for non-parliamentary conferences when the European Parliament was not sitting. The MEPs' offices would be used as bedrooms for delegates. Notwithstanding what certain newspapers alleged, I was never aware of any MEP spending the night in his office. After the first year or so, an office was also provided for each member in the Parliament building in Brussels. Richard Steele, my excellent full-time research assistant, kept much of my paperwork there and worked there when not with me in Strasbourg. He gave excellent service. Richard's salary, work-associated benefits and travel costs were paid out of allowances made to me by the European Parliament. (My own headquarters was the office I rented in West Kirby.)

MEPs were paid a round sum for office expenses in their home country; this covered office rent, office machines, cleaning, postage, staff travel costs etc. With this allowance I hired an office over Lloyds Bank in West Kirby. I insisted with the bank that I should be able to come and go at any time of day or night, weekends included. The local manager was quite happy to give me a written waiver from the bank's normal rule which stipulated that tenants could only go into the premises during bank-opening hours. When the lease came up for renewal, the new manager said that to grant a similar waiver was quite beyond his power. 'Not even Manchester could do that,' he said. The matter would have to go to London for a decision. I wrote him a letter saying what I wanted, gave him two weeks to reply, but heard no more about it. I wondered, if the bank was like this when I was trying to pay money *to* it, what it would be like if I wanted to borrow money *from* it!

MEPs received funds to employ staff, on presentation of contracts. With these funds, I employed a part-time secretary, Bridget Johnston, and a "man-Friday", David Saville. After these retired, Liz Bell and John Plows took over their functions. They all made splendid contributions to my work and took many burdens off my shoulders. Myra spent a good deal of time helping with certain correspondence, answering phone calls, arranging my diary and travelling about the constituency representing me at functions. As in the case of MPs, I was allowed to allocate a sum from European Parliament funds to Myra in return for the work she put in.

I endeavoured to reply personally to all letters I received. Bridget and then Liz signed almost all of my outgoing mail on the basis of my dictation or instructions phoned or faxed from Brussels and Strasbourg – this was before the days of personal computers. Mail arrived in great quantities. Even now the letters from Miss Timewell of Birkenhead stand out in my memory. I never met her, as far as I know, but she wrote to me regularly giving her views on the events of the day. Her comments were relevant and informative and I valued them. I replied to each letter. A further regular stream of letters came from the Forum of Private Business, a well-informed organisation based in Knutsford, supporting small local businesses. They forwarded to me copies of questionnaires sent in by their members giving their views on issues of the day. I found this briefing useful; indeed, I found all briefing useful. I cannot claim to have read every word of every document sent to me but very little of it went without being at least scanned through.

It had long been the practice for election candidates to put a photo of themselves on their headed notepaper. I took this a stage further by also having my photo on my business cards and compliment slips throughout my ten years as an MEP; I added a small map showing which parts of Cheshire and Merseyside were within the constituency. I believe I was the first MEP or MP to do this, outside election times. As time went by, I noticed a small number of others doing the same thing. I have only come across one other MEP putting a constituency map on his paper. That was Lyndon Harrison (now Lord Harrison of Chester), who took the seat off me in 1989.

For a few months I had the talented and high-powered services, at no cost to myself, of Sheila Dwyer, an American student who went on to be Assistant Secretary of the United States Senate. After she had left, I thought it would be a good idea to have a British student to work for me for a while, paid for by one of the government training schemes for young people. I thought this would be good training for an ambitious youngster. However, I was told that I would have to train such a person in certain particular business procedures which, as a politician, I did not need to carry out (such as company payroll). Moreover, I would not be allowed to choose the young person concerned, the choice being

119

made by a civil servant over whose decision I would have no say! So I had to say: 'No Thanks!' Some young person therefore lost what could have been a highlight of their education.

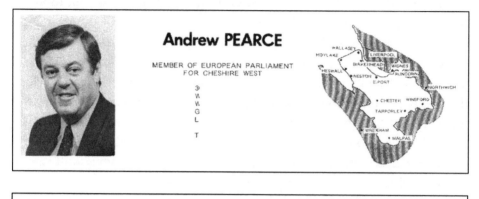

Top: My compliments slip. Below: Lyndon Harrison's letter head

MEPs received per-day and per-kilometre allowances for official travel. The jibes in the press about "all those expenses-paid trips" ignored the fact that in Britain executives of private sector companies and all British public servants and indeed journalists themselves are fully reimbursed for their travel costs. The travel payment from the European Parliament was on a swings-and-roundabouts basis, a flat fee for the first few kilometres, designed to cover the cost of a taxi to the nearest airport, in my case Manchester, thirty miles from home, and a lower flat fee for the remaining kilometres. In my first year as an MEP, my bill for air tickets alone was more than my salary after paying income tax. The Parliament's allowance would cover the costs provided that they were in economy class. Flights of long duration, such as to Africa, America or the Far East were in business class. There was also a payment to cover hotel costs, meals and local transport in the cities visited. For me, the allowance generally approximated to what I spent but I lost a good deal on every visit to London due to the high cost of hotel accommodation there and the need to travel between meetings in different parts of the city by taxi, in order to pack several appointments into the day. For most of my time, there was no allowance for travel outside the constituency other than to official parliamentary meetings. Thus, if I was invited to a meeting in London with a Minister, an MP, a businessman or some other public figure, I had to pay the travel costs myself out of my after-tax salary. So I usually turned down such invitations.

In tax terms, MEPs were employees of the Home Secretary. Therefore, we paid UK income tax on our salaries at the normal rate for employees (schedule E or PAYE). However, our subsistence, travel and administration expenses were exempt from UK tax by virtue of European law. The Inland Revenue attempted to ignore this. For some months we had to save up myriad receipts as proof that expenditure of our various allowances was actually spent on the purposes for which they were paid. I saved up taxi bills in marks, restaurant bills in krones, hotel bills in francs and so on. The matter was taken to court and the Inland Revenue lost.

MEPs received no allowances from the British government other than salary and then a pension. The levels of both were, and are, pegged so as to be equal to those of Westminster MPs. Initially, my salary was about half that of French and Dutch MEPs, though the difference has narrowed a good deal since then.[14] My parliamentary pension was, in 2009, about £7,200 a year, for ten years as an MEP plus three extra pension years which I had bought.[15] British MEPs received no other financial support from their government – yet I could benefit from free travel on Belgian railways. In several other member states, national governments gave their MEPs free travel or other allowances, as well as much higher salaries. MEPs from certain EU countries received additional pensions from their own governments.

[14] A number of MPs repeatedly castigated what they described as the large salaries and expenses of MEPs. The salaries of both were, and are, identical, as stated above. MPs are provided with offices and postage and telephone services in Westminster. They can receive expenses in relation to all their travel, some of their spouse's travel to and from London and also various staff and constituency administrative costs. In 1979, the salary of an MEP or MP was £9,450. In 1989 it was £24,107, in 2012 £65,738. (Select Committee chairmen and certain other MPs receive £14,582 extra).

[15] Since my time as an MEP, the European Parliament itself pays ex-MEPs a pension but such is not provided for those who ceased to be MEPs prior to its introduction.

Having my arm twisted

Prominent features of life in Brussels and Strasbourg are business consultants trying to influence legislation or to obtain contracts for studies and projects. Lobbyists are also much in evidence putting forward the policies of non-governmental organisations (NGOs) and the interests of the regions of Europe, including Scotland, Wales and Northern Ireland and, more recently, the various English regions. The International Fund for Animal Welfare, the European Tour Operators Association, Lancashire Enterprises (an offshoot of the County Council), the Portuguese Industrial Association and the European Banking Federation are among the large number of organisations represented in both cities. Thankfully, the lobbyists do not have the enormous influence exercised by their counterparts in the USA. [16]

Lobbying is useful – indeed it could be considered as necessary in order to keep politicians properly informed about the matters within their remit. Given the way draft legislation is processed in the committees of the European Parliament, with a strong focus on detail, the general standard of lobbying of MEPs by British business in my time, was very poor.

Businesses and journalists who express shock and horror when new laws come into force had often only themselves to blame for not having paid attention as the legislative process went along, during which time they might have been able to influence it. Many lobbyists and journalists failed to understand that trying to influence legislation when it comes before a plenary session in Strasbourg is usually pointless; this is the end of a very long process. Compromises between Groups and between the governments of EU countries have been agreed upon and incorporated in the texts by then and will not be changed. On 12 December 1987 the *Daily Telegraph* published a letter from me

[16] These are sometimes known collectively as "K Street", where many of them have their offices in Washington DC. There are said to be 17,000 lobbyists in Washington, seeking to influence federal policies. A figure of 14,000 is quoted for London but not all of these are necessarily lobbying on national matters.

in which I said, 'I can recall no occasion over the last three or four years when the Confederation of British Industry has approached me to lobby for a point of view. It should, because since July the Parliament has had a decisive say in making new EEC laws.'

The best lobbyist I knew was Mike Seymour-Rouse, a character almost too big to be true. He represented the animal welfare lobby, principally the Royal Society for the Prevention of Cruelty to Animals. He understood that a good political lobbyist is not there to browbeat or pester but rather to inform. He knew that to get people to listen, he had to be available, pleasant and really know his subject. He occupied a particular sofa in the lobby of the Parliament in Strasbourg that he called his office; he kept his files behind it on the floor. I had a meal with him once in Brussels in a restaurant offering German and east European dishes where he was a regular customer. I studied the menu and told the waiter what I myself wanted. Mike said nothing. The waiter went off. I said to Mike, 'Are you not having anything?' 'Oh, the waiter knows what I have. Always have the same thing, old boy,' he said. 'Serbian bean soup – twice.' Sure enough, a bowl of soup came for him along with my starter. Then when my main dish came, there was a second bowl of the same soup for Mike. At that time, Mike was as effective a lobbyist for the causes which he supported as any ten British business lobbyists put together.

One of the more unusual types of lobbying was that of the Mormons. They regularly sent two representatives to Strasbourg for the sessions there. They believed that the mere act of communicating with politicians would help to make the world a better place. The Mormon Residential Conference Centre in Britain, a minor stately home, happened to be situated in my constituency. It was beautifully kept, inside and outside. I visited it once or twice to talk with groups of young people from various European countries. They all looked very rich.

When I was first elected to the Parliament, I accepted invitations to dinners when invited by business lobbies whose activities were of concern to my constituency. Unfortunately many of these engagements were not at all well-organised; sometimes there would be only two or three hosts to handle ten or twelve MEPs, so some of the MEPs had only themselves to talk to. More than once I came away wondering exactly what the hosts wanted to tell us. Some of them seemed confused by the bustle and variety of languages of the Parliament. On the other hand, Japanese companies usually targeted their dinner guests accurately and made sure they received the appropriate "messages". At one lunch I went to, there was one Japanese businessman for every one or two MEPs. There was a pause between each course of the meal during which a short speech was made. Paper and pens were provided for each guest for the purpose of taking notes. How organised was that!

After a year or two of these duty dinners, often starting at half past nine in the evening after twelve hours of parliamentary work, they were in no sense a pleasure. I decided to politely refuse further invitations in Strasbourg. People wishing to lobby me could come to my office by appointment for a half hour meeting to say whatever they had to say. Many of them did not take up my invitation. Many of those who did come were professional parliamentary lobbyists, smooth "metropolitan" types, who seldom really knew their stuff. I preferred to meet the people who actually did the work in their businesses.

Lobbyists also got through to MPs and MEPs using ordinary mail. Many companies, trade associations and charities sent letters and brochures to my office in West Kirby. I tried to read all of them. When I went to London by train, I took a large holdall full of this paperwork to read on the train. I took it as a privilege to have such a wealth of sources of information. MEPs became very knowledgeable on a wide range of subjects if they read all this mail.

Demonstrators are different from parliamentary lobbyists but nevertheless are people trying to get their views across. There were demonstrations every week in Brussels, some consisting of a few hundred banner-wavers, some involving tens of thousands of people. Bands played. The European Commission received advance warning of large demos from the police and put up notices in the buildings so that staff could avoid the streets most likely to be involved. Many of the demos were purely Belgian affairs, often directed to the national Employment and Agriculture Ministries. Others concerned matters of EU-wide interest. Cheerleaders led the chanting of slogans and sometimes firecrackers were thrown. There were frequent demonstrations in Strasbourg too when the European Parliament was in session. Large groups of French riot police, the *Compagnies Républicaines de Sécurité,* kept demonstrators away from the entrance to the Parliament building. One week the IRA mounted a poster campaign in Strasbourg's main square.

People in the head offices of big companies seem to think that the more you pay for public relations services, the better the results. In fact, I thought that the reverse was often the case. I visited one particular company HQ in London. The man I had been meeting invited me to a pub around the corner for a pint. In the pub were a number of his colleagues. The pint turned into an invitation to dinner – for me and eleven executives of the company! Afterwards, cars were ordered to take each of these back to their homes in the suburbs. I went on foot to my hotel, which was nearby. This illustrates the waste of money in many London head offices and the disadvantage of them being located away from the relevant manufacturing facilities.

A public relations agency was employed by an American firm to help obtain approval for the construction of a major plant in North Wales. The plant would be seen from the Wirral and Wirral residents were thought likely to object. The Public relations agency had sent letters to Ministers and had held public meetings on the Welsh side of the Dee. It asked my advice on what else it should do. I enquired whether it had contacted all the local councils of the areas whose residents would be affected, such as Neston. It had not!

The Liverpool-based campaign organised by Roy Castle's widow for cancer research came to Brussels. Members of the Merseyside Fire Brigade erected a pair of turntable ladders twenty-five-metres high outside the Brussels Stock Exchange in a V-shape and ran up and down 355 times, the equivalent of climbing Mount Everest. The astonished passers-by applauded and put money in the collecting tins. Later the fire officers went into one of the British pubs in the city, taking the Football Association cup (or a replica of it), which Liverpool had won, with them. Glamorous Miss Something-or-other came along too. I have a photo of myself taken holding the cup (but *not* Miss Something-or-other!), for which I made a donation to the fund.

I myself received a retainer for advising a company in my Euro-constituency. This company produced a lead additive for petrol. There was a campaign for the EU to ban it. This was supported by evidence in the UK from some flats close to Spaghetti Junction on the M6 in Birmingham that lead emissions were damaging the brains of children living there. The campaign was also supported by the Germans who contended that lead emissions were causing trees to die. Neither argument carried much weight in the other country. The campaign was supported by, amongst others, the producers of raw materials necessary for the production of the catalytic converters to be attached to vehicle exhaust systems to mitigate the problem.

I provided background information to the company which produced the lead additives, at Ellesmere Port. This assisted their lobbying designed to persuade the authorities to bring in the new rules gradually to give time for new types of production to be initiated and jobs saved. A total of 2,000 jobs were at stake. I made sure that my colleagues in the European Parliament knew the facts of the case, both sides of the argument and that the company kept abreast of the various legislative stages. In the end, the new rules were much less damaging than might have been the case. Whether the removal of lead additives, and their replacement by methyl tertiary butyl and benzene is an improvement, is a matter of some debate as both these products are toxic. It may be that the new additives cause traffic pollution to hang near ground level, causing more of it to be inhaled rather than being blown away to higher levels.

I have no doubt that British industry now takes the European Parliament far more seriously than it did in my time. I have to say that in my time it did not match the "clout" of German industry lobbying Brussels as well as Bonn. This failure may have contributed to the decline of British manufacturing industry.

Brushes with British bureaucrats

I had many contacts with Whitehall. The British Civil Service had a deserved reputation for being much freer from corruption than many other national civil services. It was also viewed as reasonably efficient, especially when compared with the European Commission, a comparison Whitehall officials were often tempted to make in private. Regrettably, what we have learned in more recent times about the workings of Whitehall has changed our view about the efficiency of the British government system. Whether recent malfunctions are the fault of Ministers or officials, I cannot say. At least some parts of the European Commission, despite their reputation, have proved themselves to be capable of handling difficult issues including competition and energy issues in an effective manner.

Whitehall officials visiting Brussels for meetings with officials from the Commission and other EU countries sometimes did not match the effectiveness of French civil servants in presenting and promoting policies that favoured their national interests. British civil servants always say that they do what Ministers want and that the politicians must carry the can. But Ministers are only human and cannot know everything. Moreover, in Britain Ministers change jobs quite frequently. Ministers and European Commissioners are entitled to expect competence in the formulation and execution of policy. I have known Ministers tear their hair out at the determination of certain senior civil servants to do things *their* way, not the Minister's way. One Minister referred to his officials collectively as "Martians". Formulation of policy has often seemed more important than delivery of results. The television program *"Yes, Minister"* was horribly near the truth.

I observed that some parts of the Customs & Excise, now part of Revenue & Customs, seemed to think that their department was a law unto itself. Customs officers had tremendous powers which they sometimes used with a discourtesy and arrogance that made me think of police states. It was at Dover that I experienced most unpleasantness. On my occasional trips through the port, almost all car drivers were questioned by customs officers, sometimes none too politely. On one occasion, the floor in front of the driver's feet in every car was searched. We were delayed over an hour. When I asked whether this was because they had had a tip-off, the answer was, 'No, it was a training exercise'.

For foot passengers travelling on car ferries, the whole experience of Dover made me so ashamed of being British that I avoided admitting my nationality to foreigners if I could. Foot passengers were herded over a dirty and wobbly gangway into the Customs hall. After the Customs officers had done their worst, passengers were shepherded into filthy, bumpy buses to be taken to the railway station a mile away. I wrote to the Port of Dover authorities telling them in unmistakable terms what I thought of their facilities and the service provided. I suppose the management did not often stir out of their nice warm offices to see how the passengers fared, a common problem with British management at the time. The top man wrote back apologetically, saying that "I had a strong right hook," (verbally speaking, that is!) and that he would look into it. It pays to be rude sometimes. The port authority would blame the Customs for the unsatisfactory situation: Customs would blame the port authority. Both were bodies in the public sector.

On one occasion while we were living in Brussels, I was carrying a parcel containing a pair of my mother's voluminous knickers which she had left in our house during a visit. I intended to post the parcel on to her address in Aughton from London. The female Customs officer at Dover told me to open my bag. I did so. On the top of my belongings was the parcel. The officer, sensing blood, thrust out her chest and demanded: 'What is in that?' I paused for dramatic effect and then said, with total honesty, 'Knickers!' in a very loud voice. The woman stepped back in horror. I prayed that she would ask for the parcel to be opened but she just stood there in shock. I counted up to ten, closed up the bag and departed with dignity, leaving the officer still standing there with her mouth open.

Soviet ships came and went regularly at Ellesmere Port docks on the Manchester Ship Canal, bringing in timber and also ferrying nuclear material from Capenhurst nuclear reprocessing factory to Riga in Latvia for reprocessing. This was part of a little-known piece of nuclear cooperation agreed during one of the Wilson governments. I was invited to go aboard one of the ships with a local journalist. There lay the vessel. No immigration officers, no Customs. We went on board, up several flights of stairs and there was the captain in his cabin entertaining two or three prominent local left-wingers. We accepted a glass of vodka, chatted for a bit and left. On another occasion, I took a London journalist on board another of the Soviet ships. We were greeted as before but this time by the No 2 officer. The Captain was ashore somewhere. As we left the dock estate we saw a policeman on a bicycle. We waited. He came across hesitantly. We told him where we had been. He seemed quite put out – because there was a secret surveillance operation in progress, he said!

I was told that Soviet officials in London were not normally allowed to travel more than thirty miles from the centre of the capital. From Ellesmere Port, adjacent to the M53, one could be in Birmingham or Manchester or Leeds, the heartlands of industrial Britain, in two hours. I had been given to understand that MI5 had no branch offices outside London until recently, no doubt believing, like many in Whitehall, that nothing of any consequence happens north of Watford. I wrote to the Customs & Excise to ask why ordinary people should be harassed at Dover when Ellesmere Port seemed to be wide open to the Soviets. I do not claim to be the author of the improvements that have taken place subsequently in the way the Customs treat the public but I suppose my letter and the press publicity I achieved made some difference.

The rigours of the Customs examination I experienced at Dover did not extend to hundreds of small ports around our coasts. In many of these a notice informed people arriving on boats from outside UK waters that they should telephone the nearest Customs office. If no Customs officer appeared within a certain time they were free to continue on their way. In a Question for Written Answer in the European Parliament, in April 1986, I raised the difference between the rigours faced by tourists at Dover and the open-door policy in operation at Ellesmere Port and elsewhere. I asked the Commission to discuss the matter with the UK authorities and report the result of such an initiative. The Commission replied that it had already been involved in discussions with the UK authorities on the subject of delays at British ports, and especially Dover, to eliminate bottlenecks.

In discussing these events with some constituents, I had to disabuse them of the idea that the large friendly poodles which accompanied Customs officers meeting incoming passengers at Manchester airport, were a gesture of welcome. Apparently poodles are the best kind of dog to detect the presence of drugs. Pigs are even better but there is an understandable reluctance on the part of Customs officers to be seen leading such animals around on leads!

Euromyths and Fleet Street lies

Perhaps the biggest influence on us, and probably on British politics as a whole, is the media. Everyone in the European Parliament was troubled by the British media criticising and mocking everything the EU did, sometimes with justification but more often without; little was ever said about the EU's positive achievements. Moreover, certain Members of the House of Commons seemed to give credence to these stories.

British newspapers will invent news if they can't find real stories but take care only to do this when they think they can't be found out or be proved wrong. To print a gross untruth about Whitehall would certainly risk being found out and having future access to important people denied. To malign Brussels or Strasbourg ran little risk of such a reaction and if there was a rebuttal... well, Brussels is a long way away and nobody would take much notice, would they? Neil Kinnock, an EU Commissioner, commented: 'False rumours and lies are powerful. As John Kennedy once said, "They are able to travel round the world while the truth is still getting its boots on."

In 1995, the European Commission had received so many queries from the public about purported, but false, reports of new EU rules and regulations that it published a series of nearly a hundred Euro-myths entitled *"Do you STILL believe all you read in the newspapers?"* This set out the truth of each rumour cited and indicated where the rumour came from. One story, credited to the *Daily Telegraph* of 2 October 1993, was that the European Commission was poised to draw up an authoritative directory of Europe's aristocrats as a means of investigating the improper use of titles on bottles of wine. This was in fact the brainchild of an Italian MEP. It got absolutely nowhere. The journalist had turned the proposal of one MEP, flying a kite, into a forecast of what official EU policy was to be.

The *Independent on Sunday*, the *Mail on Sunday* and the *Sunday Express* all carried a story in November 1994 that EU law was halting the sale of English oak seeds. In fact the Commission set up standards so that anyone planting oaks as a commercial crop, the market for which demanded the trees to be as straight as possible, could know that what they were planting would, in due course, be

10 British chalet girls will be forced out of work should a draft Directive on the Posting of Workers be passed in Europe's Council of Ministers.

Chalet girls are perfectly safe. Actually there have been a number of different drafts of the Posting of Workers Directive, the most recent having been put forward by France. The drafts were largely aimed at protecting the German construction industry from foreign workers undercutting its own labour force, but national employment ministers failed to come to any agreement when this was discussed in March 1995. All the same, British chalet girls were never under threat anyway as the latest draft also sought to avoid abusive or exploitative working conditions being imposed upon workers as a whole. Chalet girls could not be described as the victims of those who employ them.

11 Mountain rescue teams will soon find life hard-going as new EU regulations force them to replace all life-saving equipment, including Land Rovers, every five years, regardless of condition.

No, the relevant Directive - on Personal Protective Equipment - does not ask rescue teams to do this. It does, however, request manufacturers to present information on expiry dates on the label, or, where appropriate, the maximum number of times an item should be used or cleaned, although this is true only of certain specialised items, such as breathing masks or fluorescent clothing that loses its effectiveness if washed repeatedly. The rule does not apply to most of the equipment used by mountain rescue teams, let alone Land Rovers.

12 British toilets are under threat from a Brussels Directive which will force the UK to allow sales of cheaper and less sanitary Spanish and French models.

Following discussions with Member States the European Commission is preparing a mandate for CEN (the independent industrial standardisation body) which will define basic requirements for sinks, bathtubs and toilets, to make sure they are safe, hygienic and environmentally sound. CEN's consultation period usually lasts about two years and might result in an 'harmonised standard' to which all

Part of an Official British government pamphlet dispelling false stories about the EU

marketable. In actual fact, nobody was banned from getting their seeds from where they liked or planting what they liked.

The *Sunday Times* of 9 April 1995 and *Today* carried the story that the traditional British toilet was under threat from a Brussels Directive and that the siphon flush system perfected by Thomas Crapper & Co in the 1880s was at risk. Less satisfactory French and Spanish models were supposedly to be marketed instead. In fact, as a means of permitting trade to flow freely from one EU state to another and in particular permitting British toilets to be sold on the continent, a 'CE' quality standard mark was set up for toilets, as for a great many other products, by a panel of independent standards bodies representing the industries concerned and designed to guarantee standards of safety and suitability for purpose.

The Commission's London office quoted a press release from a prominent firm of solicitors dated 13 February 1995, repeated in the *Daily Telegraph* a day later, the *Daily Mirror*, a day after that and the *Guardian*, two days later still, as saying that the sending of unwanted Valentine cards could trigger an avalanche of claims for damages for sexual harassment which would be contrary to EU employment law. This arose from a Commission recommendation of 27 November 1991 — four years before this fuss – about sexual harassment, which went nowhere near banning Valentine cards. This rumour was thought by the European Commission's London office to have been spread by as a commercial publicity stunt for St Valentine's Day.

The *Daily Mail*, the *Sun* and the *Star*, of 17 October 1994, all warned that traditional pizzas were to be outlawed. In fact, the Commission had produced no such law and had no intention of doing so.

The *Star* stated on 24 March 1994 that Brussels was ruling on compulsory release dates for murderers. In fact the Commission has no powers to make any such ruling and was not seeking any. This subject has nothing whatever to do with Brussels though the European Court of Human Rights, a totally separate body, might have had views on the matter.

The *Observer* and the *Star* reported in February 1994 that feeding stale bread to swans had been banned by an EU Directive. The EU had in fact done no such thing. The British Environmental Protection Act of 1990 implemented elements of EU legislation, the Waste Disposal Directive, designed to prevent the tipping of waste. The British government, obliged to put these principles into law, was perfectly within its rights to add further rules to those which it had agreed upon with the other EU governments. It was those other rules which the press interpreted as banning the feeding of stale bread to swans.

The story about prawn-cocktail-flavoured crisps illustrates another type of Euro-scare story. The EU wanted to agree to a list of safe food flavourings so that food made in one EU country could be freely sold in any other – very good for Britain, one of Europe's major producers of processed food. The Commission asked the governments of the EU countries for a list of flavourings already in use. Whitehall sent in a list but forgot to include prawn cocktail flavouring. The Commission corrected Whitehall's error as soon as it was pointed out.

Much has been said about EU officials banning curved cucumbers. The Commission did produce a regulation, Number 1677/88, laying down quality standards for cucumbers. This did not make restrictions on the size, shape or curvature of cucumbers but did lay down quality categories. In response to pressure from cucumber growers, the quality categories demanded less curvature for the sake of easier packing in boxes.

One rumour was that the EU would ban the sale of plants at church fetes. In fact, new standards were brought in to facilitate trade between EU countries but these specifically excluded sales in local markets such as church fetes.

It was rumoured that standard size Euro-condoms were to hit the market and that the compromise size of them would not be big enough for British "assets". In fact a European Standards Committee proposed safety standards, which would be voluntary.

It was stated that all boats, from the largest to the smallest, would have to carry sixty items of medical equipment at a cost of £1,800. In fact, the smallest craft would be obliged to carry only eighteen different items of equipment. Another nonsense story was that boats would have to carry 200 condoms so that the crew could have safe sex.

The EU was said to be laying down rules that in conservation areas, street lamps must be of steel and at least six metres apart. The EU has in fact no jurisdiction whatever in this matter and did not seek any.

A butcher told me that the EU insisted that every butcher's shop must have a special blue electrical light above the counter which would kill flies. I took up this particular matter up with North Yorkshire Trading Standards, the leading trading standards authority in the UK for this particular issue. 'Surely you don't think we would want to have such a device above the meat so that the dead flies would fall on the meat, do you?' they said. Investigation established that the rumour was being touted round butchers' shops by salesmen of a firm making the special blue lights.

Only recently, in 2008, a butcher told me that, because of "Brussels", he could not serve me a pork chop with the kidney attached to it – though I could have the kidney separately. The story was untrue.

A man in my local gardening shop said that salesmen had told him that "Brussels" had banned a certain garden chemical. I checked and discovered it was nonsense. Next time I went into the shop, there were boxes of the product on the shelf awaiting customers!

The Euro-myth habit even spread to France where it was said that use of maggots as fishing bait would be banned because the creatures suffered stress on the end of the fisherman's line.

The *Irish Independent* went to town on Euro-myths on 28 December 1994, condemning the British press for circulating nonsense. It quoted, amongst other stories in the UK press that Brussels was going to ban double-decker buses and make everybody on buses wear seat belts.

Between May 1994 and July 1995, the European Commission's London office rebutted almost ninety false claims about EU measures. It is bad enough that the newspapers should print this sort of thing, knowing it to be false: it is worse that certain MPs should give credence to it. It is worse still that otherwise

People might actually believe that the EU might propose changes like this

intelligent people should believe it, in response to their prejudice against the EU.

The British media knew no bounds of accuracy or balance in its coverage of the European Parliament. Here was something which, in its view, combined venality, sex and exotic locations – and which could not answer back. The media did not allow its coverage to be sullied by such things as informing the British public about what its representatives were doing on their behalf. In any case, if titillating copy could be written in a London office, why spend money sending someone over to Strasbourg or Brussels to get the facts?

"£1m Roman orgy plan for Euro MPs" was the headline in the *Daily Mirror* for a piece about a meeting of the ACP-EU Joint Assembly. (See later chapters). The word *orgy* is useful for headline writers; it is nice and short, easy to spell and, when linked to politicians, combines sexual scandal with that blend of shock and disgust that journalists think their readers ought to feel. That the word *orgy* had no correlation to reality in this case was, of course, of little significance for the journalist who wrote the piece. That it was an insult, not only to the MEPs – fair game, it seems, in Fleet Street – but to the African, Caribbean and Pacific MPs who were also present at the meeting, the parliamentary staff and the Italian government who were hosting the event, was of no moment to the paper either. Falsehood and hypocrisy were acceptable in Fleet Street so long as you could not be sued for it.

The Times quoted an example of the hypocrisy of its sister paper, the *Sun*, on 8 January 2002. "The European Commission rounded on the *Sun* yesterday, accusing it of hypocrisy for publishing positive stories about the euro in Ireland while damning it in Britain. The front page headline in the *Sun's* Irish edition on New Year's Day was "Dawn of a new €ra. Ireland wakes up to a new era today as the euro is introduced." The front-page headline of the British edition read, "Dawn of a new €rror" above a story that proclaimed the euro is born. And thank goodness Britain is not part of it." A European Commission official commented, 'Every euro-coin has two sides and so apparently has the *Sun.*'

One of the keys to Fleet Street's fun with MEPs was that the MEPs, like ordinary members of the public, could not answer back; they did not have, in practice, a right of reply to unjustified attacks by the press. Members of the House of Commons who consider themselves maligned can perhaps ask Mr Speaker to intervene. No Member of the House of Commons would intervene to defend MEPs; Downing Street would not defend MEPs either. It was open house for the "knockers" of Fleet Street. Even the BBC did not, on occasion, eschew trivial criticism although its reporting was usually more restrained.

A prime piece of Fleet Street misinformation was when one of its finest had it that there was an internal telephone number in the Parliament at Strasbourg that members could use to contact lonely secretaries who would welcome male company in the evenings. A number of other journalists tried to substantiate the story but of course there wasn't a word of truth in it. Still, I suppose it sold a few extra copies.

When we were newly arrived in the Parliament, a journalist brought a bottle of wine and two glasses to the office of a Parliament official in the Cash Office and opened the wine there. He invited the official to pour some wine and drink it, making a toast. The journalist then photographed the official drinking the wine and later published the photo as an example of how such officials spent their time.

While much of the inaccurate coverage of the European Parliament was the fault of the media, there were serious shortcomings in the way EU news was presented to the media by Commissioners, MEPs and staff working for them. The European Commission issued some of the worst press releases imaginable, though not necessarily through the fault of its press office staff. Each Commissioner or Director General liked to see a well-honed press release containing every nuance, every extra titbit of information favouring EU actions with careful explanations of problems so that nothing was exaggerated or said out of context. The outcome of this obsession with detail of these press releases was that all too often they were rejected by the media as just pap and therefore ignored.

Too many MEPs and too many of the European Parliament's press staff seemed to think that they could command attention by means of a press release on a topic of their choosing and at a time of their choosing. Not so! The matter had to be newsworthy and timely. The requirement for Conservative press releases to be approved by a sometimes hesitant Conservative Group leadership, anxious not to upset Downing Street, meant that deadlines were missed more often than not. Some of the Conservative Group's leaders were nervous about the press and terrified of the wrath of Bernard Ingham, Press Secretary in Downing Street, who fed selected cuttings to Mrs Thatcher. This fear led to a fervent desire by certain MEPs to isolate themselves from the media, even if the result was that we got no coverage at all. (Mind you, that might not have mattered to some of the Conservative MEPs who thought they had rock safe seats, but it mattered a great deal to me!) While some of the Tory MEPs would back away from answering journalists' questions, I nearly always found that if I gave journalists whom I knew something press-worthy, even if it was positive about the EU, it would restrain their desire to go digging for dirt for a while. But there was no guarantee that my story would be published.

Some of the newspapers were quite unreasonable in their slanting of the news to show the EU in a bad light. The *Daily Telegraph*, controlled at the time by their Canadian-born proprietor Conrad Black (subsequently convicted in the USA for fraud and obstructing justice), was virulently anti-EU. Several years into the 21st century, even certain senior BBC presenters seemed incapable of avoiding making sniping comments about the EU or of describing its functions accurately. There is scarcely any coverage of debates in the European Parliament yet critics of EU legislation including, on occasions "rent-a-quote" MPs, strongly opposed to anything coming out of Brussels or Strasbourg, are given time on the airwaves.

There were many outbursts in the press when the new, wine coloured "EU passport" was introduced. In fact, the travel document we have today is a British passport, issued by the British authorities according to British criteria. It's only the format and the colour that have been standardised within the EU. The passport still says on the front "British Passport". People complained about the death of the old, blue "British" Passport format. In fact this hallowed document followed a standard 1920 League of Nations design, and was not uniquely British. In 2001 the *Daily Telegraph* took up the paranoia by reporting that plans were being drawn up to replace the standard maroon EU passport, introduced in 1988, bearing a national symbol on the front cover (in our case the royal coat of arms) with a sky blue passport bearing the EU symbol of a circle of twelve stars. This, of course, has not happened! But I suppose some journalists thought it made a good story and it fitted in with the newspaper's editorial views.

The Conservative MEPs in my time never got to grips with dealing with the press. For a short time, I had a responsibility for this myself, working with a journalist on the staff of the Group. I proved that coverage could be increased if good stories were offered to the press. However, the leadership of our Group often wanted to issue lengthy elegant press releases, sometimes long after the matters concerned were in the media. I myself probably had as much press coverage as any MEP in my time. I learned that an editor uses the scissors on the bottom of a draft of an article. There is no point in putting the best news nugget at the end of an article because if the article has to be shortened, which is very often the case, this is what will be cut out. An article is not constructed logically or chronologically. Each sentence from the headline downwards expands the theme stated in the headline into a further degree of detail or explanation. Moreover, an article must contain one message, not several. You don't see an article which says: "Bloggs' stores have appointed a new managing director, and by the way a shoplifter was caught in the ladies' lingerie department yesterday". No, you have one story or the other, whichever best meets the test of being shocking or amusing. Some of my Tory MEP colleagues seemed not to have appreciated these points.

Writing headlines is one of the most difficult jobs in journalism. A headline has to give a short and clear message. Someone reading a newspaper can scan the headlines and get a general picture of what is going on. Editors like short words to cram in as much meaning as possible, so if they can find words like *fury* or *chaos* or *orgy* in a press release, such words will be used in the headline. Most journalists did not understand the EU and their editors did not often provide funds for them to travel to find out about it. Worse still, a journalist who had instructions from his editor or the paper's proprietor to rubbish the EU, had to do exactly that or damage his own career, or, in the case of a freelance journalist, not be paid for the article submitted.

The use by some British people of the word *frogs* to denote the French is clearly unflattering. So a headline, in the *Hoylake News* "Euro-MP wants frogs' legs banned" could be taken as backing for a political action I was supporting or a jingoistic insult. (In certain Asiatic countries, where most of the frogs legs consumed in Europe came from, the legs were pulled off while the creatures were still alive.) Another sprightly headline with lots of hidden meaning was *"Achtung!* All's well in the Fatherland". This followed comments I made after a visit to Germany where the difference at that time between the prosperity of Germany and lacklustre Britain – before Mrs Thatcher's effort to rid the country of socialism had fully taken effect – were clear to see. 'The prosperity of Germany is amazing,' I had said.

One day, Jacques Delors, then President of the European Commission, gave one of his orations in the European Parliament, commenting on a wide range of EU activities – some might say on most forms of human activity! Some of what he said was favourable to Britain, some unfavourable, and some did not concern Britain at all. As soon as he finished, the seven or eight mainstream British journalists in Strasbourg went into a huddle in the press bar. I watched them and after some minutes it was clear that they had arrived at a decision. I asked one of them what the line was that they would all take. 'Oh', he said, 'It has to be 'Delors attacks Britain' again, doesn't it?' And so it was across the British headlines the following day.

Early in my time as an MEP, I asked whether the then editor of the *Daily Telegraph*, Bill Deedes, would meet us as a Group and tell us how editorial priorities were determined. The day he came, the *Daily Telegraph* ran a small piece about the result of a by-election in the Australian state of Queensland. The same day, a large grant of European money had been made to improve roads and other infrastructure in Merseyside but not a word of this appeared in the *Daily Telegraph*. I asked Bill Deedes why he thought that a by-election in an Australian regional parliament was more newsworthy than a major European investment in Britain.

'Well', he drawled, 'the Aussies are our kith and kin, aren't they?'

In Strasbourg and Brussels in the years following 1979, the number of journalists allocated to follow European Parliamentary affairs was very small. By the year 2000, Brussels had the largest foreign press corps in the world apart from Washington. In the early days of the elected European Parliament, the quality newspapers usually sent someone to Strasbourg for the monthly session. The tabloids, on the other hand, were mostly represented by two or three stringers – freelances paid according to the amount of their copy which was actually published. Most of these poor souls knew that they would only be paid if they sent in knocking copy. The BBC made an effort towards balance but sometimes even it could not resist broadcasting some of the knocking stories. Its people kept themselves rather remote from the Members, which had both advantages and disadvantages.

In the earlier days of the directly elected European Parliament, it was journalistic practice for newspapers to head an article with a by-line saying "from Joe Bloggs in Brussels" or some such mention. Sometimes, one reporter would send the same story with the wording slightly altered to two different papers, using different names as authors, their own or fictitious. I can remember one particular case where a by-line of "So-and-So in Strasbourg" referred to a reporter who was actually in his house in Southend at the time.

One day, I heard of a British journalist working for a serious British daily paper in Brussels who was challenged over the accuracy of one of his reports which concerned certain events in Belgium. He replied that his paper did not have a large number of readers in Belgium who could be upset by the inaccuracy. The main thing was that the piece was in line with the paper's policy on Europe.

During the time when I was asked by the EDG to take an interest in trying to improve the press coverage of my party and colleagues, I kept a watch on which journalists were in Strasbourg and what they did. One day we heard that a hit-and-run journalist from one of the tabloids was coming out with a photographer to try to find one or more MEPs *in flagrante* and photograph them for the popular press. We were used to the technique of journalists doing one-off pieces about the European Parliament. They, as opposed to some of the regular Brussels press, could by no means be expected to even try to be accurate, let alone fair. The standard technique of many of these hit-and-run journalists was to draft their knocking copy on the plane on the way out – no doubt following the line laid down by their editors – have a few drinks in the press bar at the Parliament, go out for dinner with fellow hacks, then to bed with a long lie-in in the morning before the journey back to London.

This particular journalist turned out to be an attractive young lady with long, flowing hair and bright red trousers. She was quite a dish and clearly wanted to be seen as such. There had to be a reason for this and some of us thought we knew what it was. Redpants, as we named her, wandered round the press room in the Parliament but did nothing very special in the afternoon. The photographer was not to be seen. We heard on the grapevine that the young lady would turn up at the *Bang 'o Bells* restaurant in town during the evening, to catch MEPs doing whatever she thought they got up to. The restaurant had two adjoining rooms, both with doors leading to the street.

I waited for her in the restaurant. In came Redpants on cue, eyes agog. I decided to introduce myself and escort her from table to table in the first room. Better to be perfectly open, hide nothing and have witnesses aware of what was going on in case she printed a pack of lies. I knew most of the people there anyway, so it was all very civilised and quite proper. Redpants looked disappointed. Then she cottoned on to the existence of the adjoining room, which appeared to be an "inner room". Her eyes were agog again! Perhaps this was where the MEPs were doing whatever they got up to. But there was no joy for her there either. It was exactly the same scene as in the first room, with members and others just enjoying dinner and the *patronne* fussing round. I introduced Redpants to a number of those present. She hid her disappointment but before long said she would go back to her hotel.

Will she just go outside and invent a whole pack of lies? I asked myself. I decided to escort her back to her hotel which I did, uneventfully, and then went back to the restaurant. Many of us were still worried that Redpants would invent a story of depravity and worse. She could not go home without her story, the paper having paid her air fare, and she would submit a bill for food and lodgings. I therefore had words with both the Conservative and Labour press officers to see whether they could give her a story which would stop her inventing some tale of sleaze. The two press officers were already thinking along the same lines and one of them came up with a good story about some unrelated matter which satisfied Redpants' editor. She therefore went home happy enough and presumably got her expenses claim form signed.

If the state of the British media is a cause of real concern, television and radio have to be included in the criticism. It is sad to have to include some of the news and current affairs output of the BBC in this judgement. The BBC has been a magnificent force for truth in the world for over half a century. However, it sometimes seems to be operating in a metropolitan goldfish bowl, out of touch with the views and standards of ordinary British people, spending public money lavishly and allowing its quest for ratings to lower its standards. One or two of its presenters allowed themselves to descend into trivial sniping at the EU, arising presumably from their own personal prejudices or the result of simple ignorance of anything outside Westminster. Its London-centric habits meant that it said little about the impact of EU policies on the English regions. Yet the Corporation remains a great British asset, much better than broadcasters in most countries.

British television was very unwilling to film events in Strasbourg or Brussels or broadcast material from them. The BBC and ITV used to say that this was mainly a question of cost. There was some truth in this, especially because, in the early 1980s at least, it seemed to take a team of four or five BBC staff to film in Strasbourg, doing what one Belgian cameraman could do, thanks to the unions to which BBC staff belonged. A further factor was the high cost of transmission to London via the European Broadcasting Union networks.

I made use of the fact that an MEP has the right to initiate a line of expenditure in the draft EU budget and ask the Parliament to approve it. I worked out the cost of ten minutes transmission per month from Brussels and ten minutes a month from Strasbourg to each of the national broadcasting centres in the EU countries and proposed a sum in the EU budget to cover this. My proposal went through the budget approval system in due course and the

Pearce Line of expenditure was born. For several years this facilitated the task of those broadcasters for whom the transmission cost really had been a problem. But the BBC took umbrage at this. It said that on a point of principle, as a broadcasting organisation free from political influence, it could not accept this money. However, many principles are flexible and this one was flexible enough to permit the BBC to use the *Pearce Line* for regional news broadcasts in the UK, though not for national ones.

When a BBC or ITV interviewer was not around I sometimes made use of a self-service TV studio in a large cupboard in the Parliament's building in Brussels. At a time prearranged with one of the UK broadcasters, I went in, switched on the lights and spoke to the interviewer in the UK "down the line", to receive instructions for positioning myself and then to hear the questions put to me on camera. An unseen hand, usually in regional studios in Manchester or Liverpool, turned the camera on and off.

I took the matter of BBC coverage further and in the early 1980s I asked to see the BBC's Director General about his organisation's lack of coverage of the European Parliament. BBC personages of stratospheric importance do not see mere MEPs! However, in London I met some functionary down the line; he was in charge of forward planning of foreign news or some such grand but vague managerial territory. He was courteous but I did not get very far with him. A few weeks later, I was invited to a drinks party in Brussels to mark the arrival of a permanent BBC correspondent there. I don't think the BBC had had a permanent correspondent there before. The functionary whom I had met in London was at this drinks reception. To make conversation, I asked which hotel he was staying in. He said he was moving on to Paris directly after this reception and would be spending the night there. I asked which hotel he normally stayed *there*. I was astonished when he replied that he had never been to Paris before. How could the BBC put a man who had never been to Paris, whether to see the Eiffel Tower, watch the rugby or sneak into the *Follies Bergères*, in charge of planning news coverage of continental affairs? No wonder so little about Europe made the BBC airwaves!

During one Strasbourg session, Barbara Castle and I were due to appear together on a regional television programme to put forward the Labour and Conservative angles on a topical issue. The Belgian TV crew hired to film the interview and transmit it simultaneously to the studios in the UK prepared us, sitting next to each other on a seat in the area outside the hemicycle. Many TV stations like to broadcast interviews with something going on in the background

141

rather than with a sterile studio background. This is a happy opportunity for people who want to get on the telly by walking about in the background while the interview was taking place! The first question came down the line from the interviewer in the UK. Barbara started to answer. Stop! The British unions had blacked the transmission. The rule was that when a foreign cameraman was used, only one interviewee was allowed to be on the screen at any one time. Barbara plus me was one too many! I spoke to the TV station in the UK on the telephone. At their behest I found a British freelance journalist in the press room. After more phone calls, he was appointed to put the designated questions to Barbara and me separately, off camera. He then faced the camera alone to report that I had said this and Barbara had said that.

Radio interviews are very short, sometimes forty seconds or less. It *is* possible to get a point across in this time, provided you are very clear about your facts. When people in conferences say they need ten or twenty minutes for their speech – 'I can't get my argument across in anything less', they say – they are talking nonsense. Most radio and television interviews are very short and skilled politicians know how to use very short periods of time to their advantage. Moreover, to insist on speaking at length makes it highly likely that the editor cuts out much of what was said.

I was asked one day to be part of a regional TV programme in a Liverpool studio, to respond to questions and opinions from an invited studio audience. When I got to the studio, I discovered it was to be a live transmission. Live broadcasting increases the tension of the participants because you cannot say your bit a second time if you get it wrong the first time. However, it has the advantage that the producer cannot edit the discussion to reflect some particular point of view which he or she holds. The theory of a discussion before an invited audience is that such audiences represent a balanced cross-section of regional opinion. I found that they were largely made up of carefully selected party activists. Many Tory voluntary workers often performed badly in these circumstances; they were often less well-briefed and not as naturally articulate in front of the cameras as the hand-picked people of the Left.

On this particular occasion, a difficult but perfectly fair question was lobbed at me from the Labour side of the studio. The interviewer omitted to mention that it came from a very senior, paid, trade union official, one of several activists present. Next to the union official was a lady Councillor who was bitterly anti-police and who had been reported in the paper as having paraded alongside a pig's head on a plate in an anti-police demonstration following the Toxteth riots of 1981! 'Where I come from…' she began, as though an ordinary woman in the street.

'I know where *you* come from,' I said. The interviewer, obviously calculating the cost of a possible libel action if I went over the top, tugged at my jacket. I backed off.

Another day in the constituency, I was telephoned by a researcher of a BBC religious television programme. This was in the days when apartheid was still in operation, and the researcher urgently wanted my views about South Africa, presumably knowing that I did not favour boycotts of that country. Depending on what I said, I might be invited on to the programme. Such a possibility always causes the politician's adrenalin to flow – reach for comb, check tie is straight etc.

'Do you agree that…?' asked the researcher.

'I won't go as far as that,' I replied.

'But would you at least go as far as to say that…?' pressed the researcher.

'I would only go as far as to say…' I responded, and this went on for half an hour.

'We'll let you know,' said the researcher. She didn't. No need for the comb then. Clearly, I would not express the sentiments which she wanted the programme to broadcast. She must have telephoned around until she found someone else who was willing to express precisely the sentiments which I had refused to utter. That was what was eventually broadcast.

I had an experience worthy of those "out-take" television programmes of mistakes while filming taking place. I was being interviewed in the garden of a hotel in which I was attending a conference. First, Granada filmed me, showing me arriving up some steps at the entrance of the hotel. (This was actually after the conference had finished and I was about to leave). Then BBC North West also wanted to film me arriving, up the same steps but at a different angle. Since plenty of people watched both Granada and BBC regional news programmes, and it would look a bit odd if I appeared to have arrived twice, I suggested to the BBC that their film piece should make me appear to be *leaving* the hotel. The BBC man, Jim Hancock, put his first question. I began to answer. The church clock nearby started to chime. Start again! Jim put the question again. This time a lorry with a defective exhaust pipe spluttered by. Start again! Then a low-flying aircraft making for Manchester airport came over. Start again! This time there was silence all around us – but behind me, a couple who had been lying in some rhododendron bushes got to their feet with guilty looks and slunk off. Start yet again!

One of the difficulties with television interviews is that there is sometimes only one camera available. In these cases, the cameraman films the interviewee listening to the question and then answering, with a back view of the interviewer. He then films the interviewer asking the questions a second time, showing the interviewee apparently listening to them, nodding. A reputable interviewer makes sure that the questions filmed are the questions answered. I have never known this routine to be deliberately falsified but the episode in the hotel garden demonstrated that after two or three "takes" it is not always easy to remember exactly what the original question was.

Another television interview involved going to Manchester for a Sunday lunchtime transmission. I was reasonably good at live television, especially at answering questions. The BBC said they would send a car to fetch me from my home. I said I could drive myself. No, they insisted on sending a car for me. The BBC car arrived at my house late, having gone to the wrong address. I had phoned the studio several times to report progress. Felicity Goodey, the interviewer had switched the order of the interviews in order to accommodate my late arrival. I arrived in the BBC building, was wired for sound at once and we were off; there was no time for the usual briefing or rehearsal. It went quite well. Felicity said afterwards that, given my delayed arrival, it was a good job I knew what I was talking about in answering the questions.

There are techniques for getting on television if you want to. After one of William Hague's speeches in Blackpool as Conservative Party Leader after I had left the Parliament, I felt that the pro-EU case was just not getting an airing. The anti-Europeans had had most of the platform time. I guessed that the television would want instant comments as the faithful came out of the conference hall. I went out of the building rapidly and waited by the exit and, sure enough, a BBC person approached me.

"What did you think of the leader's speech?" asked the interviewer.

"He spoke brilliantly and left the party in good heart, BUT…. he won't take some of us along with him in his anti-Europe attitudes," I replied.

Only a small proportion of vox-pop (man-in-the-street) interviews filmed are ever broadcast. My Blackpool piece was broadcast twice on prime-time national news, but my opening remarks were cut and viewers only saw and heard the bit beginning with "BUT…" I had given them what they wanted – a usable sound-bite provided at the right time. I had flown the pro-Europe flag, in contrast to the other exit sound-bites. When you have been on television, you always meet people who tell you that they saw you – some people seem to feel that knowing someone who has been on television enhances their status. On this occasion, having of course heard only half of what I had said, the views were mixed. 'Good show! Someone had to say it,' said some. "Bit naughty that, going against the Leader," said others.

When the 1989 election approached, one which I knew I would lose because of boundary changes and the unpopularity of Mrs Thatcher, a *Sunday Express* journalist said he wanted to come up to Chester and interview me in the constituency. The Conservative leadership told me not to do this, but I ignored them. The journalist came. He told me I was bound to lose (which I myself knew). We enjoyed an excellent Chinese meal. We said little about the EU. We went back to his comfortable hotel, which happened to be having a "grab-a-granny" event that evening. The "grannies" were mostly in their mid-twenties as far as I could see. I departed quite soon leaving the journalist to enjoy his evening as he wished. He went back to London the next day and printed a very fair, friendly and well-informed account of my campaign in his paper. He forecast in his article that I would lose, which I did.

Showing the Prime Minister a map of my constituency

Sometimes I used the press to try to shake up my colleagues. Some members of the Conservative MEPs seemed to behave more like members of a club where getting on with everyone else was all that mattered rather than trying to shape events. I do not deny that one needs allies and that sometimes this requires compromises, but this does not forbid combat where it is called for. There are times when a frontal attack is necessary; it would not necessarily damage the Tories' reputation or that of the Parliament as a whole.

In January 1987 I launched an attack on a proposal to sell off some of the butter mountains to the Russians at a discounted price. A substantial EU subsidy was to be paid to reduce the price to a level which the Russians (or the French intermediaries involved in the deal) would accept. I said that this was "obscene" and "a gift to the enemy". This was reported at length in the *Daily Telegraph* which added: "Mr Pearce does not speak for the Conservative Group in the European Parliament but it is known that many British Euro MPs share his view that destroying butter stocks and ending the present system of unlimited buying of dairy products at guaranteed prices is the only politically feasible method of eliminating the butter mountain and restoring balance to production". They got it right this time!

The press sometimes used purported comments by what they called "senior" MPs to support their stories. Whether on such occasions they spoke to any MPs at all, I cannot say. However, there was certainly a number of "senior" Westminster MPs who could be relied on to criticise the EU, whether out of deeply felt conviction or just to bolster their public images. The European Parliament was fair game! Mrs Thatcher seemed not to discourage such sniping. I recall being told by a journalist much later that there were two things that Mrs Thatcher could not stomach: Scottish nationalism and Europe. The reason was the same in both cases – she was intrinsically incapable of getting control of either. She was not Scottish and did not represent a Scottish seat so she could not control Scottish politics, and in Europe, the power structure of the European Union is such that no single nation can ever control it.

In more recent years through the various memoirs of Downing Street spokesmen and spin doctors, we have come to understand what they get up to in their briefing of journalists. The spokesmen give the party line and most reporters follow it; if they don't, their privileged access to Downing Street could be withdrawn. Quite a few Tory MEPs believed that sometimes Downing Street briefed the press against them. On one occasion, immediately after having been received by the Prime Minister, our Group was reprimanded by Downing

Street for a press leak! It was rumoured later that the leak actually came from inside Downing Street itself, which, true or false, says much about the relationship between the PM and the Conservative MEPs.

I sent out one or two press releases to twenty or more local papers and radio stations almost every week. Sometimes the journalists would phone me back for more detail. Sometimes the local radio stations would ask for an interview, either by telephone or in one of their studios in Liverpool or Wrexham.

The local press is a bit of a hit-and-miss operation. In the free weekly local papers, there seems to be little logic about which stories are printed and which are not. Sometimes a story about an event is included three weeks after it took place. On one occasion a report by the chairman of the mid-Cheshire branch of the European Union of Women about a visit by members to Normandy was printed twice in the same paper in consecutive weeks. The first time it was on its own and the second time it was attached to a report of a talk which Myra gave at the same meeting but on another topic. Errors in newspapers are legion. One of the most satisfying was when I spoke at a meeting at the Liverpool Chamber of Commerce when I was a European Commission official. The (Liverpool) *Daily Post's* intrepid, if ill-informed, reporter promoted me to be a European Commissioner! Well, I wouldn't argue with that, would I? Better than being called a commissionaire – a title which has befallen a Commissioner on more than one occasion.

But for all its sins, we needed the media. Without it, how would the public know why their laws were made and what their taxes were spent on? In the eighteenth century, an MP would return to his constituency from time to time, dine with the squirearchy and consider his duties done. Nowadays, everyone has a right to know. Politicians may be driven to bask in press coverage to assuage their egos but there is also a perfectly good reason for them to try to get their words and deeds into the papers and on to the television and radio. All sorts of headlines and articles helped me to get across some small part of what I did as an MEP.

One good headline was "Euro MP to fight cruel bull horror". This was the headline in the *Wirral Globe* about one of my efforts to curb *encierros* (bull runs) in Spain. Even more glowing was the headline in the *Chester Chronicle* on 6 November 1987 "Euro chief's visit". I had never thought of myself as a chief. Sometimes the papers were indeed a little over-enthusiastic about my prowess. "Tory MEP hits out at Thatcher" said the *Daily Post* on 21 May 1989, after I had said she was wrong to vote against new EU health warnings on cigarette packets.

"Pearce and Premier" on 14 April 1989 was more flattering except for the note, which was perfectly correct, that my seat was the second most marginal in the country.

The press finds it necessary to quote the ages of people in the limelight. The *Hoylake News* had a headline in May 1984 "The EEC and our Euro-man". The accompanying photo of me in my office in West Kirby was good. But why did they caption it with "Forty-six-year-old Andrew Pearce, Euro MP for Cheshire West in his office in Grange Road, West Kirby from where he and his team are co-ordinating his election campaign." In any case they were a year out – I was only forty-five! Strange that when they quoted a reference I made to Ted Heath in the same article, they didn't give *his* age.

Sometimes the press carried out surveys upon which to build news items. These are seldom scientific, or even claimed to be, but they are bound to have an impact on readers. The *Hoylake News* carried out a survey of fifty local residents. Twenty-two per cent of them could name me. The *News* thought that this was disheartening. I didn't think it was too bad and I'm sure it was much better than the score for most of my MEP colleagues.

The media loved reporting on strikes in Liverpool. Reporters could always find Liverpool strikers willing to give colourful comments. One day, a dock strike was announced. Reporters raced to Liverpool for a story. But the Liverpool docks were *not* on strike. On another occasion, a reporter got off the train from London at Liverpool's Lime Street station, looked at the river from the city centre, saw no ships and reported that the port was dead. He did not bother to find out that the port had moved a mile or two nearer the mouth of the river where it now had up-to-date docks and handling facilities.

I doubt that any Fleet Street paper ever carried photos of four MEPs on the same page. The Turkish Cypriot paper *Günaydin* did so, however. In January 1984 it carried photos of a Dutchman, a German, a Northern Irishman and me. We four were among MEPs supportive of the Turkish position vis-à-vis the Greek Cypriots.

Listening to the voice of business

As MEP, I involved myself with Liverpool Chamber of Commerce (known as Merseyside Chamber of Commerce during a period in the 1970s and 1980s), as a means of keeping in touch with local business. I had an arrangement with a colleague MEP, Gloria Hooper, now Baroness Hooper of Liverpool and St James, whereby she generally took the lead on matters of social policy in my Euro-constituency as well as her own, and I generally took the lead on commercial and industrial matters in her patch as well as mine. I was made an honorary member of the Chamber and attended many meetings of its ruling council.

British Chambers of Commerce are not as strong as those in most continental countries because membership is compulsory over there but voluntary in the UK. In many countries, the Chamber is the route by which companies have contact with government departments. Liverpool Chamber grew to some 2,000 members, a small percentage of the total number of businesses in the city – though a much larger percentage of overall employment. This is typical in this country. In contrast, the Chamber at The Hague in the Netherlands, which I visited, had 22,000 members.

Merseyside is similar to many other British provincial cities in that the decision-makers in many of the firms in the area are scattered worldwide — London, Rotterdam, Detroit, Russelsheim, Tokyo. Such firms tend to organise their lobbying of governments from those cities or in the national capitals, not through Chambers of Commerce in cities such as Liverpool, despite having large numbers of employees in their production units there. The two Merseyside car plants, owned at the time by Ford (now Jaguar Landrover) and General Motors (Vauxhall) are prime examples. Local managers in many cases seemed, in that era, to be deterred by their distant head offices from concerning themselves with political issues even though it was they who had to implement many of the decisions taken. That is not to say that big companies based elsewhere were lacking in generosity towards local causes. I heard that when a Japanese firm set up in a newly-created borough near Liverpool, the management generously offered to purchase a gold chain for the mayor, a sign of commitment to the community. (The local Burma Star Association protested against this in the light of their members' experiences of another side of the Japanese character during the Second World War.)

The Liverpool Chamber of Commerce viewed itself as the voice of Liverpool business. There was a time when it seemed remarkably disengaged from the general well-being of the city. I attended the Chamber's Annual General Meeting (AGM) in 1982, the year after the Toxteth riots when Liverpool was at its lowest point both economically and politically. There were all the usual pomposities such as 'My Lord President, I have great pleasure in proposing the re-election of Mr So-and-So as Vice Chairman for the coming year…' Elected unopposed, of course! I waited to hear some comment on the then parlous state of the city's economy or about the Toxteth riots. Not a single word! At subsequent AGMs I spoke up about this and said that the business community should be helping to find solutions but I did not get much support. However, the Chamber did cooperate with many public bodies concerned with the local economy. I played a part in some of this activity. I often said that I wished the Chamber would speak with a louder voice in both local and national affairs.

The Earls of Derby have long played an important part in the life of Liverpool. They were Presidents of the Liverpool Chamber from its inception in 1850. The 18th Earl was President of the Chamber in my time. He did not like meetings to last more than one hour. He was prone to closing a meeting and leaving when this length of time had passed.

One day in the 1980s, I arranged to go and see Lord Derby at Knowsley, his seat in the outskirts of Liverpool, to discuss a particular problem. It was winter. I was shown into a long gallery. Lord Derby said I must be cold. I said I wasn't but he insisted and went off to 'do something about it'. He returned with a one-bar electric fire, positioned it nearly three metres from where I was sitting, switched it on and asked if that was better. When we had finished talking, he gave me a key and told me to drive to the gates of the park, let myself out and leave the key at the lodge. I got lost in the park and found myself driving over various cattle grids. Part of his estate had been turned into a safari park. When I eventually found a lodge to drop the key in, I moved very rapidly from my car to the lodge and back to the car just in case I had strayed into the safari park and some of the big game were hungry.

Merseyside County Council, bringing together some of the local government functions for a population of one and a half million people in Liverpool and surrounding areas, existed from 1974 to 1986. One of its actions was to set up the Merseyside Enterprise Forum as an occasional meeting place for particular local bigwigs so that they could discuss the local situation in a non-confrontational way. This being the era of Derek Hatton and Militant Tendency, the setting up of the Forum was an important step to try to bring sense and progress into a city rent by brutal political conflict amounting to class war. The Forum was initially chaired by John Parkes, a rare man in public affairs who judged people by their ability and commitment, not by their party label. Members represented only themselves, not whatever organisations they belonged to. I myself was a member, as were certain senior county councillors, Derek Worlock, the Roman Catholic Archbishop, and various industrial and commercial leaders. One of the reports produced under the Archbishop's guidance was "Chips with Everything", a prescient account of the dominant role which computer chips would come to play in our lives. The Forum was a talking shop – and none the worse for it. Talking defuses many conflicts and enables people to understand each other better and therefore cooperate more easily.

When Mrs Thatcher abolished the Greater London Council, the provincial metropolitan counties, including Merseyside, were also disbanded. The metropolitan counties brought a valuable measure of coordination to some of their areas' activities such as transport, strategic planning and waste disposal. Several of these functions are now handled by joint boards made up of local councillors seconded from the boroughs which took over the county responsibilities. Merseyside County Council was hated by Tory Councillors in Wirral and Sefton who found it a threat to their borough fiefdoms, though I don't think this sentiment was universally shared by the population. The existence of Merseyside County Council came under threat due to Mrs Thatcher's determination to get rid of Ken Livingstone and the Greater London Council. I obtained an undertaking from a Minister that, notwithstanding what was done in London, separate thought would be given to the justification or otherwise of scrapping the other metropolitan authorities including Merseyside. I was promised that I would be allowed to put some ideas forward before the decision was made. In fact, I was not informed that any such thought was given. Even in 2012, when Liverpool elected its first executive Mayor, the government did not seem to realise that such a mayor ought to be appointed to function for the whole Liverpool City Region, not just the City itself. The success of Ken Livingstone and then Boris Johnson, successive Mayors of London, in championing issues which concern London *as a whole* should have been a pointer for what the Liverpool area needs.

There was much discussion about whether the Merseyside Enterprise Forum could continue despite the demise of the County Council. Although the University of Liverpool took over as 'guardian angel' for a while, the Forum did not survive.

★ ★ ★

Merseyside, like many cities, has had a considerable number of unelected quangos (quasi-autonomous non-governmental organisations). The Merseyside Development Corporation (MDC) was one. Liverpool was also within the orbit of the North West Development Agency (NWDA), which handled large amounts of public funds but was subject to no direct democratic oversight or accountability. A good deal of the vaunted public consultation which took place on local plans consisted of one quango consulting other quangos and the officials of local councils. The private and voluntary sectors and private individuals were not much involved. Simply passing the bureaucratic buck around the quango circle does not mean that local opinion has been effectively sounded out. The position was made worse by the fact that certain people were on the boards or committees of several of the quangos. The Mersey Partnership (TMP) was another quango. It came into being to spearhead the drive for inward investment for the county as a whole and to run such supportive measures for tourism as existed at that time. TMP's public relations got off to a bad start when it refused the press access to its inaugural meeting.

★ ★ ★

I tried through the Chamber of Commerce and Wirral Council to increase interest in tourism. Chester City Council already knew a great deal about this and its area benefited in many ways. By 2008, people far and wide knew that the city had much to offer tourists – heritage, culture and sport. But back in 1979, it was uphill work. Many local councillors and officials did not see that there was a strong economic purpose in encouraging tourism; that it creates jobs, brings in money and improves the image of the place and that all this acts as an incentive to outside investors to come here. They could not see the potential assets which the area possessed. Many times I countered the view coming from well-heeled Wirral people that tourists should be satisfied with walking along the attractive beaches of the Dee. I used to reply: 'Fine. But they bring their sandwiches, park for free and spend nothing. What economic value do they bring?' The failure of many local worthies to understand the value and prospects of tourism in Merseyside was illustrated for me by a particular councillor in Wirral. In the early 1980s I suggested to her that trams should be brought back as a tourist attraction to Birkenhead, the first place in England to have a street tramway (in 1860). They could connect with the Mersey ferry across to Liverpool. The Councillor laughed in my face. 'What?' she said. 'Trams in Birkenhead? Tourists here? You'll never get tourists coming to Merseyside.' I and others pointed out that more visitors would come on the ferry across the Mersey to Birkenhead if more effort were made to publish and improve that town's heritage attractions. I recall a Chairman of the Liverpool Chamber commenting, with great surprise, that Dutch and Irish football supporters, in Liverpool for a match at Anfield stadium between their two national sides, spent the afternoon shopping. The idea that people visiting, for whatever reason, are likely to spend money in shops, indeed that shopping is one of the main motivations of tourism, had not dawned on him.

I attended an excellent conference about tourism in Merseyside, a few months before the city's year as European Capital of Culture (2008) came into view. It said much about TMP that the conference was organised by a local MP, Ben Chapman, and the hotel where it took place – not by TMP itself. Many of us worried whether this quango, quartered in well-appointed offices on Liverpool's Pier Head, gave value for money. There has indeed been an increase in inward investment; tourism has blossomed especially in and following 2008. How much of this can be attributed to TMP or whether the upsurge would have happened anyway is a matter for debate.

The European Capital of Culture status in 2008 brought in unprecedented numbers of tourists in what is hoped will be a permanent major part of the local economy, based on the city's heritage of magnificent Victorian buildings and its vibrant cultural life. By this time (despite continuing knocking copy from Fleet Street), the city was being reborn. A large new complex of shops, Liverpool One, has cemented the city's new role as a major tourist and retail centre. The city has overtaken cities such as Oxford, Bath and Chester in the numbers of international tourists coming in.

One looked for support for tourism in Merseyside from the national authorities. However, the national tourist authorities seemed to concentrate much of their attention on London. All too often British tourism is portrayed as being about London, with the occasional Scottish loch or Welsh castle thrown in to placate the Celtic fringe. Complaints about this bias in favour of London are usually met with the claim that most tourists want to go to London. They will, won't they, if that is mostly what is advertised! The BBC radio's otherwise excellent World Service keeps Britain's heritage and culture in the world's public view, thereby helping to attract tourists, but barely acknowledges that there are places of interest in Britain other than London.

★ ★ ★

Providing advice to individual business executives is a strange matter. I found that on a number of occasions such people would not believe the information and advice I was willing to provide free of charge but they would happily pay several thousands of pounds to obtain three quarters of the same information six months later from a consultant. The logic of this seems to be that it is easier for the executive who obtains the information to convince colleagues to follow some proposal for action resulting from it, if the firm has paid a large sum to obtain it.

Liverpool: the good, the bad and the indifferent

Liverpool was not within my Euro-constituency but it is the economic and cultural focal point of what is now known as Liverpool City Region, which includes Wirral. I am very fond of it. Many of my own Tory colleagues, much of Whitehall and most of the national media had little knowledge of it and had no hesitation in criticising it. I tried to re-educate them.

Liverpool was a tiny fishing port in the thirteenth century and was made a borough by King John, on whose instructions a network of seven streets was laid out. These survive to this day. In the eighteenth century it grew to be the key port of the British slave trade. John Newton, writer of the words of "Amazing Grace", was a Liverpool slave trader in his younger days. William Roscoe, a Liverpool MP, historian and poet was one of the leaders of the campaign to abolish the slave trade, which came to a successful conclusion in 1807.

In Victorian times, the town (from 1880 the City) was hugely successful as a port bringing in raw materials and exporting manufactured goods. It became known as the second city of the British Empire. Its cultural life was second to none outside London and its architecture, including buildings such as St George's Hall, was among the grandest in the land. The architectural tradition continued into the twentieth century with both the Anglican and Roman Catholic cathedrals being noteworthy.

As the twentieth century progressed, industrial decline of the Lancashire hinterland, horrendous wartime bomb damage, the drift of private and public sector employment to the South East and the tailoring of much national policy to serve principally the needs of South East England damaged the city. Bad labour relations and obsolete industrial facilities made things worse. The inevitable switching of much of the country's trade to European markets was a further factor.

The Merseyside Development Corporation, covering both sides of the Mersey, was set up by Michael Heseltine. It was intended not only to bring in government funds but also to make the administration of government aid more efficient. The MDC helped to clean up redundant areas in the port and make them fit for new economic development. It also helped to lever in money from the new European Regional fund, for which I and colleagues lobbied hard in Strasbourg. Cynics said that the MDC might not have been set up if the government had not decided to set up and finance the Docklands Corporation in London with similar objectives and wanted to avoid the charge that public money was being concentrated only on the capital.

I and British MEP colleagues of both parties from the north of England frequently spoke in Brussels and Strasbourg of the need for funds from the new European Regional fund to be used in our areas. Part of our lobbying resulted in the European Parliament's Regional Policy Committee holding a meeting in Liverpool Town Hall. The Committee's Italian chairman described this superb eighteenth century building with its splendid Council Chamber, magnificent reception rooms, superb chandeliers, its mahogany and its silver table decorations as *antichità splendida*. Mrs Thatcher sometimes referred in somewhat disapproving tones of all the government funding pumped into Liverpool. In fact, a good deal of this was money from the EU, not the British Treasury. Moreover, to be strictly accurate, some of the largest sums went into neighbouring boroughs rather than the city. It was welcome just the same. It was no wonder that many in Merseyside believe that the area gets a better hearing in Brussels than from our own government. (The problem of too much public money being spent for the benefit of South East England, Wales and Scotland, as opposed to being spent in the English provinces, was and continues to be a problem. For example, a raft of money which could and should have been spent in the English provinces was spent on the London Olympics).

In 1984, Britain's first International Garden Festival was held in Liverpool, strongly supported by Michael Heseltine. The idea of garden festivals came from Germany, being designed to clear up derelict land and war-damaged property and recoup some of the cost of doing so by holding a festival on the site. I wrote to Food from Britain, the quango responsible for trying to improve the woeful standard of the marketing of British food, to see whether they would arrange for the sale, inside or outside the festival grounds, of the local Lancashire and Cheshire cheeses and perhaps other products from our region such as black puddings from Bury. They were completely uninterested, possibly believing that the expected target of three million visitors would be missed. Or was it just too far north, I wondered? In fact over three million people attended and had

Liverpool suffered terrible damage from bombing in World War II, such as shown in this picture of Lord Street and South Castle Street in the city centre, taken in May 1941

a good time. After the opening ceremony of the Festival, I saw Derek Worlock, the Roman Catholic Archbishop of Liverpool, sitting in the sunshine. We were both, as I have said, members of Merseyside Enterprise Forum. I said to the Archbishop, 'I think that the European Community, as one of the sponsors of the festival, may take some credit for the lovely weather.' 'I think that's really more in my department than yours,' replied the Archbishop with a twinkle.

The Liverpool-owned shipping companies suffered the same depletion as much of Britain's merchant fleet but the port handles (in 2012) as much tonnage as it ever did. It is seventh in Britain by tonnage and is the UK's leading port for containerised traffic to North America. Yet just a few hundred dockers do the work which at one time required 15,000.

The city's population is growing again after years of decline.[17] It still has above average unemployment and many people of lower than average wages but it is vibrant and confident and looks forward to building on its renewed status as one of Britain's great provincial cities.

I put a lot of effort into obtaining wider recognition of Liverpool's ancient origins. The Calder Stones, ancient blocks that once supported the roof of the

---

[17] As in many cities, a proportion of the population has moved out of central areas into the suburbs. While the population of the City of Liverpool is not much more than half what it was in the 1940s, the population of the conurbation is slightly greater than it was in those days.

tunnel of a burial chamber, are probably older than Stonehenge. The Castle, built at the behest of King John between 1227 and 1235 as a base for military incursions into Ireland, was about the size of Harlech Castle built many years later. None of Liverpool Castle remains today but the ancient street pattern leading from it is still evident. The heavy bombardment of Liverpool by Royalist forces in 1644 during the English Civil War is a piece of history deserving better recognition.

I have enjoyed a couple of stories about Liverpool's history – though I do not vouch for their accuracy! The first came from Bob Parry, formerly MP for Liverpool Riverside. Bob told me that his mother had been the landlady of the pub across the street from where a medieval stone cross used to stand. Bob was responsible for the erection of a plaque here commemorating the "fact" that St Patrick preached there in AD 432 before going to Ireland. The second is the story that Adolf Hitler stayed in the city in 1913, with a relative who really did live here, at 102 Upper Stanhope Street. Locals in the Olde Post House pub showed me where, according to them, Hitler used to sit, adding that the French Emperor, Napoleon, who certainly did spend some time in nearby Southport, also drank there. (Some say that Southport's tree-lined Lord Street inspired Napoleon to create the *Champs Elysées*.)

Riots

By the time Mrs Thatcher came to power in 1979, the same year as I was elected to the European Parliament, Liverpool was on its knees. Many in the city were in despair and the situation boiled over in riots in July 1981.

The Toxteth riots in July 1981 followed similar trouble in Bristol in 1980 and in Brixton (London) in April 1981. I visited the scene of the Toxteth riot in what most of the locals called "Liverpool 8" and "Liverpool 7", (using the postcode nomenclature), about three days after it started. As I walked up towards the troubled area, shop owners in Leece Street, nearer the city centre, were frantically boarding up their windows, having heard rumours that fresh riots and burning would spread right through the city centre.

I walked up Upper Parliament Street to where barricades of rubbish were spread across the road. On one side of the street, there were the shells of old, grand terraced houses, the former homes of rich merchants. Some of these were burned out in the riots together with the Racquets Club, a gentlemen's haunt, and Britain's first drive-in bank, both presumably taken as symbols of wealth and capitalism. Some of the damaged properties had been lived in or used as lodging houses or drinking clubs.

On the other side of the street, the old houses had been cleared and replaced by municipal housing – buildings which have subsequently been torn down to make way for the construction of a hospital. These buildings were set back from the street by humps of earth ("berms", as the military call them) which meant that people could lob stones and firebombs from behind them and the police could not see exactly where they came from.

I decided to walk further up the street. Two men came to me and said that I could not go any further. I said that I would go inside the troubled area by this route or by some other way. The men decided that one of them would take me around. I went to his flat in Princes Avenue. From his window, I could see flames still playing in the buildings just a few yards down the road. We went along Lodge Lane where many houses were smouldering with flames.

There were large numbers of police on the streets. Police had been brought in from Norfolk, Devon, Staffordshire, Northumberland and other places, and many from North Wales. The radio systems of the different forces were not compatible with each other so some of the groups of officers were not able to speak to others. Some of the police had had their badges ripped off. The out-of-town officers in particular looked bemused by the situation. At one point, my escort and I were approached by a young man with copies of a left-wing newspaper over his arm. My escort sent him packing, saying, in terms incapable of misunderstanding, that he wasn't going to have outsiders causing more trouble.

Were these riots in Liverpool basically racial? I don't think so. I do not say that there was no race problem. There have been African families in the city for generations. Liverpool had the second largest population of Somalis in the world after Mogadishu. There had indeed been discrimination against people of African origin. It was widely believed that city centre shops would not employ black people. It was said that police would question black people outside their own area and, later, that only police from one particular police station were allowed into the Granby Triangle, an area regarded as the centre of drug dealing and other forms of trouble.

But I don't think these riots were primarily a racial affair. There were other causes. How could the African population of Toxteth be responsible for putting leaflets round various wealthier parts of Wirral advising local hooligans about forthcoming riots in their area in the coming days? I saw some of these leaflets myself. Trouble did begin where and when the leaflets indicated it would but the police nipped it in the bud.

The most immediately believable reason for the Toxteth riots I have heard advanced concerned some local pimps. These people were alleged to have started trouble in the streets in order to deter a citizen group which was campaigning to have prostitutes moved away from their area. Rioting was in the air anyway after the affairs in London and Bristol. The local left-wing activists got into the act and I think it was they who caused the real trouble. But behind this was economic despair.

I was able to compare the Toxteth riots with the second bout of rioting that year which I witnessed myself in Brixton in London. I was in London to attend a meeting and decided to go to see where the earlier riots had taken place, in Railton Road, Brixton. There were corrugated-iron barricades along both sides of the street keeping people out of the ruins of the houses that had been burned out a few weeks earlier. I walked about and talked to people. Nearly all the locals were of Caribbean origin; the only other white people I saw in these streets were 'Red Ted' Knight, a local left-wing politician, and the local vicar. Several people invited me into their houses. In one house, a man in his fifties wearing British Rail clothing told me that a couple of nights earlier the police had come into his flat, questioned him about having weapons and had thrown his belongings all over the place. They found no weapons. I heard many stories of this nature.

Towards eleven o'clock, I decided to leave the area in order not to miss the last tube train. As I left Railton Road, I stopped in a pub to have a drink and make a few notes of what I had seen. I am not a great maker of notes but the stories of police misbehaviour were, for me, so extraordinary that I wanted to write them down so that there was no question of me thinking the next day that I had imagined them. A journalist was having a drink at the other side of the bar. Noticing that I did not look like one of the locals, he came over and asked whether I would agree to speak to the editor of his paper in Fleet Street. He wanted confirmation for the editor of his own account of what he had seen which the editor had been disinclined to believe. I did what he wanted and the story came out on the front page of the paper the next day.

Then another journalist came into the bar with a broken and bleeding nose. He said that Railton Road was now ablaze with piles of burning tyres. I went cautiously outside to see for myself, and sure enough, at the far end of Railton Road, there was a wall of burning tyres. A man standing beside me said these white men had a stash of petrol bombs behind the corrugated iron barricades. Then a mob came from behind the wall of burning tyres towards us, throwing petrol bombs; petrol bombs whistle as they fly through the air. Most of the men involved were white – although I had seen very few whites earlier in my visit. We both stood stock-still as the mob approached. It detoured slightly to avoid us and continued down to the end of the street, where a phalanx of police had formed up. The police carried five-foot-high Perspex shields. There were no functioning street lights but the shields shimmered in the moonlight.

After a while, I decided to leave. I walked down towards the line of rioters, and said, 'Excuse me.' I carried on towards the phalanx of police and repeated, 'Excuse me,' to them also and carried on to the rear of the crowd. At this moment, police reinforcements from the Special Patrol Group (SPG) came through to confront the rioters. The ordinary police near me, who, I was told, came from Wood Green in North London, murmured with excitement at the arrival of the SPG. I could sense the buzz they obviously felt.

I had heard all day from the locals that people trying to defuse the situation found it very difficult to get in touch with the police. They could not get through on the phone to senior officers. In 1981, police confronting riots did not routinely wear special clothing. People were used to the idea that constables and sergeants wore helmets and inspectors upwards wore flat, peaked caps. That night in Brixton, I wondered where the senior officers were until I realised that they also were wearing helmets, with two lines of silver braid around them instead of the one line on the helmets of lower-rank officers. In the darkness, it was therefore not at all easy to spot the senior officers, which I think contributed to the inability of local people to establish contacts with the police in order to avoid further trouble.

Whether the earlier Brixton riot had racial causes I cannot say but I had no doubt at all that the second riot, the one which I witnessed, was the result of reprehensible behaviour by the police, in terms of their attitude to people and property, both during and following the earlier riot there.

The riots in 1981 in Toxteth, Brixton and other urban areas were in part due to the crumbling of life and the despair in older and poorer inner city areas. They encouraged Mrs Thatcher's government to really pay attention to this situation. The problems existed long before she came to office, resulting (in my opinion) from failed housing and planning policies in many towns and cities and, in the case of trouble spots outside London such as Toxteth, from the centralising of jobs and wealth in the capital. Efforts had been made to tackle these problems but the riots put some real impetus into them. It is not hard to find people in Merseyside who avow that the Toxteth riots were what finally gave the spur to the regeneration policies which followed using considerable amounts of UK and EU money. As Michael Heseltine said in a report which he wrote: "It took a riot…"

EU money for my constituency

I was at pains to insist that the North of England got a fair share of public money and jobs. I told anyone in the Tory party who would listen that if government largesse was concentrated on London, which too much of it was (and still is). It is no wonder that there is a regional imbalance in the distribution of wealth in the country. I was quoted in the *Today* newspaper on 26 June 1986: "Tory tells Thatcher: The North matters." Perhaps one can understand Tory emphasis on the South East because that is where most of their voters are, but I fail to understand why there was and is no effective lobby within the Labour Party for the North West.

I was asked to help with access to European funds for firms and local authorities in the Euro-constituency. Merseyside had been a major beneficiary of EU funding through the European Regional Development Fund (ERDF) and the European Social (i.e. Training) Fund (ESF), because its *per capita* income level was less than three-quarters of the EU average. Local unemployment was high; indeed, in my time, it was always higher than that of Northern Ireland. These European funds were administered by British civil servants within European Commission rules and there was in fact no great need or purpose in my intervening once the right officials had been contacted. EU money was spent on all sorts of projects. Aid for a bypass around Upton in Wirral, new lights in the Mersey tunnel, new stations and trains on the Merseyrail suburban railway, riverside redevelopment and many factory sites came from the ERDF.

The European Commission had a requirement that all areas benefiting from projects in this scheme had to display a notice saying so. In the first few years of the ERDF, this was very rarely done in England (although motorists could not fail to see such information in Scotland, Wales, Ireland, or France). I wrote many letters to the authorities about this. I am convinced that the powers-that-be did not want the source of part of the money used for such projects to be publicly known.

There may be two reasons for this. One is just blind prejudice against the EU. Plenty of people in Britain would say, 'It's only money from our own pockets coming back to us. Why should we advertise the fact that it has been to

Brussels and back?' This ignores the point that the British government and its various agencies saw no problem in advertising the fact that money for its own schemes in our area had come from our own pockets – and had been to London and back! Why is a pound from my pocket better going to London and back than to Brussels and back? People in London liked to give the impression that this was largesse from London, not from Brussels.

The second reason for not telling the public that EU money was involved arises from the concept of "additionality". This is the principle that regional aid from Brussels should be "additional" to money which the national government should be spending anyway. In many cases in Britain and in other EU countries it was not in fact additional. It was a substitute for national expenditure. Whitehall did not want to be rumbled.

I tried to publicise EU grants in my constituency with information in leaflets, speeches and press releases. I even arranged the production of two weatherproof notices 30cms (about 1 foot) long saying, "This project was part-financed by the European Community," and threatened to fix these on EU-aided project sites myself if the public authorities did not give proper notice of the source of the funding. In time, whether due to my efforts or not, local recognition of EU financing was, in fact, improved. There are now many billboards on construction sites in Liverpool proclaiming "Thank EU"!

The allocation of EU grants was made subservient to British policy imperatives. When a large sum was accorded to Merseyside for a five-year period, Whitehall decreed that a major part of it should go to training schemes. While there was indeed a need for this type of spending, there was a greater need, as seen from Merseyside itself, for spending on other types of projects, such as trade promotion. Whitehall had in mind that the UK budget for training schemes at that time was quite large and could provide the matching national funding required to support the EU grants. But matched funding for trade promotion would have had to come from the Department of Trade and Industry, which only had a small budget! Hence the emphasis on training for EU grants to the region. I had no doubt that having cash coming into areas such as Merseyside was a good thing, wherever it came from. Failure through the churlish attitude of anti-Europeans in Westminster and Whitehall to acknowledge this fact, as was demanded in regulations, risked curtailing the flow of such funds.

Whitehall wanted the EU money to be paid into the general kitty if possible. For example, some of the ERDF money was allocated to the English Tourist Board to assist tourism development especially in areas of high unemployment.

163

In effect this money went into the English Tourist Board's general funds and, although some of it did end up in the priority areas, much of it actually went to reduce the English Tourist Board's call on the UK budget. It is worth noting that several pots of EU money available to the UK were not taken up because Whitehall would not make the required matching contribution of national funds.

EU finance for a train station

As time went on, the European Commission became stricter about the objectives for which EU money was used, including greater emphasis than Whitehall usually applied to the spin-off effect of grants. As an example, EU funding went towards the widening of the Dock Road in Liverpool and its connections with the general road network. Over a couple of decades this has opened up large areas of land for redevelopment for offices and homes. I doubt that this would have happened under the purely UK grant rules at the time.

A London-based company wanted to demonstrate its commitment to the North West where it had a plant by donating money to help set up the "Catalyst Chemical Museum" in Widnes. The museum's founders could use such a gift as the matched funding which EU grants usually required. The company Chairman thought that my support as the local MEP would be useful. Even though I knew that Whitehall had more or less decided to back the project, I wrote to the authorities supporting it but this wasn't enough for the company Chairman. He came up from London for the day by train. A car was hired for him (from a firm in Manchester for some reason!), and he gave me a tour around the museum building which I found interesting. After buying me an expensive lunch, he went happily back to London. I am grateful for the interest he took.

The allocation of specific European grants for improvement of agricultural production facilities was administered in Britain by the Ministry of Agriculture, Fisheries and Food and related bodies. I could not do much about the allocation of individual grants but I did study where the grants went within the UK. I formed the impression that the MAFF office for East Anglia was winning far more grants for its region than our own MAFF regional office serving Cheshire and Merseyside. I cannot claim that my protests solved the problem but, knowing that civil servants are often sensitive to criticism, I would be surprised if my comments did not have some effect.

There were other smaller pots of European money to tap into which were not at the behest of Whitehall. I did my best to help people to find out how to access them. I spoke at a training course for women, funded by a grant from the European Social Fund, the application for which I had supported. The course turned out to be for women who had been at home looking after their young children and wanted to be "brought up to speed" so that they could start work again later, possibly running their own businesses. They needed to update their skills, especially as regards office equipment. Their main need, however, was to regain the confidence and knowledge to enable them to succeed in the modern business environment. I think the course did them some good.

For many years there have been, quite rightly, complaints about fraud and misuse of European funds. In my time as an MEP I was amongst many calling for better management of such funds. While the European Commission must take some of the blame for this, a good deal of the use of such funds is in the hands of the EU countries. The Commission's auditing of this has become tighter in recent years but member state governments are slow to cooperate, not only because of fear of exposure of their own poor management but also because resulting repayments are net outflows of money from the national treasuries. There have been faults with the handling of EU monies for agricultural subsidies in all member states. One such example was that of the UK Rural Payments Agency which carries out the payments to farmers in England. The payments to farmers under the 2005 budget, which should have been reimbursed by the EU, were late and missed the deadline for doing so. This meant that a cost of £54.9m which could have come from Brussels, had to be borne by the UK taxpayer. In October 2009, the UK National Audit Office reported that the Rural Payments Agency, had "scant regard to protecting public money". It was estimated that it cost £1,743 to process each claim in England whereas the figure for Scotland was £285. The problem with the English office was said to be the complicated system adopted by Margaret Beckett, the Minister responsible at the time.

The system for supervising payments to farmers in Northern Ireland was officially described as only "partially effective". The European Court of Auditors reported that in the year 2005-06 the Regional Development Fund expenditure for North East England was defective because of non-retention of expenditure records. There was no evidence of day-to-day management checks or evidence of any checks by the (UK) paying authority. UK officials acknowledged that not enough priority had been given to day-to-day management checks. The UK reported 1,666 irregularities (including possible fraud) in 2007, an increase of eighteen per cent by number and 125 per cent by value compared with 2006. It was reported, for example, in July 2009 that Walsall Council's failure to provide an audit trail for European Regional Fund cash may have cost taxpayers between one and four million pounds which would have to be refunded to Brussels.

Similar problems, irregularities and fraud occurred in all EU countries. It was announced in July 2006 that the European Commission was to reclaim €161.9 million of CAP money from Greece, Spain, France, Ireland, Italy, Portugal and the United Kingdom in a bid to correct the improper allocation of EU farm funds. The point to note is that, as far as payments under the Regional, Social and Cohesion Funds are concerned, the systems of payment and subsequent audit that were defective were mainly in the hands of officials of the member state government, not of European Commission staff. The Commission is, however, open to criticism for not insisting that the member states install proper accounting systems and subsequent audits. The examples I have given are more recent than my time in the European Parliament. There is always a time lag in audit work. But the problems were already manifesting themselves in my time. I was not a member of the Parliament's Budget Control Committee, then getting into its stride, so was not directly involved in the rooting out of this maladministration.

£54m European Union grant released for Merseyside regeneration projects

A damaging freeze on European development aid meant for Merseyside has been lifted – allowing £54m to be released for key regeneration projects.

In March, the European Commission slapped a temporary ban on all European Regional Development Funding (ERDF) announced for England, after an audit found "irregularities". It was the second time in three years the Commission had thrown doubt on grants earmarked for projects across England's poorer regions, because of tendering errors and faulty documentation.

And it threatened £54m earmarked for Merseyside – the last slice of £250m pledged over the seven-year period between 2007 and 2013.

Now Communities Secretary Eric Pickles has claimed the credit for "swift action" to restore the flow of regeneration funding, through "tighter controls on projects".

And, controversially, he suggested the rescue flowed from the decision to bring the process "in-house" – following the announcement that the North West Development Agency (NWDA) will be axed.

Mr Pickles said: "The ERDF programme has been plagued by a legacy of poor administration and fines that dates back to 2000.

"The Coalition Government has overhauled the management of these schemes, bringing them in-house and successfully minimising the liabilities.

"The measures this government has taken have been recognised by the European Commission which has just announced that payments for the ERDF programme will restart, allowing vital regeneration work to continue."

Among the projects part-funded through ERDF grants are:

The Echo arena and BT convention centre, which opened in 2008 at the former Kings Dock.

The Mersey Waterfront revival project – including the cruise liner facility, at Princes Dock.

The "Visitor Economy" project, led by the Mersey Partnership, to attract more tourists to the city region.

The construction of the Floral Pavilion Complex in Wirral.

Mr Pickles said his department had inherited potential liabilities for ERDF projects estimated at £236m – money allocated to councils that the Commission was refusing to refund – but this had now been reduced to £172m. Of this figure £38.1m "cannot be recovered", but ministers are still seeking to recover the remaining £133.9m.

The DCLG's annual report vows to get tough by targeting projects that have "failed to comply with the requirements of the grant".

Earlier this year, a U-turn saw 40 NWDA staff transfer to work directly for the DCLG, but questions remain about how projects will receive the "match funding" without which applications will fail.

Co-funding must come from the £950m "regional growth fund", which is three times oversubscribed in its second cache, with decisions due in weeks.

Meanwhile, organisations in Merseyside have been fined almost £20,000 for failing to display the EU logo after receiving grants.

(1980s)

Life in Brussels

I lived in Brussels with my family full time from 1974 to 1979 while I was working in the European Commission. Then, as an MEP, I visited the city frequently up until 1989. I lived there again Monday to Friday from 1994 to 2002, while once more working in the Commission. I became very familiar with the city, or at least the centre and the parts near the buildings of the European Parliament and the European Commission, and had many insights into how Belgians lived.

When I started work in the European Commission in 1974 I lived in a hotel in Brussels and then in a studio (a single room with a shower and toilet in the corner behind a curtain) for a few weeks before Myra came over to join me. I learned that although the term *un flat* exists in French, it tends to mean a place occupied for an hour or two for moments of passion rather than somewhere to live.

While living in the hotel, I had an early experience of Brussels' superb standard of restaurant food. I went to a tiny restaurant near the hotel. The *patron* worked in the kitchen and served at table as well. He was enormous; he had no neck and his chest started from his chin, full flush all the way down. I ordered a meal. At the next table, a middle-aged woman was tucking into a bowl of something. After a while she sat back exhausted and asked the *patron* to keep her meal warm. After a quarter of an hour or so, she asked for it to be brought back and tucked into it again. I asked the *patron* what it was. *Fricassée des fruits de mer*, was the answer. So on my next visit to the restaurant, I ordered the *fricassée* and asked for some *pâté* as a starter. 'You can't have anything before the *fricassée*,' said the patron.

'But I'm very hungry,' I said.

'Nothing before the *fricassée*,' he insisted. I gave in and waited for the dish to appear.

The *fricassée* turned out to be a combination of prawns, shrimps, mussels, coquilles St Jacques, half a lobster and palm hearts in a creamy white sauce generously flavoured with whisky, all sitting on a small bed of rice. Halfway through, I began to appreciate the problem displayed by the woman on my earlier visit. Perfect but exhausting! Sadly, the little restaurant isn't there any more.

When Myra and two of our children came over to join me, we rented a house in the leafy suburb of Boitsfort (Bosvoord for Flemish speakers). Shortly afterwards we bought a large house nearby, an old property backing onto the 11,000-acre Forêt de Soignes (Zoniënwoud in Flemish). It was on the other side of this forest that Wellington made his stand at the battle of Waterloo.

Myra fitted in well with other Brits, Danes and Irish who had moved into the city after their countries joined the EU. Brussels offered shopping facilities, medical care and general cleanliness considerably better than was usual in the UK at that time. Two of our children were born in Brussels – acquiring in theory a duty to serve in the Belgian army for national service. We quickly found friends who had children of the same age as our two older children. At that time, people working in the European institutions were a minority of the Brits in Brussels. There were many other Brits there, mainly working for international companies, several of which had their European headquarters there. Our daughter Sarah went to the local French-speaking infants school in Boitsfort and then to the European School. A close friend was Michael Welsh, who later became an MEP. He was a producer for a British amateur dramatics group in Brussels as well as having a day job in a large commercial company.

Coping with languages is always a top priority for people living abroad. But many non-Belgians live for years in Brussels without using French, let alone Flemish. Most Belgians in Brussels speak English and German as well as their own official languages. Our local shopkeeper, Roger, was an example of this. He spoke English and German as well as French and Flemish but had never been to either England or Germany. (The standard of the food he sold was of unbelievably high quality compared to what we had been used to in the UK in the 1970s.)

Myra began to be able to say simple things in French; my own French improved from what I retained from school. Like most Brits of my generation, I had been taught French in a ridiculous way, fussing over obscure grammatical rules that most French people don't use but offering virtually no practice in actually speaking the language.

We soon learned to use English, not French, when we knew we were talking to Flemish speakers. Many French-speaking Belgians cannot speak Flemish.

With the FA Cup won by Liverpool, which was shown off in Brussels

Many Flemish-speaking Belgians *can* speak French but will not do so. The Belgian Civil Code that governs much in daily life was only translated into Flemish in 1961. There was a Flemish-Belgian in my office in the European Commission who, as a child, had been forced to attend a French-speaking school and who had been in the Belgian army in World War II with Flemish troops under a French-speaking officer; most of the troops could not understand the officer!

You don't have to speak foreign languages to live in Brussels, and some of the Brits there didn't, though I don't think we should take any pride in this. There were said to be over a hundred English-speaking social, political, cultural and sporting associations in the city, ranging from the English Comedy Club, the Royal Brussels Cricket Club and the Australia Society to the Liberal Democrats, the Masons and the Decorative and Fine Arts Society. The British & Commonwealth Women's Association had its own club house. The British Community Association in Brussels acted as a link between the various societies and raised funds for charity among retired British people in the city. The British Ambassador to Belgium hosted a reception each year for the British Community Association around the time of the Queen's official birthday. There were other British diplomatic missions in Brussels: to NATO and the EU. The last of these is the second most important post in the British diplomatic service.

When I became an MEP, we sold the house in Brussels and moved our home back to the UK. On my frequent visits to Brussels for parliamentary meetings, I stayed at first in hotels but later rented an apartment or, to put it more accurately, the partly-furnished top floor of an old house built for a nineteenth century merchant. My accommodation was sound-insulated from the lower floors by a layer of soil between my floorboards and the ceiling below. The space I occupied must have housed some noisy industrial process. I had one large room, with a shower in a curtained-off corner, plus a kitchen.

When I went back to work in the Commission full time in 1994, I rented an apartment with two living rooms and a kitchen on the ground floor. The bedroom was below street level and it was so damp that the bedding became very heavy with moisture if I did not have the heating on frequently.

Brussels is a conurbation of nineteen boroughs with a total population of about a million, about two-thirds the size of Merseyside. Belgians in the country as a whole are split about 60:40 between Flemish and French speakers, plus a small number of German speakers in a border area taken from Germany after the First World War. However Belgians in Brussels itself are split 20:80, the French being the majority in terms of mother tongue. These figures relate to Belgians only. I heard estimates that thirty per cent of the inhabitants of Brussels were not Belgians, some being from other European countries and a great many more from Morocco, Turkey and other parts of Africa and the Middle East.

In Brussels train departures are announced at stations in one language first on certain days of the week, and in the other on the alternate days. Announcements on the train are in the language of the part of Belgian through which the train is currently passing. I advised constituents coming to Brussels by car not to try to show off their French in Flemish-speaking parts of the country.

The modern city includes what was called in the nineteenth century the *New Town* on higher ground. This has broad boulevards, some of which replaced the medieval town walls. It has fine residential areas and not so grand residential areas. The city has an excellent road system, some of it tunnels. The Commission's X-shaped building, the *Berlaymont*, the Council of Ministers' building which looks a bit like an aircraft hangar, and the elegant new Parliament Building overlooking a park are grouped near the Rue de la Loi.

There is an Anglican pro-cathedral (a church to be upgraded at some future date to cathedral status with its own Bishop) in the city, situated in the nightclub district. There is a Church of Scotland church and also various other Protestant churches with British and American links. One of the city's Roman Catholic churches had regular mass for English speakers.

Some of the British residents in Brussels had been there many years. At the Anglican Church I met a very old British lady who said that she had received the *Croix de Lorraine* – French version of the Victoria Cross – personally from General de Gaulle. She had been an interpreter for the British and French High Commands during the Normandy landings in 1944. I also met an elderly Belgian woman who had escorted RAF aircrews, downed over Belgium during the Second World War, to the French border. This was part of an escape route to Spain and freedom. Another old lady told me that during the war she had lived near the Gestapo headquarters in Brussels' fashionable *Avenue Louise*. She regularly saw the bodies of people who had been put to death there taken away on a truck early in the morning. The story is told of a wartime Belgian RAF pilot who, in defiance of orders, poured machine-gun fire into this building, flying vertically downwards so as not to hit civilians in nearby houses.

★ ★ ★

Some time after I ceased to be an MEP, *The Times* started to print an edition in Charleroi in the south of Belgium. This would be in the shops in Brussels by 7am together with the Frankfurt edition of The *Financial Times*. There were at least three weekly publications in English published in Brussels. *The Bulletin*, an English language magazine, was almost compulsory reading for expatriates. It contained summaries of Belgian news, theatre and cinema listings and notices of social and cultural events. The *European Voice* was a digest of political events in the EU institutions.

I had a letter printed in the *European Voice* in 2002 about the fact that Liverpool had been knocked off the board game *Eurocracy* because Neil Kinnock, known as the Welsh Firebrand in the newspapers, wanted Cardiff there instead. I wrote, "This is typical of the way a fine provincial English city such as Liverpool is ignored in favour of the noisy Celtic periphery of the UK. Liverpool is far better known than Cardiff, has better art, architecture and music, is more interesting, commercially important and exciting, has supremely better football and probably contains more people of Welsh descent than Cardiff". The *European Voice* headlined it "Liverpool 1, Cardiff 0".

The *Parliament,* the third weekly publication in Brussels printed in English, ran features about MEPs of all nationalities. The advertisements in it were placed by a wide variety of political and commercial organisations. To name but a few, in one edition I noticed some by The Institute of Population-Based Cancer Research, the Metropolitan Transport System of Barcelona, PKP Cargo, a Polish company specialising in rail freight, the Packaging Recovery Organisation Europe, a group of four electricity transmission system operators and the narrow gauge railways of northern Spain among others, all seeking to get their points of view across. Such is the importance which the world of business now gives to the European Parliament and the European Commission.

There seems to be a law for everything in Belgium. Brits joke that in the UK you can do anything you like unless there is a law to stop you. In Belgium they say you can't do anything at all unless there's a law which says you can. The story is told of a Scandinavian girl trying to get a bike onto a tram.

'You can't bring that on the tram,' said the driver.

'Why not?' asked the girl. 'There's no notice to say I can't.'

'There's no notice to say you can,' came the answer. It's all a question of the penal code. Most bars have notices on the wall about the avoidance of drunkenness, not that there is much of it anyway. You are not allowed to be drunk – because Article number so-and-so of the penal code says you must not!

Belgian police are not like British police. Many people say they are best avoided. Reporting crimes, other than where one is directly affected oneself, is something to avoid. You can end up causing more difficulty for yourself than the amount of good you do. I observed a particular police technique when there were some riots and arson attacks not far from my flat. Turks were attacking Kurds or vice versa. The crowd confronted uniformed police, verbally but not physically aggressive. Behind them, plain-clothes police, distinguishable only by small armbands, were hitting some of the demonstrators with short truncheons. The Brussels police and members of the national gendarmerie are very experienced in dealing with demonstrations and can produce razor wire and water cannon at the drop of a hat. They are not always very gentle.

I attended a ceremony to mark the anniversary of the entry into Brussels of British troops led by Field Marshal Montgomery in 1944, near the end of the Second World War. Armoured cars of the (British) Household Brigade and tanks of the Welsh Guards had entered Brussels followed by other British units and the Belgian Brigade. Following skirmishes, the retreating Germans had tried to take 1,500 political prisoners with them by train but Belgian railwaymen prevented this. The British had set up a headquarters in the secluded royal park at Laeken as protection against the exuberance of the Belgian welcome of flowers, beautiful girls and strong beer. (Records show that the British troops had to be protected from the attention of ecstatic Belgian girls.) But there was no protection against five German shells which landed in the park. The anniversary was celebrated by British troops marching in Square Montgomery, a large traffic island named after the Field Marshal. The city was ablaze with plastic carrier bags bearing the Union flag that evening.

July 21 is Belgium's National Day and its citizens make a big thing of it. One such day, faced with the necessity of doing some work in my office despite it being a holiday, I was faced with a serious noise problem. A squadron of jet fighters tore across the sky above my office; then a wing of Hercules transport aircraft; then a fleet of bombers. Then various bands followed, marching and playing their instruments in the street below my window. I gave up trying to work. This was just as well because the finale was a procession of tanks from each of the countries which make up the Euro-Group military force. The clatter

An official pamphlet

of the tank tracks on the tarmac, the roar of the engines and the blasts of hot air emitted sideways from their engines were formidable. On subsequent National Days, I arranged to be well away from Brussels!

The National Day is not only a symbol of Belgium's place in Europe and the world but also a reminder that it is one country even though most internal matters are handled by the three federal regions – Flanders, Wallonia and Brussels. Each of these territories is fiercely determined to defend its own powers. Voting in elections is compulsory for everyone on the official list, which means all Belgians. Foreigners can apply to be entered on the list if they wish.

Each party offers a list of candidates. The proportion of each party's list which is elected is in proportion to the number of votes cast. But, unlike the otherwise rather similar system used in the UK Euro-elections in 1999 and subsequently, the voter can vote for *any* candidate on the list. (The system used in the UK for these purposes gives the political parties control of the order of names on their lists and therefore the likelihood of each candidate being elected. The Belgian system allows the voter wishing to support a particular party to choose which of the candidates on that list he will vote for. This difference is of great importance in the determination of the power of political party bosses.)

PART III

*Links with African, Caribbean
and Pacific (PAC) Countries*

Joint Parliamentary oversight of aid and trade

During all of my time as an MEP, I was fortunate enough to be involved in the African, Caribbean and Pacific (ACP)-EU Joint Parliamentary Assembly which was set up under the aid and trade treaty called the Lomé Convention. I was one of four vice-presidents; there were two from the EU side and two from ACP countries.

The EU had a highly developed policy to aid the economic development of countries in the third world. With hindsight, the promotion of democracy, the protection of human rights and the avoidance of corruption should have been major elements of this but at the time the received wisdom was to concentrate on provision of financial assistance for infrastructure projects, social policy schemes and agriculture. The European Parliament committee, of which I was part, the Development and Co-operation (D & C) Committee, was intended to monitor these polices. However, there was a good deal of posturing by socialist MEPs from various countries, including Britain, and an unwillingness to challenge the conduct of even the most inefficient and corrupt African governments. The committee did do a certain amount of good. I was a member of the committee for ten years and became quite knowledgeable about its remit. Members of the D & C Committee carried out the EU role in the ACP-EU Parliamentary Assembly.

The Convention was signed in 1976 and replaced a similar treaty called the Yaoundé Convention which had been in force since 1963. Lomé is the capital of Togo, the portion of former German Togoland which became a French colony before achieving independence. Yaoundé is the capital of Cameroun, a former German colony which was later ruled partly by Britain and partly by France before achieving independence. In 2000, the Lomé Convention was replaced by the Cotonou Agreement, which embraces seventy nine developing countries in Africa, and the Caribbean and the Pacific regions as well as the twenty-seven EU states.

It was said that the ACP-EU Assembly was too large. At first sight, it was. The problem was that it was set up so as to have an equal number of parliamentarians from the two sides, the ACP and the EU countries. In the beginning far fewer ACP countries were involved so the Assembly was much smaller. The number of delegates has increased as additional countries joined the Convention. In my time as an MEP there were sixty or so developing countries which benefited from this arrangement. They were former colonies of the European powers, mostly of Britain and France. To reduce the number of ACP representatives would be to choose between ACP countries, difficult because they were independent, sovereign and equal states. To have fewer EU than ACP representatives would be seen by the ACP countries as a breach of the equality of the two sides. It would have made the Assembly simply a scene of conflict between two blocs rather than a meeting place where delegates from many countries could debate issues on their merits and not according to bloc views.

Supporters of the Convention stress its humanitarian purpose. Others might point to the success of EU policy during the Cold War years in keeping Soviet influence largely out of the areas concerned and preserving Europe's ability to trade there peacefully on terms beneficial to both sides.

The aid program for the ACP countries is run by the European Commission under a special budget agreed by Britain and the other EU countries, and separate from the general EU budget. The Commission also provides for relief of customs duty on ACP exports coming into the EU.

The ACP delegates were supposed to be MPs but in reality some were diplomats. When I later visited Nigeria I was told that the Nigerian embassy in Brussels did not pass on the invitations to the ACP meetings to their parliamentarians because the Ambassador himself wanted to attend as a delegate. The delegate from Ethiopia had never been elected to anything. I was told that he had held a high post under Emperor Haile Selassie, and then a top job under the dictator Mengistu. When Mengistu was thrown out, the delegate retained his place as Ethiopia's ambassador to the EU under the regime which followed. He later became chairman of the ACP ambassadors to the EU. He was very charming. His children were at a good school in Brussels, and he wanted them to be able to continue their education there. Some of the ACP delegates were representing countries where real democracy did not exist so they had to speak with care. But most of the delegates from Caribbean and Pacific countries and several of those from former British colonies in Africa really were MPs in their own national parliaments.

Twice a year, members of the European Parliament sat with parliamentarians from the ACP countries in the Joint Assembly to debate general co-operation and specific trade and human rights issues. Views were exchanged not only between the EU and the ACP bloc but also among delegates within the two blocs. British and French socialists often joined forces with African representatives in criticising the actions of the then Conservative British Government.

The ACP MPs from countries with little long-term parliamentary experience attending these joint events had the opportunity to learn something about democracy and freedom by observing the behaviour of the Members of the European Parliament. On a good day, MEPs acted with a mixture of respect for the rules and the rights of others and insistence on their right to speak freely. They criticised the actions of their own executive, the European Commission, without in any way denying its right to exist. The European Commission was fair game for criticism from both ACP and EU parliamentarians but most ACP MPs and some of the MEPs were reluctant to utter a word of criticism of the governments of the ACP countries. I myself never refrained from criticising waste, corruption and abuse of power in the ACP bloc or anywhere else when it seemed necessary to do so. I never suffered as a result. Indeed, I felt that I gained respect from several sides for doing this. My interventions in debates were seldom ignored or forgotten. I was often asked to tell delegates in advance when I intended to speak so that they could be present in the debating chamber to hear me.

From 1979 onwards the plenary meetings of the Joint Assembly were held alternately in an ACP country and then in an EU country. The first meeting was in Freetown, in Sierra Leone, just a few months after the first European Parliament elections. This produced a chorus of criticism from the press about European Parliament "junkets". One of the Conservative MEPs due to attend was asked by a journalist how she could justify the use of taxpayers' money to go on a junket like this. She was taken aback by this and replied that if that is how it was going to be, she would not go. The press had a field day! Few asked about the aid offered to developing countries under the Lomé Convention; few asked whether there should be parliamentary scrutiny of such expenditure and none asked why it was acceptable for civil servants and UK MPs to go to conferences, to join in information visits or to visit the projects over which they were supposed to exercise supervision and yet wrong for MEPs to do so. However, I myself was very clear why I was going; I said so to the press and received no criticism directed at me personally. Journalists' criticisms of our efforts to supervise and guide EU aid to Africa meant that the public only got to know about the suffering we were trying to alleviate when journalists themselves visited the crisis locations; it was as though nobody was aware of the problem until the media became involved.

The much-criticised use of luxury hotels and their conference facilities by delegates needs to be seen in context. In many African countries, there were only a few hotels, often French-owned, which offered clean and safe accommodation and food. To stay elsewhere would pose a strong likelihood of illness for Europeans not acclimatised to local food; sometimes there was a real risk of serious food poisoning due to poor hygiene. Also, in certain countries, walking to and from small hotels, away from the central areas of cities, there would have been a very real risk of physical assault and robbery. Moreover there had to be means of producing, copying and distributing the documents discussed in the debates. To have telephones that worked in at least some of the rooms was a necessity and not all hotels could provide these.

If every conference had been held in Europe, costs would have been cut for the EU side but increased for some of the ACP delegates. It would have impaired the political goal of treating the ACP countries as partners rather than clients of the donor countries. Rather than criticising the cost of the Assembly, it would have been more useful to point out that if the whole ACP-EU relationship had worked better than it actually did, some of the starvation and bloodshed which has occurred might not have occurred. People who criticise aid being given to developing countries have to explain what response they would have given to the widespread popular concern about bloodshed and poverty in Rwanda, Congo and Darfur. They would have to explain how they would have reacted in the 1980s if the Soviet Union had made greater inroads than it did into countries from which Europe and America obtain vital minerals and foodstuffs.

That is not to say that economies could not have been made in the organisation of the ACP-EU meetings. I saw no reason why the meetings held in Europe could not always be held in Brussels where full conference facilities were available all the time. I said so on many occasions. The practice of holding them in different European locations was costly even though host countries such as France usually paid some of the expenses. Eventually sense prevailed and the meetings in Europe were thereafter always held in Brussels.

I also said that it was folly to take interpreters for all the community languages. Almost all of the ACP representatives used English or French as their European language. I did not see much value in MEPs who could not speak

English or French attending these meetings because, although there would be interpretation inside the conference halls, such MEPs would not be able to converse with the delegates elsewhere. The conversations on the margins of the conference were a very important part of the proceedings. I and some of my colleagues succeeded in getting the languages used in the ancillary meetings reduced to English and French but we could get no further than that.

Parliaments in West Africa

My first meeting of the Joint Assembly was in Freetown in Sierra Leone on the west coast of Africa. The radical Italian MEP, Marco Pannella, began his disruptive efforts for which he had started to become infamous in Strasbourg sessions. His pantomimes in Strasbourg may have had some genuine political purpose in the context of the contorted politics of Italy, but in Sierra Leone they had none whatsoever. His technique was to draw attention to himself by disrupting parliamentary procedures with obscure points of order. These rules of procedure, conceived for meetings of MPs delegated to attend before 1979, were simply not good enough to cope with Pannella's verbal assaults.

The Assembly's EU Co-President, another Italian, Giovanni Bersani, lost control of the proceedings one day and I took over the task of presiding. I gave Pannella enough rope to hang himself, knowing that the ACP delegates viewed these meetings as important, thereby meriting dignified behaviour. I told him that if he did not behave himself, he would be ordered from the room. He continued to be disruptive. I therefore ordered the entire staff of ushers, which consisted of one elderly and very dignified Italian and one younger Irishman, to escort him from the room. To my surprise, he went.

Naturally I could not preside when I wanted to make a political speech myself, which I did several times in each of the sessions. I concentrated on speaking on three subjects. The first of these was on the need for European aid to the ACP countries to be administered efficiently. I said that it was not good enough for the EU to dole out the money at the request of the ACP countries only to find that large sums ended up in the Swiss bank accounts of their ministers and officials. I said that there had to be plans for efficient use of the money, proper accounting and full audit afterwards. I further stated that aid should help to foster private businesses in the ACP countries; it should not be squandered on socialist projects which, even if not tainted with corruption, had little hope of achieving worthwhile results. I noted that many Africans had the natural attitude and aptitude of the small business man or woman, and little sympathy with the socialist nonsense of collective farms, state industries and so on that were inflicted on them by some of their Western-educated leaders.

This sort of talk in such a forum was novel to say the least. Many of the died-in-the-wool socialist MEPs thought I was some kind of heretic in such a place, or believed that their reputations demanded that they side with the ACP delegates. Yet I found that quite a few of the ACP delegates either agreed with what I said or could see that, even if they disagreed with me, I was free from the insincerity and condescension of some of the European socialists. That said, I never had any personal arguments with even those self-same socialists, unlike some of the more remote, more upper-crust of the Conservative MEPs.

Speaking time for all the delegates had to be limited. The Nigerian delegate, the Ambassador, liked to argue that despite the conference rules, he should have more speaking time than other delegates because he represented a bigger country. He did not get his way.

The French had made plans to hold a reception for the ACP delegates attending the conference in Sierra Leone. I saw no reason why they should be in the driving seat so, as leader of the British Conservative MEPs there, I had a word on the plane on the way to Sierra Leone with Barbara Castle, who led the British Labour MEPs on the visit. I asked if she would support having a less lavish British and Commonwealth reception to counterbalance the French one. She replied smilingly, arms tucked up under an airline blanket, 'Of course, good idea.' The European Co-President of the conference, Giovanni Bersani, did not like the confrontational approach about the proposed receptions, so he decided to hold a presidential reception for everyone as well! The three receptions took place on the same evening in adjoining function rooms in the same hotel. I stood outside the door of our room, like a night club doorman, entreating all Commonwealth delegates, and indeed any others, to come in. I and one of the Commonwealth Africans made short speeches. After the speeches were over, Barbara Castle appeared. 'Is this your grotty little reception?' she asked. 'Are there any black faces left for me to talk to?' she demanded.

This may all sound rather silly but it signalled to the Commonwealth ACP delegates that the Lomé Convention did not just belong to the French. Many enduring friendships were made and several useful connections were cemented for later use when gathering support on issues under debate. Much of Britain's general isolation in the EU in the Conservative period of government was made worse by our own ministers' unwillingness to make such connections, to horse-trade and to actively seek friends.

Getting to Sierra Leone had not been much of a problem for me, but it was a different kettle of fish for Richie Ryan, an Irish MEP and former Minister in the Irish government. On the way to the meeting from London, he intended to change planes at Lagos. He slept on the plane on the way and woke suddenly to find that the plane was on the ground and that it was daylight. He grabbed his things, got off the plane and walked across the tarmac. There was nobody in the terminal so he decided to wait until the place woke up. When it did, he found he was not in Lagos but in Kano, in the north of Nigeria; unbeknownst to him, the plane had made an unscheduled stop. It cost him several hundred pounds to get the next plane to Lagos. Arriving in Lagos with most of his money spent, he telephoned the Irish Embassy. The Nigerian voice who answered the embassy phone said he had never heard of the former Minister. 'What you say your name is?' it enquired. 'Ryan,' replied the MEP. 'Doesn't sound Irish to me,' said the voice, and slammed the phone down.

Before setting off from the UK for this conference, the media had started the stories about "junkets" such as "MEPs on junket in Africa at taxpayers' expense". The *Liverpool Daily Post* had a major article on 16 February 1981 which began: "Euro-MP Andrew Pearce last night hit back at Barbara Castle over her attack on a Parliamentary trip to West Africa next week. Mrs Castle, leader of the Labour party group in Brussels, called on all British Euro-MPs to boycott the trip unless expense allowances and staff were cut back. She said that, although the meeting would be useful, the total cost was unacceptable when there was so much hunger in the developing countries and when people had to cut back at home too. Mr Pearce, who represents Cheshire West, is to lead the trip to Africa. Last night he said he had been trying for a year to get the number of MPs reduced."

I went on to say that Mrs Castle was one of those who should be dropped, commenting that she should not go because she had not been involved in the preparatory work. I added it was important to supervise how some of the £1,000m a year, which the EU gave out through its aid programme, is spent. The paper concluded with a quote from Jim Scott-Hopkins that he was astonished at Mrs Castle's hypocrisy and that he could not remember Mrs Castle objecting to her allowance when she went on a similar visit earlier to Tanzania.

The BBC decided to join in the chorus of criticism and sent their reporter, Brian Barron, and a British camera crew all the way to Sierra Leone from Nairobi on the opposite side of Africa to report on the event. I mention the fact that the camera crew were British because at that time it seemed to take four or five British technical staff to support an interviewer, thanks to trade union rules, whereas just a couple of non-British technicians would do the same job for other broadcasting organisations. However, having said that, the BBC did sometimes employ continental camera crews in foreign countries to reduce costs.

Brian Barron interviewed me in sweltering heat outside the conference hotel and asked me about the purpose of the trip. 'To help monitor and direct the EEC aid programmes,' I replied, 'and to debate current issues with MPs from ACP countries with a view to keeping Africa friendly to Europe in the face of attempts by the Soviet Union to take over western trade and political interests in the area.'

'Do you get all expenses paid?' asked the BBC man, clearly uninterested in anything important.

'Yes', I said, 'just like any other politician, civil servant, businessman or journalist. My salary could not possibly cover several such trips – and in any case why should it?'

'Some of the members' wives are here. Does the taxpayer pay for this too?' he asked.

'Some members' wives are here, including mine. I paid the whole cost of my wife's travel myself. I see nothing wrong with wanting to be with one's spouse. Most happily married people who are away from home a lot would say the same.'

This, I emphasise, was the BBC, supposedly a source of serious journalism. Some of the UK press was full of stories about the sufferings of Africans from drought, war and economic mismanagement but this interview was not concerned with what we MEPs were trying to do about it. Many of my constituents told me that they saw the interview on the *Nine o'clock News*. I know of only one person who was critical of my performance. 'You should have been wearing a tie for the interview,' said the dear lady.

Some of the journalists on the trip, several of them all-expenses paid by the European Parliament, even though the coverage their papers gave about the subject matter of the conference was just about nil, were hoping to find the casino at the conference hotel full of MEPs at times when they should have been in the conference hall. They were disappointed. 'Worst week we've had in a long while,' said the casino staff. 'Haven't seen any of them in here at all.' That was not in the papers afterwards, of course. There happened to be a tourist

187

from my constituency in the conference hotel while we were there. He told me afterwards that a couple of the journalists stayed on at the hotel for another week after the conference was over, enjoying the pool in the hot sunshine.

The conference itself progressed uneventfully for the most part, except for the Pannella incident. Several ministers of the Sierra Leone government were in prison on corruption charges at the time but those who had particular parts to play in our conference were let out at the appropriate times.

On that first visit to Africa, to Sierra Leone, I was interested to find that the receptionist of the British-owned hotel where we stayed was a British born black woman. She had gone to work in Africa partly out of solidarity with fellow people of African origin. I asked her about the standard of the local labour force. She told me very honestly that she had soon discovered that it usually took two or three Africans to do the work of one European, of whatever ethnic origin, a situation which I found in most of the African countries I visited. Local staff looked tired and languid and it seemed as if they did not understand the purpose of the work they were asked to carry out. I saw one man making slow polishing movements close to a window he was supposed to be cleaning but his cloth made no contact with the window. I asked myself many times why this should be so. Local staff had every reason to try to do satisfactory work in order to hold on to their jobs. There were a hundred other people eager to take over their jobs if they got the chance. It is not a matter of race or ethnicity because black people brought up in western countries live and work with the same range of skills and effort as white people, as the hotel receptionist amply demonstrated.

One factor is education, in the broadest sense. An African living in a hut made out of packing cases and corrugated iron, surrounded by rubbish and half a mile from the nearest water tap must initially find such jobs as polishing plate glass windows in a hotel rather pointless. A second factor could be diet. It cannot be simply lack of protein. I met villagers in Rwanda and Burundi who never ate animal products of any kind. They live satisfactorily on bananas, plantains, maize, and beans. In contrast, I met Masai people in East Africa who never ate vegetables, having a diet exclusively of meat, milk and animal blood. In West Africa, dried fish is sometimes available at times when meat is scarce or too expensive. A further factor is simply exhaustion. In South Africa, I was told that a domestic servant had to walk two hours to and from home either side of a twelve-hour working day. Yet another factor is language. Europeans visiting Africa forget that English is the second language of most Africans or maybe the third or fourth language for people living in areas populated by more than one tribe.

During intervals in the conference I went into Freetown. Sometimes Myra came too; she had a friend there. I visited the City Hotel which featured in Graham Greene's novel *The Heart of the Matter* as the Bedford Hotel and where the author is said to have stayed on the second floor. At the time of my visit, the ground floor was a bar. I was told there was a brothel upstairs. A monkey sat on the bar or swung in and out of the window. I made a friendly gesture to it. 'No touch de monkey. De monkey drunk,' I was told.

Myra and I went around the city, which it was at that time safe to do, with caution. I saw a man with two delightful young monkeys, one under each arm. I consider myself quite good with dogs so I extended a friendly hand towards one of the monkeys. It bit me; no pause for thought – just bit me! I had to go for a tetanus jab.

After ACP-EU meetings, there were usually opportunities to visit places in the country concerned and in neighbouring countries to try to judge the effectiveness of EU aid-funded projects. I went to see a couple of agricultural projects in Sierra Leone. One of these was a project to teach new ploughing techniques. An elderly Scottish expert was solemnly marching up and down a field of rich soil behind a plough which he steered so as to control its depth and direction. The plough was pulled by a pair of oxen, yoked together. Nothing remarkable about this, you may say, but this is not how the Africans had been doing it. Their way was that the man pulled a single ox which pulled the plough. This method did not produce straight ploughing lines, with the result that some of the land was not turned over; it did not ensure that the ploughing was at the right depth in the ground so that the surface soil was turned over but not mixed with the infertile subsoil below. The Scotsman's efforts had increased output by thirty per cent in one year, we were told! The problem was trying to persuade the locals to carry on with the new method after the aid worker left. The risk was that they would relate the higher yield to the presence of the aid worker rather than to the techniques he used.

I visited a project to set up new dairy production. We were told that in colonial times there had been steady, if limited, production of milk but that the animals had succumbed to disease after independence. New cows, considered to be immune to local diseases, were being introduced by the EU project. Our driver told us that life for ordinary people was better when Sierra Leone was a British colony. It had got a great deal worse since I was there.

On my way back home from Freetown, I had a couple of night's stopover in Abidjan in Ivory Coast. (Myra went home directly.) Ivory Coast was viewed at that time as one of the most successful former colonies. I met government Ministers and officials. Each time a French official was also present. The Minister or senior official would conduct the formal part of our conversation; the Frenchman would deal with all points of detail. I stayed in a good quality French hotel. As usual the French ensured that, for the rich and for foreigners at least, the physical quality of life was safeguarded, unlike many former British colonies where standards collapsed after independence except for the new ruling classes. It was safe to walk out of the hotel in the evening. I passed the finely-robed and splendidly turbaned "ladies of the night" standing under the trees, causing no trouble once one's intention not to do business with them was made clear.

Many of the former French colonies around the world used special francs from 1945 onwards. These francs had a fixed rate against the francs inside mainland France. A similar link was made with the euro when it was introduced, a euro being worth 655.957 Africa francs and 119.33 Pacific francs. The system means that monetary policy, including much of the control of inflation, is carried out in cooperation with the French government which itself now acts in line with the rules of the European Central Bank. This has tempered desires in the former French colonies to tolerate or even encourage the rampant inflation and large-scale devaluation of currencies as occurred in many former British colonies.

My next stop was at Lagos in Nigeria. Inside the hotel, for safety's sake, I had to be escorted by an armed man from the lobby to my room. I met a number of Europeans in the city of Lagos, mostly oil industry people. They lived in a compound outside the main city, protected by men with sub-machine guns at the gate of each house. I visited a United Nations agricultural research station at Ibadan, a city of over two and a half million people, about a third the size of Lagos. This visit involved driving through the endless, filthy shanty towns of Lagos and then through the similar townscape of Ibaban until we reached the research station. This establishment was a haven of peace and luxury, behind stout iron railings, with fountains playing in ponds and set in well-trimmed lawns.

Another ACP-EU conference was held in the city of Lomé. The European Parliament had paid for some television crews to be at the conference. I was determined that we should get some coverage for this money and not let the British journalists just sit about or send unsuitable material back to London. The EU had financed new harbour installations there, so I arranged a rendezvous with a TV team on a harbour tugboat. When I boarded the launch, I realised that the German Minister for Development Aid, Frau Adam-Schwaetzer, who had spoken at the Assembly, was also on the tugboat. The British TV crew did not want to know anything about her. They tried various ways to get the shots they wanted of just me. Not once, but several times, the TV men asked the Minister, with that lack of charm that seems to come naturally to certain media persons, to get out of their way so that I could be filmed. Some months later, during the German presidency of the EU, Frau Adam-Schwaetzer was on the front bench in the Parliament in Strasbourg. I caught her eye across the Chamber and she gave me the tiniest finger wave over the edge of her desk.

I decided to visit the little communist-style dictatorship of Benin on my way back. I was invited to be interviewed live on the local TV station, which was opened specially for this purpose, this being a Sunday. There was to be a discussion, I was told, but I was not told who else would be there. The "discussion" turned out to be a grilling about my views on South Africa, being questioned for an hour and a half, live and in French! The Beninois were very keen to demonstrate their anti-apartheid principles and, as a member of Mrs Thatcher's party, they viewed me as some kind of devil. For all Benin's condemnation of South Africa, it sold its entire oil output to it.

After this meeting, I went with a locally based female EU official to see a project to improve fish stocks in Lake Ganvie. The lake is several square miles and about thigh deep. People lived in houses built on stilts with platforms connecting them and visited their neighbours by boat. Fishing was done using nets held in place by poles driven into the lake bottom. The lake was also a sanitation facility for the local people as I realised when one of the fishermen not far from us crouched down and performed nature's functions in full view.

One ACP meeting was in Brazzaville, in the former French Congo. Our hotel, owned by a French company, was fine, except that the bedroom windows were sealed and the bedroom doors would only stay open if a chair was propped against them. This became critical during the ten-hour period when the electricity was off and the air conditioning therefore did not work. Without the bedroom door open, the sweat poured off me. With the door propped open, I had to stay awake for fear of robbers.

From Brazzaville, I went across the Congo River for a day in Kinshasa in the former Belgian Congo. The Congolese police casually, but not *too* hard, beat various people in the queue for the ferry with truncheons, seemingly to pass the time. In Kinshasa I saw a mixture of wealth and poverty. It was widely held in Brussels that Mobutu, the former dictator of Congo, had four large houses in Brussels and others in Switzerland, so that was evidently where some of the EU development aid went to.

My MEP companions on visits to Africa obviously included Germans. The British are generally thought to be poor linguists but the German Christian Democrats as a group were worse, although there were some notable individual exceptions. Prior to 1914, Germany had a number of colonies in Africa. (Getting them back was one of Adolf Hitler's demands.) One or two of the German MEPs expected to find Germanic traces in these places, people preferring to speak German, but we met none, much to the chagrin of the German MEPs. When some of the former German territories were put under French administration after World War I, the French took deliberate steps to get rid of German cultural influences. English just spread of its own volition, as it has done in so many places.

South Africa – seeking a peaceful transition

At every ACP-EU session, the EU in general and the British Conservatives in particular were assailed about alleged support for South Africa. I made my views clear on many occasions. I condemned apartheid without reservation but said I believed that those who advocated boycotts and armed intervention were wrong. I believed that political pressure from both inside South Africa, and also from outside it, would bring about change peacefully. And this is exactly how it turned out in the end. I noticed that those ACP countries most strongly in favour of economic and military intervention were mostly those farthest away geographically from where such operations would take place. I also noticed that a good many of the countries condemning oppression of black people in South Africa had worse regimes themselves. It was of course evident that the standard of living of black South Africans, however much below that of whites in their own country, was considerably better than those of most people in most other African countries.

Among people striking sanctimonious postures on this subject was a French European Commissioner, Claude Cheysson. On a visit to a neighbouring country, which required a change of aircraft at Johannesburg airport, he insisted on sitting in the airport lounge all night rather than checking in at a hotel and therefore stepping on to apartheid-contaminated soil.

The European Parliament received requests from ACP countries, led by Nigeria, to send a team of MEPs to investigate allegations of South African military attacks on neighbouring countries, "front-line states" as they were known, and accepted to do this in view of the calming affect which such missions can sometimes have. European socialist MEPs, not least the British ones, were eager to join this cause.

On these visits I was usually the only participant who had actually been to South Africa or who knew much about it. I visited South Africa several times in my time in the European Parliament. The South African government had offered me a fact-finding visit of their country. I was very cautious about accepting this because of what I had heard about trips for MEPs to Israel organised by the government there.[18] So I accepted the invitation on condition that I could choose my itinerary and that I would not be accompanied except when travelling by car was the only means of getting to a particular place. The South African authorities accepted this and honoured the deal.

I asked for briefings from various South African government officials and experts. The white South Africans were very hospitable and good company but they wore blinkers. Most had no idea of the poor quality of life and the sometimes squalid conditions of the great majority of their fellow countrymen. It was not generally as dreadful as the lives of many people in the "liberated" former colonies elsewhere in Africa suffering under Marxism-spouting despots, but it wasn't good. I had an example of standards of the lives of the black population when I went to an area of new housing near Cape Town. Hundreds of single-storey concrete shells of houses, three or four metres square, had been put up and connected to drains and water mains with a tap and a lavatory provided. But putting in doors and windows and the rest was for the new tenants to do themselves. This was viewed as an improvement compared to where the people had lived previously, and indeed it was.

I went to Soweto, which stands for South Western Township. The townships were built at the peak of the apartheid years to force black people to live outside the white areas. Since the white areas contained most of the industry and commerce, the black people inevitably faced long and overcrowded train and bus journeys to work. Soweto didn't have ordinary street lights; it had huge lamps on enormous poles of the type used in railway marshalling yards in Britain. These were on all night, so there was never any darkness outside people's houses. In cold weather, houses were heated by burning soft coal which left a pall of smoke all over the neighbourhood. There were very few shops or eating places. I was shown with great pride the first Kentucky Fried Chicken in Soweto. Brightly lit, it seemed to be a monument to a better world which had not hitherto generally struck this blighted place. Soweto had well over a million people in it.

By contrast, the whites lived in levels of luxury almost incomprehensible in Britain. Even bus drivers, for long an occupation restricted to whites, lived

---

[18] When considering an invitation to visit Israel, I had been shown a report of an earlier visit to that country by a joint group of British MPs and MEPs. One of the MPs had taken it upon himself to declare the group's support for Israel. The whole proceedings had been recorded verbatim and typed out. I would have nothing to do with this way of doing things and did not accept the invitation. I have never been to Israel.

in pleasant detached houses with gardens and, quite often, swimming pools. The richer people lived in spacious modern well-equipped houses with large well-tended gardens. Nearly all whites had servants of some kind. Some of the whites I talked to had no idea of the distance that their servants had to travel to work each day, sometimes on foot; nor were they aware of the primitive conditions in which they lived. Many of the richer whites who went to Europe on visits were surprised at the lack of servants and considerably lower standard of living of even fairly well-off Europeans.

The mutual lack of understanding between the races was illustrated for me by a white woman working in a European owned bank. The word had gone out that toilets were to be desegregated – all the female staff would use the same facilities. The white staff then found that the toilets were in an appalling condition because black female staff had been standing on the seats to perform their functions. Some of the white staff then had the sense to explain that western-style toilets were designed for people to sit on, not to stand on or crouch over. This solved the problem. (Squat toilets can still be found in various parts of continental Europe and it *is* appropriate to crouch over these.)

On one occasion, mentioned later, when my luggage had failed to arrive on the plane on which I was travelling on a visit to Mozambique, I needed to buy some clothes when I reached South Africa afterwards. In South Africa, suits are often sold with the legs not cut to length – this is done for you after taking your measurements. This task was duly completed, thanks to a kind tailor, in about half an hour. I subsequently went to see the tailor in his house in the wealthy white suburb of Sandton. The house was well protected with barbed wire, locks and chains. His wife told me how she had employed a black woman as a daily lady for many years. This lady had made her own way to and from the tailor's house until she developed an ailment which prevented her walking such a long distance. The tailor's wife agreed to ferry her by car to and from her home in the black township of Alexandra. She was utterly amazed and shocked at the poverty, dirt and violence in which the people lived there. She just had no idea of the difference between the very comfortable, if sometimes insecure, life of the Whites and that of the black people, even though she had driven in her car past Alexandra on many occasions.

It seemed then in the 1980s that the richer Whites, including large numbers of English speakers, would make out all right when apartheid ended because they had professional skills which most blacks could not match. The rub was really beginning to come to the white manual workers, very often Afrikaaners, when their jobs were opened up to other races and the wages adjusted to suit.

Government officials explained to me in great detail how the full apartheid system, introduced in 1948, had worked and how they were trying to modify it. What they couldn't see was that the best solution was just to leave people alone to get on with their lives, recognising that people are people whatever the colour of their skin. The Afrikaaners thought they had to have a regulation for everything. Everybody had to be classified as one of four racial groups – White, Black, Asiatic or Coloured (mixed race).[19] There were endless specifications about who was what and what members of each group could do. The absurdity of this classification was brought home to me when I visited a former British diplomat who lived near the city of George on the Wild Coast between Cape Town and Durban. It happened to be the day of the first election for the Parliament set up for "coloured" people. These were mixed-race descendants of people who had lived around Cape Town for generations. They were thoroughly westernised, in contrast to some of the black population, many of whom came from very primitive home conditions in South Africa or in neighbouring countries. My host took me into the polling station, which was an exact replica of a British one. There he introduced me to some of the locals who were sitting about. They knew him but he did not know them.

'Now, my man,' boomed my host to one local sitting quietly having a beer. 'Have you voted?'

'Me?' said the man. 'I'm not voting today. I'm white!'

In fact, the whites and coloureds in this area lived cheek by jowl in perfect harmony. But the high priests of apartheid in Pretoria just couldn't stop making more and more rules. The word priests, in the more literal sense, leads me to say that it beggars belief that many supposedly Christian clergy running whites-only churches had convinced themselves and their congregations that God intended people to be organised in racial categories.

On one occasion I was given a poster for an earlier election to the whites-

---

[19] I have used these terms in this book, distasteful as they are, because the pattern of life in South Africa in the apartheid years and in Rhodesia/Zimbabwe where, de facto, similar provisions applied, was completely built around such discrimination. The effects of this on people's living standards will still be there for a good many years. In the United States, segregation, which was much the same thing as apartheid, may be said to have come to an end in 1964 when President Johnson signed the Civil Rights Act. However, the effects of segregation on the lives of many black people there are still evident today and will remain for some time into the future.

only parliament, as an example of South African politics. It said: "Vote for an honest white policy. Vote HNP". This was an appeal by the Herstigte (Reconstituted) National Party, a rigidly pro-apartheid breakaway from the larger National Party.

On my way back from South Africa, the government there booked me on South African Airways. This airline was prohibited by most African countries from flying over their territory so flights had to go right around the western coast of the continent, non-stop. When we were in the vicinity of the island republic of Cape Verde, one of the plane's engines caught fire. We safely made an emergency landing at the airport there and about 250 of us were transported to a hotel in shifts in two mini-buses, the only vehicles available. We waited while a meal was cooked. The meal turned out to be lobster and we consumed the hotel's entire stock of it. The airline contacted British Airways who sent a relief plane from London for us. This replacement flight was diverted from Heathrow to East Midlands Airport due to fog! It takes a long time to get from East Midlands airport to Liverpool by train on a Sunday!

Many MEPs did not want to hear the truth about South Africa. My comments in a debate on 7 July 1988 were typical of my attitude: 'Mr President, there are far too many people here who go on about sanctions as being the only way to bring influence to bear upon South Africa. What I want to propose is that there should now be, for the first time, a meaningful dialogue where we in the Community begin, as we have never done so far, to say what we actually want to happen in South Africa. It is so easy to moralise; to tell them they are wrong. Let us tell them what we want. Let us be constructive. Let us get peaceful change that way.'

I do not pretend that fine words from me had any direct effect on subsequent events. Yet there really is such a thing as a climate of opinion. In the real world of politics, certain views become accepted as the general view or at least recognised as the majority view. I tried to do my bit to make people see the truth about Africa in general and about South Africa in particular. My views on South Africa usually brought what the minute-writers in the European Parliament call mixed reactions, that is to say a mixture of applause and boos. But did we ever hear criticism from the left when black governments in Africa and elsewhere treated their peoples far worse than the South Africans treated their people? Rarely a murmur!

I suppose it is tempting to want to "go with the herd" in politics. Certainly many politicians do – and get promoted for not rocking the boat. On many questions, I did not "go with the herd". On issues of the developing countries and regarding South Africa, I was largely in tune with my fellow Conservatives and many of the other MEPs. However, I was more outspoken than most and I believe that being outspoken does have an influence on general opinion.

A brothel and an anti-aircraft gun in Angola

The ACP states had proposed that a delegation be sent to examine the consequences of attacks by South African military forces which they said had taken place in neighbouring countries, what they called the "front line states". These visits were undertaken by a group of six or seven MEPs and some ACP delegates plus staff for interpretation and planning the logistics. We visited each of the front-line states in turn. We had to produce a joint report but were free to say what each of us as individuals wanted to say as we went around. Perhaps, diplomatically-speaking, the making of these journeys was of more importance in African terms than the report itself. The media sneer at this sort of thing and of course it can be a waste of money if the people involved do not genuinely show interest and build bridges. In retrospect, we should have taken some media people with us: that would have avoided all criticism! In my view, the visits made a contribution towards peace-making in southern Africa and perhaps helped to inform opinion in Europe about the real situation – though not in Britain because the British press was only interested in the cost of hotels and what it called "luxury junkets" and not in the slightest about the objectives of the visits or whether we achieved them.

One such visit was to Angola. In this country, one political faction was sustained by Soviet and Cuban military aid, the other was pro-western. In fact, as I was told, the conflict had tribal origins, going back to slave-trading days. Some of the tribes had traded with European slave merchants and sold members of other tribes, whom they viewed as being inferior, as slaves.

We were to look for the truth about stories of South African raids into Angola. I don't think anybody really had any doubts that such acts across frontiers by land or air had taken place but the African members of the ACP-EU Assembly were keen to demonstrate the fact and to have Europeans admit it.[20] The trip was

[20] This conflict was not a small scale skirmish. Angolan troops backed by more than 25,000 Cubans fought major battles with the South African Army involving aircraft and tanks. There is little doubt that the Soviet Union and the United States supplied the weaponry.

going to take place whether I went on it or not so I accepted the invitation to be part of it. I was probably the only member of the relevant European Parliament committee who believed that there was right and wrong on both sides of the argument about South Africa; I also possessed a thick enough skin to speak my mind. I wanted to expose the hypocrisy which criticised white on black violence but turned a blind eye to black on black violence.

Our visit to Angola started in the capital, Luanda. The Portuguese colonial administration had left Angola in 1975 after the fall of the dictatorship in the home country. When they left after more than a century of colonisation, hardly any Africans had been trained for the simplest of tasks in daily life; very few could drive a vehicle, for instance. And when the Portuguese left, they took anything moveable with them, leaving the towns and the farms empty. For example, they took most of the usable cars and trucks so the Africans had virtually no means of carrying out the daily functions of life.

The harbour was a maritime junk yard. Port facilities were so chaotic after independence that foreign ship owners would only send cargoes in ships which they did not want back, one-way ships, if you like. We met a German harbour master who had been employed, using foreign aid money, to remedy the situation. While he had indeed made substantial progress, chaos was still the only way to describe it.

We had to travel in a coach to the town of Lubango which was on the edge of the area where we were told that acts of war by South Africa had taken place. This had been a Portuguese garrison town. We were accommodated in what had been a brothel serving Portuguese soldiers and which, after their departure, had apparently continued similar activities for the benefit of the locals. For our one-night stopover, such trade was removed from inside the building though we did see shadowy figures lurking around outside which rather confirmed what we had been told about it. The MEPs and the European Parliament staff with us were allocated shared bedrooms. Christopher Shaw, then a trainee but a brilliant interpreter, and I were to occupy beds in a small bedroom. We put our luggage on the beds.

There were about twenty-five in all in our party, including Angolan politicians, staff and media people. Washing facilities consisted of one single basin of water for all of us, for washing, shaving etc. The MEPs and our Angolan hosts dined in the hotel restaurant. I dined with Christopher Shaw and Winnie Ewing, the Scottish MEP. The food was, let us say, interesting but no doubt the best that our hosts could provide. Bedtime approached. Winnie went up to bed but returned shortly afterwards with a gaunt face complaining loudly that there were 'wee beasties' in her bed. She determined to spend the night in the restaurant with another MEP in our party, Luciana Castellina. Christopher and I decided it was time to go to our bedroom. It was midnight and we were to be called at four o'clock in the morning. When we got upstairs, we found an African man in my bed and another in Christopher's. Our luggage had been put outside the door. We decided to see which rooms were still unoccupied. We found a room with various pieces of television equipment on the beds. We dumped the TV cameras in the passage outside the room, moved our luggage in, bolted the door and went to bed.

After our early call, we went down for breakfast. Winnie and Luciana were sitting cross-legged waiting for an escort so that they could attend to some urgent demands of nature. They said they would not feel safe using the hotel's facilities. Christopher and I escorted them down the hotel steps through the crowd of what were presumably the building's normal clientele and stood sentry while they did what they had to do behind a clump of bushes in the remains of a fallen-down building.

Our cavalcade of vehicles to take us to the war zone arrived. I was to travel in the last vehicle with a French Socialist MEP, later a member of the French National Assembly, Gérard Fuchs. In front of us were various Land Rovers and other vehicles including a small truck with an anti-aircraft gun roped on to its rear platform. Gérard and I had a Land Rover pickup of a certain age with just a bench seat. I sat in the middle, Gérard on my left and the corpulent driver on my right. The road was long and straight. Soon after setting off I noticed that our driver would take aim at a point about five degrees off the direction of the road and grip the steering wheel tenaciously on that course but with eyes clearly wanting to close. Several times I jerked the wheel to get the vehicle back on to the right course. Beginning to be worried, I suggested to Gérard that we should sing to keep the man awake. He agreed but sing what? We found that the first verse of *Frère Jacques* was the only song we both knew so we sang this through half a dozen times.

The driver spoke to us but as he didn't speak English or French and neither Gérard nor I spoke Portuguese, we could only guess that he was trying to ask us whether we wanted a comfort stop. We didn't but after getting the message two or three times we thought it politic to say that we did. We all got out. The reason for the stop became clear. The driver relieved himself of what sounded like half a gallon of beer! We told the driver to get in the back of the pickup. Gérard and

In war-torn Angola

I decided to toss a coin for which of us should drive on. I lost and took the wheel for the next fifty kilometres. Now, Land Rovers are superb vehicles but this one had a mind of its own – one headlight pointed to the Milky Way, the other to the ditch on the left-hand side of the road. The steering wheel had play in it; I fought it while I was driving and managed to get it to do most of what I wanted. The rest of our cavalcade had not waited for us. We caught up with it, anti-aircraft gun and all, a couple of hours later by which time daylight had come. We duly inspected various shot-up buildings and were shown a small display of equipment said to be from a South African aircraft which had been shot down in the area. This consisted of personal items the pilots might have carried.

When it came time to go back to Lubango, our driver, who had sobered up, announced that he was about to run out of fuel. We came past an Angolan army post and drove in. The driver had deep conversations with the army people in charge and then proceeded to fill up the Land Rover by swooshing petrol into the filler pipe from a bucket. Gérard and I stood well back in case the Land Rover went up in flames. While doing so, we noticed a soldier taking off his uniform behind a 'berm', a bank of soil, right down to his underpants. He re-dressed in civvies and then we understood that the deal was that we got the petrol if we gave this man a free ride back to Luanda.

The next day we were taken to another place and shown more so-called evidence of South African air attacks; the intention was to demonstrate how widespread these attacks had been. On inspecting the material closely, I observed that it was exactly the same material as we had seen the day before – little tears in the labels, tubes of ointment bent over in a particular way and so on were identical. The Angolans had simply moved the "evidence" from one place to another.

"Roughing it in the cause of justice" said the *Sunday Mail*, going on to report me, correctly, as saying, "It's an interesting experience cleaning your teeth with a bottle of beer!" "MPs in cat-house" said the *Sunday Times*, catching up with the others.

The *Liverpool Daily Post* reported that Winnie Ewing had asked the driver of her vehicle for a toilet stop during a long and bumpy ride. The driver, the paper said, had replied that it would be unwise to stop at all in case they were shot at and that she had gritted her teeth and continued the journey.

In Strasbourg in December in 1985, I said: 'I want to see free elections in Angola. I want to see peace there and greater prosperity. I certainly want to see the Soviets and the Cubans and all their ghastly military apparatus removed'.

The ambassador's trousers

Another visit to a former Portuguese colony was to Mozambique. A party of five MEPs, two interpreters and an official assembled at Charles de Gaulle Airport in Paris. We checked our bags in for the flight to Maputo, formerly Lourenço Marques. I myself arrived safely in Maputo after a reasonable night on the plane: my luggage did not arrive at all. I was looked after by the British Ambassador for the couple of days during which we held talks with government Ministers. I had no fresh clothes to change into and it was hot and humid, and my clothes began to be smelly.

It was impossible to buy anything at all then in that sad and impoverished country; the shops and market stalls were totally empty. The local people had virtually nothing and so it was quite impossible to buy clothes. I asked the Ambassador if he would lend me some. He kindly obliged, which was fine except that his waist measurement was twice mine. I used safety pins to put some very large tucks in the clothes he lent me, which did the job until I reached South Africa and was able to buy new ones.

(The story of the missing suitcase did not end there. Nine months later I received a postcard couched in terse French from the Paris Chief of Police. It invited me to remove my suitcase from his lost property office in suburban Paris. I duly went along to this enormous warehouse. There were about five counters for picking up lost umbrellas, six for suitcases, four for handbags and so on. My case was there. Nothing was missing. Where it had been I have no idea.)

In Mozambique we were shown the hotels and restaurants which used to serve white South Africans when this was a luxury holiday place before communism set in. It is nice to know that some years later Mozambique was admitted to the Commonwealth, the only member of it never to have been a British colony.

While in Mozambique, my colleagues and I went for a visit into the bush. We arrived in a village immediately after a raid by guerrillas had taken place. A woman had been beaten and was still bleeding. We were assured that this was the result of South African attacks. However, someone said to us afterwards that the beating could have been done by the local political leaders just to convince us MEPs of their case. We saw there, not for the first time, the superb work of Roman Catholic missionaries, mainly Irish nuns, providing the only medical services which were available to the local people.

Another visit was to Zambia. Our hosts wanted us to visit the Zambezi at a point where, on one bank of the river, there is a short stretch of Botswana, a few hundred metres long. This was squeezed between Rhodesia (under sanctions in the pre-independence days when my visit took place) and Namibia. Zambia had been accused of breaking sanctions by allowing vehicles to cross the Zambezi into Rhodesia. The purpose of our visit was to ascertain that the traffic was in fact going to Botswana, not Rhodesia. Half a dozen MEPs and some MPs from other African countries were to be the witnesses.

The ferry, or pontoon as it was called, was a floating platform big enough to carry one lorry. It was pulled across the slow-moving river by cables. In one direction we could see Rhodesian territory. In the other direction we could see an absurdly provocative and heavily armed South African soldier sitting on top of a pole in the Caprivi Strip of Namibia. We crossed the river. I discovered that the chief of the Zambian highways department, who had come to supervise the crossing of our party, came from Liverpool. While we discussed the merits of Everton Football Club, the rest of the party moved towards the Botswana frontier post which was set back a few hundred metres from the river. The corporal of the Botswana Army came out and demanded to know who had authorised the visit.

'I'm the Zambian Minister of Finance,' said one of our group. 'I say I don't need authorisation.'

'I'm a corporal in the Botswana Army, and I say you do,' was the reply, whereupon we were all put under technical arrest. However I saw nothing particularly unpleasant happening. After a while it was sorted out but some of our group fled back to the pontoon; it could not move because its driver was also under arrest. We were told afterwards that the Botswana authorities thought we were South African spies.

When we got back to our hotel, a major Fleet Street daily paper rang from London. 'Can we say you were held at gunpoint?' they asked. I said it had not been thus. They went ahead anyway. The *Chester Evening Leader* went the same way. "Euro MP held at gunpoint," it said. The *Daily Telegraph* said we were detained for about two hours, adding: "Euro MPs in Botswana muddle". The

Daily Express went the whole hog: "Day the MPs' gravy train ran off the rails" was their headline. The *Liverpool Daily Post* reported that Winnie Ewing had tried to stop the Botswana soldiers taking her camera and that scuffles had broken out. It reported that Luciana Castellina, the Italian MEP, was bitten by a monkey on the way back. (It missed the sole clarification demanded by one of her colleagues after the incident as to whether the monkey was all right).

In 1986, a delegation of MEPs went to Swaziland. Mbabane, the administrative capital, had the reputation of being a resort for white South African men who liked consorting with black women, which was not allowed in their own country under the apartheid rules. However, our hotel, which was superb, had removed the "business" ladies and some of the gaming machines for the night we stayed there. The splendidly clad Swazi warriors and some of the even more elaborately dressed members of the Swazi royal family were much in evidence in our meetings. There was a minor diplomatic crisis when one of the British Labour MEPs in our group missed some of the talks we were having. He had been contacting local Swazi trade unionists. Our hosts were not pleased.

It had been agreed previously that some political figures from South Africa, from the Prime Minister, P.W. Botha and the Dutch Reformed Church to the African National Congress, would be invited to this meeting so that they could exchange views with the ACP delegates about their country's future. "We need to hear the S. Africans…" the *Times* of Swaziland headlined its report on 30 January 1986. However, a number of other ACP countries such as Benin and Liberia blocked any idea of dialogue with representatives of the South African government so the exchange of views did not take place.

Our visit to Botswana was pretty routine. It was one of the more successful countries in Africa and had profitable, large scale beef production. Very long fences had been erected across the dry terrain to keep the cattle separate from the wild life. This seemed to upset the natural grazing routines of the latter, much to the consternation of environmentalists. The meat produced was for making corned beef, which has to be made from very lean meat. Most of the corned beef for the UK market had traditionally come from South America but trade controls made it much easier now to obtain supplies from Botswana, which in any case had ideal climatic conditions for the cattle. We visited a huge butchering and canning plant where the supervisory and managerial staff were almost all South African. The Botswana authorities sometimes felt obliged, for the sake of black African solidarity, to join in the "bash South Africa" cries but they knew which side their bread was buttered and took quiet steps to make sure we knew that.

In a debate in Strasbourg in April 1986, I said. 'There seem to be three matters at issue: the supply of meat to the European Community, which is the least important of them; the protection of wildlife in the country; and the economy and therefore the jobs and incomes of the citizens of Botswana. We sympathise with the Government of Botswana in struggling with these various priorities, which to some extent compete with each other. We think that the fact that they have been able to conform to European standards of hygiene and marketing of their beef, is something on which they should be complimented. At the same time their care for the problems of wildlife in their country also deserves our sympathy'.

I had met the Speaker of the Parliament of Lesotho in Luxembourg, and we had made common cause in the Joint Assembly in opposing the frequent attempts by the French to run everything their way. Later when I went to Lesotho with other MEPs, we were shown into the gallery of the Parliament. The Speaker interrupted the proceedings, welcomed us, and introduced each of us in a light-hearted way to the Members of his Parliament. He described me as "fiery". I noticed that the Lesotho Post Office had produced special stamps to celebrate the 75th anniversary of Scouting, a compliment to Britain. Poor Lesotho was beset on the one hand by attempts by the South Africans to treat it as a colony and on the other by internal factional rivalry.

Zimbabwe was also on our route later on. I had met President Mugabe briefly at the United Nations in New York just after Zimbabwe became independent in 1980. Four or five MEPs had attended a UN plenary debate on third world matters. This involved being seated on the main floor of the debating chamber, quite an honour.

We were looked after by Claude Cheysson, European Commissioner for such matters. One of the MEPs was a Belgian, who was a journalist as well as a politician. At a briefing before the plenary session, we met with Cheysson in a side office. I and the Belgian repeatedly asked for certain information from the Commissioner, which he refused to give us. I was seated on a sofa with the Commissioner, with a space between us. After several minutes of demand-and-refusal, I noticed that the Commissioner's hand, with a piece of paper in it, was sliding surreptitiously towards me along the sofa. I picked the piece of paper up cautiously and found that it contained the information which I had been asking for. The Belgian was not made privy to it.

As Mugabe passed through the corridors of the UN building, everyone around him then was ecstatic about the fact that independence and freedom under a democratic government had been achieved. His progress was like that of a Messiah.

Some colleagues and I visited him in Harare after independence. A map in his secretary's office still bore names such as Northern Rhodesia (now Zambia), Nyasaland (now Malawi) and Southern Rhodesia (now Zimbabwe). We did not know then what a thug Mugabe would become in later years.

It is surprising how fast things in Africa have changed. When I was at university in the 1950s, my professor, Daniel T. Jack, was a member of a Royal Commission whose report resulted in these previously separate colonial administrations being brought together in a federal structure. Then Zambia and Malawi were given independence in 1964 as separate countries and Ian Smith took Southern Rhodesia, or Rhodesia as it became known, into illegal independence. Later, Rhodesia became independent under a majority black government and a change of name to Zimbabwe. At that time, black citizens of Zimbabwe had one of the highest living standards of the black populations of any country in Africa. Not any more.

I experienced Zimbabwe's economics in the 1980s in a supermarket in Bulawayo. Certain things were in short supply due to the sanctions in force. All of a sudden there was a mainly female scrummage around a member of staff. I stuck my open hand through a ruck of female waists, and after half a minute, a packet of detergent was thrust into it. I was a winner! The people with whom I was staying were delighted to receive this product.

Zimbabwe's capital city was called Salisbury, the name being changed after independence to Harare. Harare had previously been the name of a particular part of the city, which is now called Mbare. I went to this part of the city with a couple of colleagues. I had heard the expression "beer halls" and decided we would go to one to find out what they were. This one was a large room, clean and orderly. We tried the local beer which was extremely bitter. I don't know what it had in it but you could almost chew it. The system was that you bought a jug of beer and passed it round to whoever you were next to – at least that is what they told us! We suddenly found we had a lot of friends we didn't know we had.

Another conference was at Arusha in Tanzania. This country, despite having great ethnic diversity, had previously been a peaceful but backward country. Nobody had much but everybody had something. Economic reforms taking place at the time of my visit meant that the shops were now full of goods but few people had money to buy them. Unemployment had begun to appear, in contrast with the situation in more socialist times when everyone had a job of some sort, and therefore an income, but nobody was even comfortably well-off, except of course the ruling politicians and officials.

My colleague MEP Richie Ryan had another unfortunate experience in Arusha. The conference delegates were accommodated in two hotels about 150 metres apart. When delegates wished to go from one hotel to the other, they were supposed to be escorted by a soldier armed with a rifle, for safety's sake. Avenues had been mown in the long grass between the hotels to facilitate walking, but these were not in a direct line from one hotel to the other. Richie would have none of the soldier escort and insisted on setting off on his own, taking a straight course through the long grass. He soon discovered that a horizontal web of barbed wire had been constructed between posts about thirty centimetres off the ground to oblige people to walk on the mown paths and not to approach the buildings except by the doorways. But the grass had grown through the wire which was therefore invisible. In plunged poor Richie – and received multiple scratches to his shins and tears to his trousers. He followed the mown path from then on!

In Tanzania some of us met former President Kaunda. Part of the country, Tanganyika, had been a German colony, before being taken over by the British. The rest, Zanzibar, had been a British protectorate for years beforehand. The former President talked to us about the need for the state to control land, labour and capital; he sounded like a textbook of late nineteenth century left-wing economics. After leaving office alive and peacefully – a rare event in Africa – he was said to have been astonished at the low living standards of the people of his own country.

Due to the difficult terrain and poor condition of most roads in these countries, the most common and suitable vehicle used for transportation to various areas outside the cities was the Land Rover. I cannot praise this British-made vehicle enough! Up to the time of my travels at least (the 1980s), there was no four-wheel-drive vehicle to touch the Land Rover. On one visit to Africa, the wife of one of the German MEPs complained that she would not travel in a Land Rover; she wanted a Mercedes saloon, more luxurious and, of course, German. She had to make do with a Range Rover, not as good on difficult terrain as the Land Rover. The Range Rover hit a slippery patch of road and nearly turned over. Our old Land Rover was completely steady. While the

Range Rover was put back on the road, one of the German MEPs with us, a rather short-sighted man, tried to photograph a local man with a spear who was urinating behind a bush. The man was not amused and the German was lucky to avoid a serious incident. This reminded me of yet another trip in an open-top Land Rover. We had been told not to film Masai warriors as we passed them along the road. But a French staffer would not to be told – until a large spear was brandished very close to his stomach.

The economic position in Tanzania was made worse by demobilisation of soldiers and there began to be danger from penniless men roaming the countryside away from their home villages. But I should not exaggerate the danger. Myra and I were able to hire a taxi to the Kenyan border and another from there to Nairobi, capital of Kenya, in complete safety. There were no bus or train services. Nairobi at that time was one of those places where, for visitors at least, safety demanded remaining inside the western hotels in the evening or going elsewhere by taxi.

Another visit was to Uganda. This was a country of great beauty and agricultural potential. It had been riven by brutal conflict between the tribal groups inside it, an example of how the boundaries fixed in colonial times bore little relation to ethnic realities. At the time of my visit, the brutal dictator Idi Amin, had come and gone but the evidence of the conflicts of his time were all around such as the bullet holes with which the walls of Entebbe airport were deeply pitted. The country's leader at this time was Milton Obote, widely regarded as corrupt. His position was being challenged by Yoweri Museveni who had played a part in the expulsion of Amin. When Museveni later became President, he was regarded as better than his predecessors despite involvement in a bloody campaign in the Luwero Triangle and later in the genocidal wars which spilled over the frontiers of Rwanda, Burundi and Congo.

The European quarter of Uganda's capital, Kampala, must have been a beautiful place in colonial times. Vegetation was lush, flowering trees prolific. By the time of my visit, the surface of the boulevards had been scoured away by the wheels of vehicles and rain so that as our car squelched along, the kerbstones alongside us were a foot or more above the level of the ground on which vehicles drove. The lamp posts drooped, leaned or lay prostrate on the verges. I was accommodated for the first night by the EU Delegate (Ambassador) to Uganda. Bedtime was preceded by an elaborate ritual of locking and barring windows and ensuring that the bells and whistles were in working order in case help from residents of other nearby embassies had to be summoned. Mobile phones had not been invented then and the ordinary phones did not work.

After breakfast the next day, I waited for my four British MEP colleagues to pick me up for our visit to industrial and agricultural projects financed by the EU. I did not know it but my colleagues were waiting for me at the British High Commissioner's house. Eventually contact was established, and this materialised in the shape of two short muscular Glaswegian military policemen in T-shirts who came in a British Army Land Rover to the house where I was waiting. One of them said: 'You've to come wi'us. You get in the back. If I say 'Get down', you get down between the seats'. I did not argue. It was reassuring to know that I would be between armour-plated seats.

We set off, roaring through Uganda's capital city with a blue flashing light on the roof and a machine gun with Glaswegian fingers on it pointing through the side window. We inspected various facilities receiving or needing aid, including an electricity generating plant where the ageing equipment was valiantly kept going by British engineers.

In the entrance of the European Commission's office sat a very large and muscular former British soldier, obviously holding a weapon beneath the desk. His arms relaxed when he was sure who we were. One of the European Commission's staff there was an Irishman whom I had known in Brussels. He told me that for weeks he had slept under his bed for fear of being hit by stray bullets flying about during the night. The European Commission's office building was adjacent to a building where Idi Amin's thugs had tortured their prisoners. The driver who took me round to meet various government officials refused point-blank to drive past this place because of his memory of the screams he had heard when Idi Amin was still in power.

I joined a couple of other British MEPs for the second night, staying at the British High Commissioner's house. The High Commissioner's wife made a meal for us. She said she had been searching the shops all morning to find food for us. When it came to bedtime, the High Commissioner said: 'Try not to leave anything downstairs that you might need during the night. You see, we have these armed fellows and if they see movement in the house and they don't know who it is... well, you see the problem, don't you? On the other hand, if you see someone on the balcony of your room during the night, don't worry at all. My chaps would have dealt with them long before they got there if they were up to no good.'

Around the Sahara

I went on a visit to Western Sahara, which had been a Spanish colony until Spain became democratic after Franco's death in 1975. At one time it contained more Spanish soldiers than local people! It is vast, sandy and dry, although it did rain slightly during our visit, and this was the first rain for months! Our party of six went by plane to the capital, La'youn (*El Ayoun* in Spanish). We were led in a group along the wide main street which was lined by almost the entire population, all wearing traditional dark blue capes, despite the heat. We were invited to take notice of the desire of local people that a sovereign state should be set up for them, rather than acquiesce to demands by Morocco that *it* should take over the territory.

While at dinner in the open air, I was approached by some English-speaking people who had come across the border from nearby Algeria. They said that they had been at Algerian camps for the training of terrorists and that they had mixed with men of the IRA, the Basque ETA group and terrorists from Italy and Germany. They said that the Americans could take satellite photographs in which they could recognise particular individual terrorists but that the terrorists somehow knew when these satellites would be overhead and hid under cover so that they could not be seen.

The courtesy of Arabs can be quite extraordinary. An example of this was when a sheikh at the reception in the evening of our visit was wearing a magnificent woollen cloak which was probably well over a hundred years old. A woman MEP was full of admiration for the colour and soft texture of the garment and its fine decoration. She expressed her praise repeatedly. It is the custom in those parts that if an honoured guest praises an article three times, the owner must give it to him or her. Despite the embarrassed MEP's protestations, she had to accept the cloak. The reception included a ceremonial meal. The main dish was a succulent roasted lamb, its legs in the air, presented on a bed of mint. The idea was that everybody pulled off chunks of it with their fingers. Apparently as a mark of esteem to a particularly honoured guest, I was invited by the sheikh to pluck off and eat an ovine testicle. It tasted gritty.

We went on a trip in a French helicopter to view the border with Morocco. We flew very low over the undulating mountains of sand and rock to keep below the level at which ground-to-air missiles could operate. We sat on a sideward-facing bench opposite an open door. There were no seatbelts so we had to hang onto the seat to avoid being catapulted through the door when the helicopter altered course abruptly.

Another war-torn area that I visited more than once was Ethiopia and Somalia. Mogadishu, the capital of Somalia, was then an unpleasant place and has subsequently become the scene of brutal chaos. While visiting northern Ethiopia we found it convenient and much more comfortable to stay at a hotel in Djibouti, a former French colony, strategically located at the entrance to the Red Sea, where France maintained armed forces. In Ethiopia, our party was received by Colonel Haile Mariam Mengistu, the dictatorial and Marxist Head of State. He did not like our visit but had little choice but to receive us in view of the amount of aid which the EU sent to his country. We sat on two sides of a table, the Head of State at the top and our group sitting on chairs slightly angled towards him. The atmosphere was tense.

Diplomatic niceties can either convey or hide real messages. My own comments in the meeting and those of one or two of my colleagues, expressed in clear but diplomatic tones, were about peace and freedom. The wars which Ethiopia engaged in at various times with Somalia and Sudan brought great suffering to its people. I wish I could say that the comments of some others of my colleagues had been as a direct as mine. I was never sure whether the lack of boldness was due to diplomatic nicety. It may also have been due to fear of the familiar left-wing nostrum that the history of colonialism meant that Europeans should never criticise Africans.

Ethiopia itself is the only country in Africa not to have been a European colony for any length of time although Eritrea, formerly an Italian colony, was joined to it for some years. Ethiopia as a whole was attacked by Italy in the late 1930s. When socialism and Soviet influence spread across Africa in the post-colonial period, Ethiopia fell under strong Soviet influence. One of the Soviet ideas foisted on Ethiopia was that of the state farm. At one such place I visited, I could see ten or more defunct combine harvesters dotted about a vast landscape which should have been bearing wheat crops. The Soviets had brought in the machines but had not supplied enough spare parts and had not trained the locals to use them. Some of one year's crop therefore could not be harvested, and some of following year's crop could not be sown because the machines intended for these functions, were unserviceable.

The fields had been ploughed in such a way that they were not completely level. This meant that when the combine harvesters were working, their blades were too high to cut that part of the stunted wheat which was growing in the hollows. In one field, the previous year's wheat in the hollows which had for this reason not been harvested was growing better than the newly-sown wheat. Despite the general dereliction of the farms, the large posters bearing slogans trumpeting the virtues of Mengistu and the merits of Marxism were all in excellent condition.

It is an understatement that Ethiopia is a dry country. It may barely rain at all for several years, yet when it does rain, much of the water runs straight off the ground because the earth is too hard to let it seep in. Big dams may be the answer in some cases but they are expensive to design and construct and would require a lot of piping. I visited a site where the alternative solution of terracing was being introduced with EU aid. Local manpower is used for this. There is no need for expensive machines and scarce diesel fuel. The hillside terraces hold the water long enough for the ground to absorb it by preventing it simply washing down the hillside, taking topsoil with it. This is an example of what the experts call "appropriate technology", technology using local resources that are either free or available at low cost.

Another example of appropriate technology which we saw was the planting of trees which grew very quickly in arid conditions for use as firewood. Sources of fuel for cooking are in almost as short supply as water. Another crop, a particular type of bush whose branches can be intertwined to produce a kind of living hedge through which goats cannot stray, was grown in rows, creating animal enclosures or small fields. Yet another system brought in by foreign aid schemes was the installation of solar-powered pumps to bring up precious water from small wells.

Since the 1950s when African countries were obtaining their independence, there has been general agreement not to contest the frontiers established by the colonial powers, however illogical they may be in terms of ethnic groupings. To begin to contest these frontiers would be to open frightful prospects for conflict. One exception to the sanctity of frontiers was that between Ethiopia and Somalia which was fiercely and bloodily contested for many years, for the reason that its exact position was unclear. Apparently a British Army General drew a line to represent this frontier on a rather small map with a rather blunt pencil. The resulting line, when translated into a line on the ground itself, is said to be nine miles wide in places! The conflicts over the position of the frontier raged for years, spurred on by Ethiopia's Marxist regime on one side and the Somali dictatorship on the other. Fighting groups rampaged across the barren land, engaging in a little camel-trading at the same time. The inevitable result has been tens of thousands of refugees.

Our visit started in Mogadishu. It was appallingly hot there. We discussed the problems of getting supplies of food to displaced and hungry people in the camps up country. The problem was not so much the shortage of food but the lack of means to transport it to the camps. We were told that 31,000 tonnes of food donated by western countries, destined for famine relief, had been sitting on the docks in nearby Djibouti for months for lack of transport and that 4,000 tonnes had been thrown away because it had gone bad. Large tins of EU butteroil (butter with the moisture removed) had exploded in the forty-degree-plus temperatures on the dockside. We were repeatedly told that gifts of trucks were of more value at that time than gifts of the food itself. We stressed this point to the European Commission on our return. But the fact remains that asking charitable organisations to donate trucks does not get the same willing response as asking for food.

On my visit to Mogadishu docks it rained, an extremely rare occurrence. The sacks of grain lying in the open just got wet. (My presence in desert areas seems to cause rain. As well as raining during my visits to Western Sahara and Somalia, it rained during a holiday in Egypt.)

We heard of a hospital in Mogadishu which is held as an example of how not to give aid. An Italian aid project, the hospital was a multi-storey building with all the latest technology. Soon after it opened in a blaze of glory, the electricity failed, so the water supply did not work and neither did the sewerage system nor the lifts. The whole place became a festering and unusable hulk!

Our group were to sleep in a government guesthouse. Lunch at the guesthouse was gastronomically "difficult". We were due to dine that evening in what had been an officers' club. A female German United Nations worker said that the risk of food poisoning was such that we were bound to be ill if we dined there unless we disinfected our stomachs with lots of whisky. We said that, if necessary, we would drink whisky; even the teetotallers in the group agreed. But where could we get the whisky? Somalia is a Muslim country and although not forbidden, alcohol was not widely available. The German woman said she had whisky at her house and we could go round there to have some.

215

However, there was some shooting going on outside the guesthouse and we were forbidden to leave the building. Our German friend then said she would go and get some. She went home and returned half an hour later with whisky, ice, soda and glasses. She poured out portions about four times the size of an English double. We all drank, except for one person. We went to the club and all survived unharmed, except the man who didn't drink the whisky. He became seriously ill and spent months in hospital.

By the time of this visit, much was being done by the United Nations, the EU, the US and other organisations to make life in the refugee camps bearable. Indeed, life in the camps was becoming more bearable than their previous peacetime nomadic life, for some of the women at least. Their men folk were still roaming the land to make war, to trade or to tend their camels but the women and children could now live in relative comfort in their huts. Water was becoming available from the solar-powered pumps. Wheat and rice were delivered to the camps under the various aid projects. The amount delivered was more than the people in the camps needed so some of it was sent back to Mogadishu by the refugees, where it was sold for cash on the black market. The refugees could then buy little radios for use in their huts, cigarettes, cans of beer and other goods.

Not only can long-term aid bring about a dependency culture, it can also destroy local agriculture. Local farmers could not obtain a living income when the prices of what they produced were undercut by wheat delivered free under foreign aid schemes. Some of the food aid sent is in the form of butteroil, which is used for cooking, especially when that has to be done with no water. Butteroil was sent in large drums and after the tops had been cut off the drums, it was ladled out to individual women using whatever receptacles were available. I saw the bottom half of a plastic washing-up liquid container used to slop the butteroil out of the drum – slop is the word, with a good ten or twenty per cent going on the floor. (Butter oil, as opposed to any other kind of cooking oil sent as food aid, was a by-product of the EU's farm subsidy system. This kept up prices for EU farmers by buying up excess milk production and turning it into two products which could be kept for a long time – skimmed milk powder and butter or butteroil. The aid therefore helped European farmers as well as impoverished Africans.)

A lot of the wheat was sent in big sacks, the sort of sacks which, when full, an old-time Liverpool docker would handle with ease, but far too heavy for a half-starved Somali woman to pick up. So the women dragged the sacks along the ground. This caused many of the sacks to catch on rusty bits of metal embedded in the ground and to tear. Out trickled the life-saving cereal. I noted that the Somali men did not help their womenfolk with moving the sacks of grain. Most of them just sat and watched, fingering their rifles. Indeed, in many African countries the women do the work and the men – well, they do the fighting if one of Africa's many conflicts is going on nearby. They may hunt a bit and who knows what else? I spoke in Strasbourg of the need to use smaller, stronger sacks. This suggestion ran into problems with the intervention agencies such as Britain's Intervention Board for Agricultural Produce. These agencies bought in, stored or sold surplus European cereal production. It appeared that convenience of handling the wheat when used as food aid had not been considered and rules to facilitate this had therefore not been imposed on the farmers. To transfer wheat from large sacks into small sacks would have been extremely expensive.

EU food aid in Ethiopia

The EU sent a great deal of food and other aid to Third World countries, particularly in Africa but this hardly ever got into the news – what good news does?

What I learned on these visits paid dividends in the meetings of the ACP-EU Assembly later on. After the first two or three meetings, it became a regular event to hold a formal meeting first with the Somalis and then with the Ethiopians, to discuss current affairs. To the practical mind of westerners, this may not seem much but to senior people from countries torn by drought and bloody strife, to be able to have a dialogue was helpful. It had the effect of toning down the rhetoric exchanged between the two sides in the plenary debates.

Another result is best described by quoting part of a speech made by my Conservative MEP colleague, Margaret Daly, in the European Parliament on 13 June 1988: 'For a number of years the Parliament has passed resolutions calling for the release of ten imprisoned members of the family of the former Emperor of Ethiopia… At our last meeting in Togo, after very lengthy talks with the Ethiopian representative, Mr Bersani, joint-president of the ACP-EU Assembly, and I were informed that our plea for the release of the prisoners on humanitarian grounds would be considered at the highest level. We gained the support of many ACP colleagues in this. Members will have seen in the newspapers that, after 14 years of imprisonment, the seven women prisoners were released on 21 May… I would like to place on record my thanks to Mr Bersani who gave up many hours of his time to help on this. I would also like to thank Mrs Ewing and Mr Pearce who gave their unfailing support through some very tough talking indeed.'

In 1987, the Heswall (Wirral) branch of Amnesty International asked me to make representations on behalf of a prisoner in Somalia, Omar Arteh Ghalib. I had had a number of contacts with Amnesty and was impressed by the fact that the making of representations to various governments did sometimes have a real effect in liberating prisoners of conscience. It may sound improbable that legal process can be swayed by lobbying, but the point is that in despotic countries, men and women are imprisoned, not because they have broken any law, but because it is in the personal interests of the rulers that they should be incarcerated. If enough external pressure is brought to bear, it may be in the interests of those rulers, from the point of view of obtaining foreign finance for their people or for themselves, or simply to attract attention, to liberate the prisoners.

Across the oceans

One of the meetings of the Bureau – the management committee of the ACP-EU Assembly – was held in 1987 on the Pacific island of Samoa, formerly known as Western Samoa from its days as a British colony, to distinguish it from the American-administered half of the island on which it is situated. I asked the question, "Why go all that way?" The point is that in any international activity there is a need for the partners to have an understanding of conditions in the areas where activities were to take place. Moreover, there is no good reason to insist that it should always be the ACP delegates who should bear the long-distance travel cost.

I had to spend a night in Sydney on the way. I took a taxi from the airport. The driver, who said he was Greek, asked me what I was doing in Oz. I explained about the ACP-EU meeting. 'Oh, yes', he said, 'I heard all about that on the radio.' Can you imagine the BBC broadcasting anything about a European conference like that? I was due to stop over in Fiji and meet some people there but they were having a revolution and there was shooting in the street near my hotel so I had to stay indoors.

The conference was in the Parliament House of Samoa in the capital, Apia. My principal memory of the small, modern parliament building designed to house forty-seven members was that it was infested with ants. I bought some anti-ant powder and made a *cordon sanitaire* around my seat.

I went on to Rarotonga in the Cook Islands, a tiny New Zealand dependency about nine miles in circumference in the Pacific. I was mystified when I first saw its flag. This contains the British Union flag in the top left-hand corner and a white circle of fifteen white stars on a dark blue background in the remainder of the space.[21] I thought it was some futuristic portrayal of a European Union dominated by the British! The island is a tropical paradise. I

---

[21] I was amazed to learn that the American state of Hawaii, which I have not visited, has a large (British) Union flag in the top corner. The territory was under British influence in earlier days. The flag is said to blend the British and American flags in a way acceptable to both at the time.

spent a day there and hired a bike and rode around the island; nice and flat and with places selling cold milk every so often. I found that the routing of my air ticket home entitled me to a stopover in Tahiti at no extra cost. Tahiti is another paradise. Superb scenery, French food and unbelievably beautiful singing by children on the ferry back from Bora Bora. Whereas the British transferred total sovereignty to most of its former colonies, France did likewise for most of its Empire but maintained a number of them, including French Polynesia, as notionally part of the mother country.

The Parliament building in the Cook Islands

Another Joint Assembly meeting was held in Jamaica. I found that by adding a little of my own money I could get to the conference via Miami. I purchased at a very reasonable price a special tourist air ticket which gave me ten flights within the region, mostly to and from Miami. The journey on to Jamaica accounted for two of these flights. Myra flew to Jamaica directly, at our own expense. We stayed in one of the hotels on the lovely north side of the island at Montego Bay. Kingston itself is not at all lovely. A street robber there was so bold that he cut the strap of the handbag of one of our female delegates with a machete. Fortunately the machete missed the woman's arm.

I had a one-night stopover in Haiti. This was a dangerous place. People handed out leaflets advertising voodoo events. I was followed around the capital, Port au Prince, by a very persistent man trying to get me to go to one of these: he would not take no for an answer. I found myself passing a building displaying the British royal coat of arms – the office of Her Britannic Majesty's Honorary Consul, who was a Belgian businessman – and quickly ducked inside to escape from my follower. The Consul made a phone call. After half an hour, he said it would be all right to go. The very persistent man was no more to be seen.

I also had a stopover in San Salvador, capital of El Salvador. This dictatorship was desperately poor; there was an over-bearing feeling of gloom and danger. The only exploring I felt I could safely do was to go by taxi from the one western hotel to another. As in so many of these impoverished and destitute places, there was a grand motorway named after the president from the airport to the capital, no doubt paid for by aid from the US, the EU or elsewhere. The airport was flyblown, the motorway tollbooths were empty, there was virtually no traffic and the motorway itself had weeds growing on it. However, the postcard I bought showed the motorway in tip-top condition with traffic flowing and decorative shrubs growing well on the central reservation.

A further official visit intended to contribute to peace-making was to Surinam, formerly Dutch Guyana, on the north east coast of South America. This sugar-producing land had a mixture of Asian, African, European and native-American peoples, constantly at each other's throats since independence. There was a feeling of desperation, of impending bloodshed in the air, and evidence of attacks on, and reprisals by, the public authorities. The sugar canes, on which the entire economy depended, had not been fully planted that year because of the violence.

Our delegation tried to bring about rational debate between the warring factions. The simple process of dialogue between these people seemed to be impossible without the presence of outsiders acting as referees. Surinam is a long way from most large countries other than Brazil, which was apparently not viewed as friendly. The former colonial power, Holland, did not seem to be held in a very good light. One of our group, a Dutchman, while clearly interested from the point of view of his own country, had to stay somewhat out of the limelight. I myself, as a Brit, never experienced such problems in former British colonies.

We did have one concrete success. We were told that in the little prison in Paramaribo, the capital, the uncle of a senior politician and two EU citizens were among those held on questionable charges. We asked if we could visit them. After making the request several times, they realised that we were serious and agreed to our request. The inside of the prison was very clean, and we saw nothing to indicate ill treatment of the prisoners. One prisoner called out to us that he was the politician's uncle. We interviewed the two EU citizens. The charges against them seemed very uncertain. We asked for their release and a couple of weeks later they were freed. I learned a small lesson about some of my colleagues on this prison visit. When we were invited to go inside the cell block of the prison in a group, as official leader, I led the way. I looked round and found myself alone. My colleagues plucked up courage when they saw that I had not been put in irons.

We held discussions with the government and all the political factions in Surinam, both separately and together. Nobody thought that our visit could solve the problems of Surinam, but I think our visit made a contribution to the search for peace and democracy, if only for a short time. Whether it was our business as Europeans to intervene in their country, even when they pleaded with us to do so, as they did, is open to argument, but I had no doubt again that the presence of free-speaking, free-thinking, unbiased people trying to help did make some difference. The Surinamers begged us to go there again but the European Parliament had no funds for this so no further visit took place in my time.

The British media downplayed the effect of courtesy visits such as this, yet people in Surinam, and in other countries which we visited, welcomed us and offered overwhelming thanks when visits went well. I have no doubt that such visits spread a little oil on troubled waters. Moreover, they helped us MEPs to better understand matters on which we were required to vote.

ACP-EU meetings in Europe

The "home" meetings, to use a football term, of the ACP-EU Assembly took place in various cities including Luxembourg, Biarritz and Berlin. In Luxembourg, I was among senior members of the Assembly to be received by the Grand Duke. The journey to the Grand Ducal Palace was one of the few I have made in a convoy of large cars escorted by motor cycle police. We were thrown all over the place inside the car in the haste to get to the palace. Why, I don't know, because we arrived early. When I occasionally see on television VIPs arriving in a cavalcade, I always try see if they have a greenish tinge as a result of the speed at which these cavalcades sometimes travel.

One of the Joint Assembly meetings was held in West Berlin; this was before the wall came down. The meeting took place in the Bundestag, the building which had been the Parliament before World War II and has now resumed that role following the reunification of Germany. I was determined to show the Africans, the socialist ones especially, what a Marxist state looked like in reality. I selected a vantage point inside the building from where one could see the East German guards patrolling the dog-runs and the barbed-wire enclosures on the East Berlin side and peering through binoculars at us over the wall on the western side. However, when the day came to invite some of the Africans to see this, all the East German guards had been removed. The communists obviously did not want to show their African clients the reality of what they offered.

When it was Britain's turn to host a Joint Assembly meeting, London was thought of by many as the natural venue, not only because it is the UK capital but also because it is the headquarters of the Commonwealth. The British government, however, refused to offer any assistance, and without such assistance, the event could not take place because of the constraints of the European Parliament's budget. Winnie Ewing, the Scottish Nationalist MEP, was however able to arrange for the meeting to be hosted in Inverness by courtesy of the authorities there. One or two British Ministers managed to make the journey to attend the meeting and it was delightful that Princess Anne was present. The Princess gained much praise for her knowledge of development issues. When problems of etiquette and procedure arose her charm and poise shone through.

Simone Veil with the Crown Prince of Luxembourg on her left. Giovanni Bersani on the far right in the back row, with ACP delegates

In her speech she complained of the multiplicity of agencies intended to help developing countries. In one small such country she had found that eighty agencies were present. 'What were they all doing?' she asked. She complained also of inappropriate aid. 'Like one very large set of disc harrows in the middle of the desert. No tractor or diesel for hundreds of miles. If that is aid, then I do not think they need it,' she was reported as saying in The *Scotsman* of 24 September 1985.

Obviously the contacts with the leaders of many aspects of our nation's life were not a fraction of what they would have been had the conference been held in London. Janey Buchan, a Scottish Labour MEP, criticised the conference in the *Daily Record* on 24 July 1985 by saying it was a pity that none of the debates were to be made public. The paper quoted my response which was that it had always been intended that the whole conference would be held in open session available to the public and the press. It was thus held.

★ ★ ★

Politicians of all nations, of different creeds and cultures, speak with authority on many things, but when it comes to overseas aid and development of Third World countries such as those I visited in Africa, I firmly believe they cannot do so with authority unless they have seen these countries with their own eyes. I was fortunate enough to have that opportunity. Some of the things I saw were extremely distressing; some were frightening; some were puzzling until situations and reasons were explained to me, and some were of great credit to fledgling independent countries trying their best under very difficult circumstances. All this information helped me to speak of the reality of the situation in Africa and elsewhere, and to avoid the empty sentimentality and left-wing slant which characterised so much comment on it. We cannot change what happened in the past and there is no point in trying to make people alive today feel guilty about what their ancestors may or may not have done. What we have to do is to be clear about what should be done in the future.

PART IV

After The European Parliament

Whitehall, Budapest and Toxteth

After my defeat in the 1989 Euro-election I had to look for a job. For a politician to lose his seat is not only a political misfortune; it means that he or she is out of work and without a source of income. A number of MPs and one or two MEPs who lost their seats were immediately offered "ornamental" or "grace and favour" jobs in company boardrooms, to which they occasionally brought relevant experience. I was not so favoured. My experience might have qualified me for a job in a lobbying firm or in a trade association but these were nearly all based in London and neither my financial nor family circumstances made this an attractive prospect.

I was, however, fortunate to be pointed in the direction of Littlewoods – the stores and mail order side of the business, not the football pools. The company had stores in most major British towns and cities focused on selling clothing to middle-aged women for their families. My job, a real one not just an ornamental one, had two parts.

The first part of the job was working as a lobbyist with other UK retailers on various issues. These included persuading Whitehall and Brussels to take a liberal view on setting quotas for clothing imports. My previous experience on these matters, both while working in the European Commission and as an MEP, were obviously relevant. It was a specialist topic. Not many people in the private sector knew what "basket exits" were – jargon for the import level at which limits might be applied – but *I* did! These were vital issues in maintaining the best balance between importers and retailers on the one hand and UK producers on the other.

I performed much of my lobbying through the British Retail Consortium and sometimes represented the British retail sector as a whole in meetings at which European Commission officials in Brussels sought the opinions of the trade. Whereas European producers wanted imports kept down as far as possible, retailers wanted an end to limits on how much clothing they could import. Most importantly they wanted to ensure that the door would not be

229

slammed shut on imports without advance warning because much of their stock was ordered from Far East suppliers many months in advance and brought to the UK by sea. I was quoted in *Fashion Weekly* as saying, "It would be bad for retailers if we were to imagine that we were in a free market and then have the whistle blown." Consumer organisations tended to take the retailers' side in these matters.

I was also lobbying to protect retailers from possible European Commission follies in consumer and environmental protection. *Ignorance* is perhaps a better description of the phenomenon than *folly*. The Commission just did not always have experts who understood how its proposals would affect retailing in practice. Whitehall often didn't either, although the German civil service certainly did.

A small delegation from the British Retail Consortium went to the Department of Trade & Industry to argue against certain provisions in UK regulations implementing an EU Directive. Each EU state normally had two years to incorporate EU Directives agreed by Ministers into their national laws, often by amending existing national regulations covering the matters concerned. Whitehall was notorious for adding extra provisions to what had been agreed in Brussels and then sitting back while the British business community blamed Brussels. This process is called "gold-plating". We asked why Whitehall did this. 'This is how we do things. The law must be precise so that infringements can be curtailed, with certainty, if necessary, in the courts,' was the answer. Most of our delegation thought that British civil servants had desk drawers full of new rules of their own invention which they wanted to bring in and that they just waited for an EU Directive to tack them on to, blaming Brussels for any criticism.

The second part of my job at Littlewoods was trying to bring to fruition the company's wish to purchase shops in Eastern Europe when the authorities there began to privatise their economies after the fall of the Iron Curtain in 1989. Littlewoods' interest in Hungary began with John Moores, son of the firm's founder. He already had a representative in Hungary who helped with his exports of bull semen, of all things, from the UK to Hungary! The objective of this was to improve the quality of Hungary's livestock. In return, Hungarian wine was shipped to the UK. I went to Hungary and the Czech Republic many times with a colleague, a ladies' fashion buyer (a man), and also to Poland and to the former East Germany, studying the options for purchasing retail stores.

Budapest and Vienna had been the joint capitals of the Austro-Hungarian Empire before it collapsed at the end of the First World War. The neo-gothic Parliament building in Budapest fronting the Danube reminds one of the Houses of Parliament in London. The main suspension bridge over the Danube was designed by Tierney Clarke, who designed the bridge over the Thames at Marlow. There had been a slow process of economic reform in Hungary, almost from the rebellion against the Russians in 1956. By the time communism finally collapsed, there were quite a few privately owned shops alongside the dreary state shops, but the general perspective of the shopping streets was grim. In common with most communist countries, there seems to have been a terrible shortage of paint and there was a general atmosphere of greyness and of nothing ever being repaired.

The Hungarian language has no relationship with other European languages, apart from Estonian and Finnish, having arrived in Europe with Asiatic tribes who settled in these three regions. I tried to learn a few phrases but even some of the most commonly used words, such as *viszontlátásra* meaning *goodbye*, are fairly complicated. Hungarian is spoken without accented syllables; the sound flows smoothly and musically. Most of the officials and business people we met spoke English. If they did not I mostly got by with a few words of German and the use of gesticulations. Black market money dealers could speak enough German or English to change German marks into *forints*, the Hungarian currency. Nobody wanted English pounds.

There had been two big chains of retail stores in Hungary, one owned directly by the state and the other a kind of cooperative but still within the public sector. The high-ranking civil servants charged with selling off these businesses after the end of communism seemed to be looking after their own financial interests in the disposal. It may sound odd that former communist officials should have the instincts of businessmen, but after all, in the communist days, there was no way forward for an ambitious and able young man or woman except through the party. While battalions of silly students in Britain viewed communism as a fine example of organising life to benefit mankind, to those who had to live under it, it was no more than a corrupt and inefficient political system imposed on them by Stalin, his successors and their secret police.

At this time, the beginnings of western commercial activity could be seen in Hungary. Marks & Spencer's goods could be obtained in Györ at the western end of Hungary. German mail order goods could be ordered from catalogues available in certain shops and sales booths, the goods being delivered some days later to central points for pick up by the customers. There was a roaring trade in a particular brand of western jeans at one of the new shops in the most fashionable shopping street. There was a queue outside, all day and every day, people being let inside a dozen at a time. This firm made its jeans, or had them made, in many countries, including Hungary. Fashion-conscious Hungarians were determined to purchase jeans which had been imported into their country, even at higher prices than Hungarian-made products of the same brand. I never found out whether there was really any difference.

The restaurants in Budapest were either new, western-style luxury restaurants within new hotels, with prices to match, or traditional lower-priced Hungarian restaurants in dark rooms with heavy curtains at the doors to keep the winter cold out. There was often gypsy music to be enjoyed; the slightest indication of pleasure by a customer brought graceful but firm solicitation of a tip. I was surprised to learn that red peppers, the basis of much Hungarian cooking, are native of the Americas, not of Europe.

I went to the town of Nyíregyháza at the very eastern extreme of Hungary. My train left Budapest very early in the morning and the police were still clearing out the hundreds of people who had slept the night there on the station floor. I took a quite reasonable express train as far as Miskolc, a shabby industrial town, one of the largest in Hungary. Buildings there needed painting as desperately as those in the capital. Then I travelled onwards in a train which was something of a museum piece through the hills and forests of eastern Hungary. Nyíregyháza had one hotel and one restaurant of any standing. It was a frontier town abutting Romania and close to Ukraine, and it was the centre of a small established free-trade zone where Hungarian, Romanian and especially Ukrainian businessmen went about their business. I never discovered why three communist countries, with almost totally state-controlled economies, needed a free trade zone.

I was attacked by two men in a street in Budapest one evening. As in a car accident, time seemed to stand still. In this never-never time I considered what to do and remembered advice to shout as loudly as possible. I did so and hugged my jacket to me. The men only managed to wrench one document, my air ticket, from my pocket before fleeing. When I got back to my hotel, which was nearby, the receptionist said, 'Excuse me, Sir, someone has just found an air ticket with your name on it in the street outside.'

My Littlewoods mandate also took me to several cities in what is now the Czech Republic. For one trip heading for Brno, I decided to fly to Vienna and then go by train via Bratislava, in what is now Slovakia. I took lunch in the dining car on the train. The pork chop was not bad but the peas had just been seared so they were slightly burnt on one side and cold on the other. At this time, not long after communism collapsed, the western price levels, which came to apply to most things that travellers buy, had not yet replaced the old price structure, at least not in this dining car. A glass of beer cost about eleven pence and the main course not much more.

I arrived in Bratislava to find the currency exchange office closed for renovations and nearly everything else closed because it was Sunday. I had no local money and no means of paying for a taxi to the hotel which I had reserved. I had been told that Czechoslovakia, although being better off than some of the other east European countries, had a particularly tightly controlled economy and I had no intention of infringing the currency rules, by changing money in the street with an illegal dealer, something that could be very unwise. I explained the problem to a passer-by in a mixture of English, German, Russian and hand-waving, asking where I could change money. He kindly took me to my hotel in his car.

I went for a walk before dinner. Great numbers of people were streaming from the churches after evening service. Most queued for trams, privately owned cars being a rarity. There was an eerie silence in the streets; almost no traffic. Nobody in the tram queues said a word; they just stood there. Then you could hear the tram coming from three or four stops away.

During the communist era, the Czechs had built one enormous retail store in each major city, three or four in the capital. Sometimes these had been built right on what had previously been the town square or a park. There were not many other shops and no small privately owned shops like those which I had seen in Hungary. Each time I went to the huge main store in Prague, it felt like rush hour on the London underground because of the number of people using the escalators.

Much of the way the shops were run was as they had been run under the communist system before 1989. Within each huge state-owned store there were small areas of particular merchandise, each in effect fenced off by display stands and seats. It was like several small shops within a shop. Each group of staff was responsible for any losses of their merchandise, the value being deducted from their wages, and so they were fiercely territorial in making sure that there was only one way into their area. Staff insisted on serving the customers. My Littlewoods colleague got into very hot water with one lady assistant because he wanted to browse by himself. Our host dismissed the problem by saying that this particular assistant was Russian!

In western countries, retailers accept a certain level of "shrinkage" – theft of and damage to goods. To the Czechs, no such idea was permissible. All stock which had not been officially sold was considered to be in stock, and moreover in stock at its original value, even if it had been there for over a year and fashion had moved on. Each state factory set the price at which it sold goods to the retail store. The government set the price at which each state store sold the goods to its customers, without reference to what it had paid for them. The concept of a trading profit or loss could not exist.

Some of the prices were amazingly low. Good quality trombones were a giveaway, if you happened to need one, that is! Excellent glass was dirt cheap and so I bought a large glass vase. I checked that it was carefully packed for my return British Airways flight, marking the package "fragile". When I got home, I found it was smashed to smithereens. I did get compensation for this breakage and so bought another one on a later trip. This time I insisted on taking it into the aircraft's cabin with me.

While preparing for the visit to Brno, I learned that the Bren gun, which I had "played with" during my national service, derived its name from the name of the city of Brno, where it was designed, and Enfield where large numbers were manufactured.

My colleague and I stayed in one of the best, but not very good, hotels in the city. The hotel lounge was a large room with a square bar counter in the middle. The "ladies of the night", a phenomenon as common in the communist world as elsewhere, all sat round the walls of the room, not near the central bar. I asked why this was so and was told that in the communist days, there were closed circuit television cameras filming who was talking to whom at the central bar. The seats along the walls of the room were out of range of the cameras.

I went to Warsaw. One of the consequences of Poland's transition into a candidate for membership of the EU was the arrival there of a number of western supermarkets, mainly French, causing disquiet among the small shopkeepers who thought that this was unfair competition. The French were much quicker off the mark in going into Eastern Europe than the British but there is now a strong British retail presence there.

My colleague and I had a trip to Lodz, which was described in the nineteenth century as the Manchester of Poland. We stayed in a hotel of very faded grandeur with plenty of the nineteenth century still evident. We had adjacent bedrooms, each with a tiny balcony above the cars parked below. In the middle of the night, for no reason known to me, the balcony of my colleague's room fell off and went right through the roof of the car parked below. Fortunately it was not our rented car. We made another impact in Lodz; the silencer fell off the rental car. Having appointments and a return flight to keep, we just roared on from appointment to appointment.

During my time at Littlewoods, I was selected to fight the 1992 British general election campaign in Ellesmere Port & Neston as the Conservative candidate. This seat had been held by the Conservatives in 1987 by a majority of 1,853. Given the national mood against the Tories, it would be a hard seat to hold.

Campaigning in Ellesmere Port & Neston

I did not win the election, receiving just under forty-three per cent of the votes against the forty-six per cent obtained by Andrew Miller, who became the new Labour MP.

While at Littlewoods, I was appointed a governor of Nugent Roman Catholic Boys' Secondary School in the Toxteth district of Liverpool even though I was not a Catholic. The school is named after Father James Nugent who lived and worked among poorer families in Liverpool in the 1860s. Liverpool's Roman Catholics had to close several schools in inner parts of the

235

city in the 1980s as the population there declined; this was a difficult task which they only partly succeeded in accomplishing. Nugent School, set up at that time, had never attracted as many as half of the boys from neighbouring Roman Catholic primary schools and never filled more than half of its own places.

The year I was appointed a governor of the school, some nine Conservatives were proposed for appointment as governors of Liverpool schools. I was the only one of these who was at all well known. Amazingly, I was the only one of the nine to be appointed. I wondered whether a mistake had been made and that it was intended to appoint all the others except me!

There were many unemployed people and single parents among those who sent their children to the school. The national curriculum insisted that they learn French. Much as I supported increased command of languages by British people in general, I could not see the point of teaching these boys French. Hardly any of them would ever use French in any job they might get in the locality, and they would have been far better served by learning to read and write English correctly.

I asked when they held Mass in the school. When told that such services were not held, I suggested that they should in fact hold one. It was agreed to do so. The day it took place was the day when the first national league tables for the performance of schools were published. Nugent School came bottom in the whole country. Granada TV's regional news wanted to come and film the Mass in the school hall as part of its coverage of the league table story. The Head had to have a couple of practice runs before the cameras went live so that the boys knew what to do.

The school was threatened with closure because of the low number of boys enrolled. At one meeting about this, the Roman Catholic Director of Education in Liverpool was present. The large number of Roman Catholic schools in the city meant that he was a person of considerable influence. Political correctness was just rearing its nasty head at that time. The Director knew all the approved phrases, 'equal opportunities for boys of all social classes, creeds and colours,' he intoned. A very dark-skinned mother next to me spoke up, 'It's all very well saying all that but what about us blacks?' *Black* seemed to be a forbidden word in the world of political correctness, although *white* was fine! Yet plenty of people of African origin in Liverpool routinely called themselves black.

There were plans to combine Nugent with a Roman Catholic girls' school nearby. However, whereas our boys were entirely working-class, some of the girls at the other school were from the middle-class leafy lanes in the outer suburbs. Moreover, Nugent had a number of Muslim boys, limited to about twenty per cent of the intake. Many Muslim parents, like Roman Catholics, prefer single-sex education.

I used to walk up to the school from the city centre for meetings on summer evenings. Women would come out of their houses to ask what I wanted there. When I told them, six or seven of them would escort me to the gate of the school. I had to leave the board of governors when I decided to return to Brussels. Nugent subsequently closed. I felt that society had completely failed the boys there.

Littlewoods asked me to represent the company in Liverpool Chamber of Commerce. In 1993 I was instrumental in the holding of a Chamber of Commerce "Made in Liverpool" exhibition in the city's St George's Hall. The idea was for local businesses to show their products and services. We had language students on hand to make sales calls on behalf of local business people in the appropriate languages to potential customers on the continent. The linguistic side worked well but many of the businessmen and women, apparently unused to prospecting for new customers, were vague about whether they were phoning to fix an appointment, to ask if a catalogue was required or to determine what products would be of interest to them. It seemed to be as much a lesson in basic salesmanship as in overcoming the language barrier.

I had noticed that across the street at the Liverpool Museum, a banner proclaimed "Made in Liverpool", the same words as the theme of our exhibition. In fact, this banner at the museum referred to an exhibition of Liverpool-made pottery in the museum, the city having been a major centre of pottery manufacture in the late eighteenth century. With the idea of making a connection between the two exhibitions, I tried to borrow a cup and saucer of Liverpool pottery from the museum. The museum said that they could not possibly lend me a cup and saucer, despite wholesome guarantees of security, because it would take at least nine months to plan such an exercise!

Within the Chamber, I joined with a few other members under the leadership of a local businessman in setting up the European Business Development Group within the Chamber. This specialised in encouraging local small businesses to export to other European countries and offered advice on how to do this. I wrote a series of articles in the Chamber's journal about individual local companies that had done this, paying each one a visit to hear their stories. Their reasons for wishing to export to the continent were varied indeed, as were the means whereby they conducted successful business. Their initiatives owed less to textbooks on management theory than to coincidences and good fortune.

'I met a Dane in a bar in Hamburg and he said he had done good business in Spain so why didn't I have a try?' was one starting point.

'My wife is German,' said another.

Some of the successful businessmen visited their continental customers frequently, often combining trips with visits to friends and family. At the other extreme, one successful businessman had never been abroad on business and seemed to do very well using the services of the British embassies and consulates in the countries where he conducted business.

The Chamber was very conscious of the city's maritime links, past and present. The Chamber and the Royal Navy collaborated to promote Merseyside business abroad through *HMS Liverpool,* a destroyer. I went to a reception aboard the ship in the docks in 2004 for exporters and government export promotion officers.

After some time, Littlewoods decided that its destiny did not lie in Eastern Europe so my services were no longer required. I therefore activated my right of return to work in the European Commission, having been technically on unpaid leave for my period of service as an MEP. I began working there again at the beginning of 1994.

Brussels yet again

On arriving back at the European Commission, I was asked to take up a position in the Tourism Unit, as its Deputy Head. I was later appointed Deputy Head of the Commerce Unit, concerned with retailing and wholesaling in the same Directorate General (DGXXIII or Enterprise Directorate General as it became).

The EU did not have a remit to plan or regulate either tourism or commerce. It does not seek such a remit. What the Tourism and Commerce Units primarily did was to ensure that other policies for which the EU had a responsibility (a *compétence*) did not, without good reason, impede the work of companies in these sectors. It was to ensure that EU policies generally applied to these sectors in an appropriate and sensible manner. For example, the Commerce Unit liaised with the Competition Directorate General when EU anti-trust rules were applied to the retailing of cars.

The EU has long had policies supporting small and medium size enterprises (SMEs). The Tourism and Commerce Units had a role of helping firms in their sectors take best advantage of these policies. The Commission's purpose was to identify and spread "best practice" – profitable ways of running such businesses. The EU could operate as a useful forum for exchanging ideas on what works and what doesn't in a whole range of fields. Projects receiving financial support from the European Commission with this end in view were submitted by consulting companies who responded to published calls for proposals. In order to qualify and be awarded EU funds towards their costs, consultants had to demonstrate how their projects would improve the quality of services provided and protect and create jobs.

For example, knowledge of 'yield management' schemes in tourism, by which hotels vary prices to match demand levels, not only by the season and the day of the week but also according to the number of bookings taken, were publicised by DGXXIII long before they became common practice. The concept of "destination management" was the subject of other DGXXIII campaigns to help SMEs. Destination management recognises the fact that a tourist is not only drawn to a particular attraction or a particular hotel but by the entire experience of the holiday, information, transport, safety, cleanliness and so on.

My arrival back in the European Commission in the Tourism Unit was in strange circumstances. Allegations were being investigated that the then Head of Unit and his Deputy were involved in bribery. The investigations of these problems were far-reaching, thorough and slow to become publicly known. *The Times* reported on 22 March 1995 that "up to £300,000 is understood to have been paid." It added that the Commission had lifted diplomatic immunity protecting three officials, and granted authority to the Belgian police to enter the Commission's headquarters, which was normally out of bounds for the police.

The *Financial Times* reported the development of the affair on 6 January 1996 as follows: "Two European Commission officials in Brussels and the wife of one of them have been arrested in connection with a bribery scandal involving European Union tourism subsidies. Mr George Tzoanos, a Greek who headed the Commission's tourism department, his wife and Mr Pascal Chatillon, a Frenchman who worked with Mr Tzoanos, are under investigation for several alleged crimes, including the awarding of EU tourism subsidies to companies in return for "illegal commissions" that often amounted to several hundred thousand ecus. According to Belgian fraud officials, companies in several EU member states sometimes paid more than ten per cent of the total subsidies awarded them by the officials. French authorities have arrested two company executives in connection with the case."

The *Guardian* reported on the same day that police had searched the officials' homes. It said that police became involved only when the British Tory MEP, Edward McMillan-Scott, issued a formal complaint after the Commission failed to take action. On 28 February 1996 the paper said that the Greek government, under heavy pressure from Brussels, had ordered dozens of companies to give back £1.9 million of EU funds misappropriated between 1990 and 1993. Tzoanos and Chatillon were both sentenced to prison terms. The *Guardian* reported on 28 February 1995: "Greece cracks down on villas built by EU aid cheats."

Exposure of these circumstances within the European Commission took place before I took up work there again. Publicity in the media came some time later, after my return.

My work in the Tourism Unit took me to several parts of the EU to speak on behalf of the European Commission. One country I visited was Slovenia, formerly part of Yugoslavia and now an independent country. I had to speak at a conference to open a tourism development project part-financed by the EU as part of the effort to put this country on its feet economically. This project was not in the skiing area for which the country is famous but in the quiet Dolenjska countryside, ideal for walking and promoted as "Europe's Sleeping Beauty". Tourist maps and guides in English and German were provided. A brochure for foreigners emphasised the country's ancient Roman garrison, its life under the Hapsburgs and during attacks by the Turks, but not its most recent overlords, the Serbs, who ruled Yugoslavia, of which it had been part. The brochure showed beautiful castles, old monasteries, vineyards and rivers. The local language was difficult and some of the place names such as Krka and Crnomelj are hard for English speakers to pronounce. But many of the younger people speak English.

A team of foreign and local experts were gathered for the conference. One of the EU experts was a former director of a major Scottish museum. The Scot asked one of the Slovenes in charge of the local museum how long the present exhibition had been there.

'About eleven years,' was the answer.

'Have the exhibits changed in that time?' asked the Scot.

'No' said the Slovene.

'Is there a cinema in the town?'

'Yes'.

'Do people go back and see the same film month after month, year after year?'

'No,' said the Slovene, 'we change the film every two weeks.'

'Well,' said the Scot, 'why do you think people will want to come back and see the same exhibition for eleven years?'

'Oh,' said the Slovene. Obvious, you may say – but something is only obvious when you know it!

According to locals, the wooded valley had a population of bears, deer and wolves. 'We'll advertise it for hunting,' they said.

'Steady on,' we replied. 'If you do that, you will have protestors and environmentalists against you. Why not organise animal viewing; plenty of tourists will come for that.'

The consultants also explained how, while congratulations could be offered to the neat and tidy appearance of the frontages of the hotels, tipping rubbish on open ground around the back of the hotel, as sometimes happened, would be a kiss of death for their businesses if tourists saw it.

The European Commission's headquarters in Brussels, the Berlaymont (before renovation after 1999)

Another project supported by the Tourism Unit with EU funds was to help Americans search for their ancestral roots in European countries. This included references to passenger lists for ships leaving Liverpool, currently stored in Merseyside Maritime Museum. The project was called "Routes to the Roots" and received 61,000 ecus from the European Commission.[22]

I spoke at a tourism conference at Palma de Mallorca. I was told that 13 million Britons took holidays in Spain every year. I had not been to Mallorca before so I asked the local tourism office to give me a quick tour around the place by car. The pubs in some parts advertised "Big screen: Everton v West Ham" or "Fish, chips and a mug of tea" just like an English resort but with sunshine. In other parts of the town there was an even stronger German influence, especially as regards the bars and the beer sold in them.

I made a speech at a conference on the Greek island of Rhodes. I arrived at about eight o'clock in the evening and went to find out where the conference hall was. I then had a meal and a drink with some British holidaymakers and went to bed. I made my speech at nine o'clock in the morning, and caught a plane home about two hours later. They call this seeing the world!

One project aided by the Tourism Unit was to improve signage and guide books on routes to Santiago de Compostela, the pilgrimage route to the city where the body of St James is said to be kept. This received 60,606 ecus. Another was to encourage tourists interested in music to consider a three-centre

---

[22] The European Currency Unit (ecu) was a predecessor of the euro.

holiday taking in concerts of Mozart's music in Milan, Vienna and Prague, cities in which the composer had lived. This received a grant of 964,031 ecus.

Another project was to spread interest in towns with medieval walls, the idea being that tourists who enjoyed visiting one walled town might go and visit others if they knew about them. This project was run by someone from a college in Bristol. Chester, in my own Euro-constituency, was involved.

I was instructed to speak at a tourism conference in Bad Blankenburg in what had previously been the Soviet zone of Germany. I was told that this was a resort where the East German Olympic team had trained. I flew to Erfurt via Düsseldorf and on then by slow local train to my destination. I had asked the train guard to tell me when we got to Bad Blankenburg but he fell asleep and failed to do so. I managed to see the station name boards when we arrived there. Nobody was about, the time being after 11 pm. Everything was dark and closed. However, after a long walk I found the hotel and roused the staff but there was no food available at that time. I had had nothing since breakfast! In the morning I opted for a lift to the conference building but this meant missing breakfast at the hotel. On arriving at the conference venue I asked about breakfast. It was finished. I walked towards some other buildings nearby and one of these proved to be the station at which I had arrived the previous evening. I found a truckers' café. Food at last! I had a frankfurter with onions and a piece of rye bread – the nearest to bacon, egg and toast on offer.

I gave my speech and had to leave before lunch was served to catch my train. The station had three platforms and no one knew which platform the train would come to. The time for the departure of the train came and went. Some twenty minutes later the train appeared, a huge steam locomotive pulling about twelve carriages. Two or three men with cameras leaned out of each open window. Nearly all were British railway enthusiasts. They had hired the steam locomotive instead of the usual diesel to pull a normal scheduled train on this particular day.

Some years after Sweden became a member of the EU, the European Commission sent me to speak at a tourism conference some distance to the north of Stockholm. Our hosts were demonstrating their cultural tourism offer. We delegates were swept up into a trip on a lake on a Viking boat on which we had to do the rowing. I imagine that the ancient Vikings were somewhat fitter than we were. Our hosts sought to enliven the occasion with Swedish jokes, which did not help. I think you have to be Swedish to understand Swedish jokes.

The night I spent there was the shortest night of the year. As midnight approached, we were invited to watch the erection of a tall, straight tree trunk, which served the same sort of purpose as an English maypole. I had left Brussels airport on a flight at about half past seven that morning, made my speech in the conference, rowed with the Vikings and was to be picked up at half past six, the following morning, by a taxi to take me back to the local airport. I therefore went to bed as soon as I could after the tree ceremony was finished but I could not resist watching the red glow of the sun which never sets there at that time of year. I understood that the other delegates were afforded a late start the following morning after their evening exertions.

Tourism represents about seven per cent of UK gross domestic product. This compares with about four per cent for the chemical industry and two per cent for the motor industry.

After moving to the Commerce Unit, I addressed a conference in Kiev in Ukraine just before Christmas one year. As was the case with several of my trips, I was given very little notice of having to go there and had difficulty in obtaining a definite hotel booking by telephone beforehand. I trudged about in the Kiev snow to find the hotel whose name I had been given and was relieved to find that a room was in fact reserved for me. This was in the early days of Ukraine going its own way after the demise of the Soviet Union. There were notices in the airport in English as well as in Ukrainian (though not always Russian) but not much English seemed to be spoken elsewhere. The Russian I had learned all those years ago in the Royal Air Force came in handy, Ukrainian being a somewhat similar language.

It snowed most of the time I was there. The street sellers congregated round their stalls in the pedestrian tunnels underneath the main boulevard. They sold anything they could get their hands on. One stall might have Marlborough cigarettes and a few Walt Disney toys, others canned food, a pile of magazines or bottled drinks. Westerners told me that caviar was the thing to buy but it was expensive even there and was not something I viewed as one of life's necessities.

The conference was about setting up a Chamber of Commerce run by the newly arising business community and about helping local firms that wanted to export their goods. The state officials were very resistant to letting go of their privileged positions running the existing state-controlled Chamber. The owners of the new small businesses, several of them run by women, were scathing about the Chamber and wanted it to be independent of the government. I saw here, as elsewhere, how the former communist bureaucrats who had carved out lucrative empires for themselves in government ministries (including the security services) were intent upon carrying their privileges into the new privatised era. The EU gave Ukraine 410 million euros between 1991 and 1997 from its TACIS programme.[23]

In January 2000 I spoke at a conference in Warsaw. This was organised by the Polish Foundation for Small and Medium Size Enterprises and was part of the preparations for Poland to join the EU, which it did in 2004. I described the means of assistance for SMEs from the European Commission including the setting up of EuroInfoCentres which provided a wide range of information about legislation and grants. I made a report as usual after the trip. In this I referred to the European Commission's stated intention to help Polish retail and wholesale firms to modernise and to compete with the French and other retailers which were preparing to set up branches in Poland. Aid for the provision of staff training schemes would be part of the project. I noted, however, that such schemes could not be organised because there were no Commission staff available to do this and that funds allocated in the 1998 and 1999 EU budgets were largely unused due to the lack of such staff. (The Commerce Unit contained about a dozen staff in all). This was one of a number of cases where EU member states or individual MEPs voted for policies and projects which responded to their political objectives but prevented the European Commission recruiting sufficient staff to manage them properly. There are no political brownie points to be gained from increasing staff!

I went to check on a project near Huddersfield that was designed to demonstrate how to tackle some of the problems faced by small food wholesalers. As the number of independent food retailers declined in the face of the development of the big food chains, so the market for the wholesalers who served them declined also. The idea of the project was to analyse the items which each retailer put in his trolley when he went round the wholesale cash-and-carry warehouse. They were to be analysed by type, quality and pack size. This was to be related to the characteristics of the area so that promotions could be tailored to local market circumstances. In this way, the wholesaler would be helping the retailer to offer goods which would maintain the loyalty of customers, even in the face of competition from supermarket chains.

Another of the Commerce Unit's projects was to assist an agricultural co-operative at Cremona, in Italy, with a project to increase sales in the USA of Provolone cheese made in the region. The idea was to have a computerised

---

[23] TACIS is an abbreviation of "Technical Aid to the Commonwealth of Independent States" i.e. aid to countries formerly in the Soviet Union.

order centre, drawing off quantities of Provolone made by several or many of the hundred or so producers, always to a strict and identical specification. This would enable much bigger orders to be accepted.

The Commerce Unit drafted a European Commission White Paper on Commerce setting out options for coping with the changes affecting the market. I contributed to this. A "White Paper" is a British term for a document explaining the government's legislative intentions on a particular topic. It is much easier to understand than the draft legislation itself. A European Commission White Paper is broadly the same. In French, EU White Papers are called *livres blancs (white books)*.

Apart from helping to write the text and getting it approved by other Directorates-General in the European Commission, finding suitable photos to illustrate it was an interesting task. The Commerce Unit had no budget for having photos taken for this purpose. We therefore had to obtain stock shots from a Belgian photographic library, keeping close watch on the costs involved and potential copyright problems. We had to ensure that the photos showed shoppers in the stores. Many of the stock shots, taken with architecture and store layout in mind, were completely devoid of customers, hardly what a project aimed at improving profitability in retailing required!

Another of the Commerce Unit's activities was helping European Commission measures to force the banks in 2002 to reduce their charges for credit card transactions across the EU's internal borders.

The European Commission was early in the promotion of Corporate Social Responsibility (CSR) – the idea that firms should behave honestly and responsibly with regards to employees, customers, suppliers, local communities and the environment. It published a document about this in 2002. It was not inventing new ways of doing things but seeking to spread information about them. CSR has proved in some contexts to be not only useful in its own right but also a valuable tool for corporate public relations and as part of the bargaining process between companies, trade unions and pressure groups. It is regrettable that CSR is also used by certain large companies as a marketing tool, displaying their corporate virtue to customers, clients and financiers. This can mean that the good works funded are focused on cities where they will be most visible to the people whom they wish to impress, such as MPs, civil servants and private sector bigwigs.

The Commerce Unit played a small part in preparations in the EU countries which were to adopt the euro. Our particular role was urging retailers to order the equipment they would need, such as tills, in good time so as not to find out at the last minute that supplies of the machines had run out. The *Irish Times* reported me on 12 June 2000 as saying, "Retailers have to train staff, modify their cash machines and they are going to have to think about their price points such as £7.99.[24]

The euro (conversion) amounts are not just nice round amounts, and the government would not like retailers to increase their prices up to the nearest round figure." In fact the introduction of the euro went remarkably well in the retail sector and the forecasts of confusion and inflation were proved largely unfounded.

I spoke at a conference of the European Federation of Conference Organisers, one of the many trade associations which maintained contacts with the European Commission. One of the objectives of such encounters was to provide business sectors with a way into the complex Brussels machinery of decision-making that affected them.

I was involved in organising a European Day of Commerce. Part of it was to highlight trends and problems in retailing. One problem was the plight of small shops, especially in rural areas, in part due to the rise of hypermarkets. There were remedies potentially available which looked easy to understand but which were politically difficult to implement. For example, in Ireland, country pubs have traditionally been combined with shops but this was not common in the UK where post offices, however, are often found in shops. In France, postage stamps are usually sold in tobacconists' shops. Most shops in Germany were closed on Sundays except those selling goods necessary for travellers. Most of these situations were the result of national laws, sometimes enacted to deal with situations which had long since ceased to exist. New combinations of different kinds of retailing could help many small retailers to survive.

Another topic was the reluctance of many policy makers, including some in the Commission's department responsible for agriculture, to realise that these days it is the big supermarket chains which determine the design of many products, not manufacturers. If environmentalists want to do something about excess packaging, for example, they must speak to the supermarket chains who specify every detail of products they choose to buy from manufacturers. Very few manufacturers have the clout to deal with such problems without the supermarkets' agreement.

A further aim was to put a spotlight on the possibility for retail chains to trade across the EU's internal frontiers and set up in each other's internal

---

[24] A price point is a supposedly attractive number such as £1.49 or £29.99.

markets, a process which had then hardly begun but which has since developed rapidly through acquisitions, franchising and agencies.

I also helped to organise a conference jointly with officials of the French government to exchange experiences about preserving the vitality of towns and cities in the face of out-of-town shopping centres drawing trade away from them. The EU neither had, nor sought, any power over where shops are built. It does however try to ensure that funds from the European Regional Development Fund used for urban development took into account the impact of new developments on existing town centres and were coordinated with national subsidy schemes of this nature.

It is often said, rightly in many cases, that the French get what they want in the EU. Where true, this is not surprising because they come forward forcefully with a clear viewpoint, agreed by all elements of their government. By comparison, the British and certain other nations often expose their internal differences in public, including sometimes the policies of Scotland and Wales when they differ from those of England. In helping to organise this conference about town centres, I was able to see how the French arrived at such clear positions. I was present at a planning meeting in Paris at which some twenty officials from French ministries, government agencies and chambers of commerce were present. Each representative spoke clearly and forcefully and there was then vigorous debate about conflicting views. At the end, however, astute chairmanship brought the meeting to common positions on all the essential features of the conference. A united view was reached and nobody questioned it thereafter. The conference, in Lille in 2000, was a considerable success. A thousand delegates attended. The French government paid most of the cost.

The use of consultants for demonstration projects brought its own set of problems. A situation we found on a number of occasions was a consultant recycling for the EU work already done and paid for by another client, albeit with a few cosmetic alterations. We used computer techniques to check whether sections of reports submitted to the Commission had already been done and paid for by the Commission. Another point to watch was whether a report was based wholly on desk work, the study of published material, when we were paying for new field studies. Yet another problem was where a consultant was contracted to use named expert staff and tried to get away with using more junior staff or even students.[25]

---

[25] One definition of a consultant circulating in Brussels is a man who borrows your watch and then charges you when you ask him to tell you the time!

It was not my job to criticise the basic policy of carrying out demonstration projects. Almost all public expenditure carries a risk of waste or even fraud. On the other hand, unless one adopts a completely *laissez faire* attitude, the public interest may require that the authorities take action to improve business sectors where competition alone does not seem to bring about improvements where these were clearly needed. If businesses in the EU were not competitive, there were plenty of firms elsewhere to take the business.

The Commerce Unit was consulted by the European Commission's Directorate General for Competition policy about plans to prevent car manufacturers restricting the sale of new cars to showrooms owned by the manufacturers themselves or bound by restrictive agreements. Such agreements would ban the sale of other makes of car, and lay down such details as the size of floor space and whether a coffee machine was provided for the use of clients. This made the price of new cars higher than it would otherwise have been, and reduced consumer choice. A prospective buyer should have the choice of buying a car in an upmarket showroom selling only one make of car, or from one which sells several makes of cars or from one which focuses on low prices. We were at pains to show that the hypermarket chains might be in a position to offer new cars much cheaper than the traditional car showrooms.

A problem with this was the provision of after-sales service, especially when most first services are done under guarantees. If the car manufacturers could restrict after-sales service to their own premises, they could easily oppose the price challenge of other dealers. The ability of a firm to sell something to a customer but then to place restrictions on that customer as to how he sells it on is basically against the principles of competition law. An example of the pressures applied by certain manufacturers was an insistence that garages could only use particular types of test equipment supplied by the manufacturers themselves. This issue sounds complicated and bureaucratic but consumers need their interests to be taken into account against the wiles of manufacturers determined to screw every last penny out of the market. The Commerce Unit was one of the conduits by which the much bigger Competition Directorate General kept in touch with the realities of the situation.

I worked on the WEEE Directive – Waste Electronic and Electrical Equipment. This is the law which, among other things, says that old and unwanted television sets and refrigerators can only be thrown away in designated locations where they have to be properly handled. This is in order to recover some of the components for re-use and to dispose of the rest in a manner where the environment will not be damaged.

★ ★ ★

I spoke at a conference in Helsinki. The conference brought together employers and employees in the Finnish retail sector, the first time they had ever sat down together in such a conference. I was a neutral focal point between the two often conflicting sides. A little background research emphasised that Finland is not, as many people believe, part of Scandinavia. The term Scandinavian is usually taken to mean the Swedes, the Danes, the Norwegians and possibly the Icelanders and the Faroese. Add in the Finns and you have the "Nordics". The Finns like people to be clear about this.

They get irritated that their country is often left off the weather map of Europe. They get even more irritated when people say that the accession of Poland to the EU brought the EU up to the borders of Russia. Finland, which joined the EU with Sweden and Austria in 1995, has had a border with Russia since it became an independent country. It was actually part of Russia, a Russian Grand Duchy no less, from 1809 until 1917 when the Russian Revolution took place and the Finns gained their independence. In earlier times, Finland had been part of the Swedish empire and to this day some six per cent of the population, mainly around its coast, are principally Swedish-speaking. The whole country is officially bilingual, meaning that all dealings between citizens and the state can be held in Finnish or Swedish. I was not aware of any tension between the two language groups.

The Finns, normally rather silent people, talk constantly on their mobiles. The telephone seems to produce a loquacity which is not otherwise evident.

When I speak at meetings, there is almost invariably a flood of questions at the end. This is either because my words were fascinating and provocative or because the audience did not understand a word I had said. (I prefer the former explanation!) At this particular conference in Helsinki, I was warned by the conference organiser, who was from the Swedish-speaking minority, that there would be no questions. I did not believe her, but sure enough, after I sat down, silence! I was told afterwards that my speech was good. But they just didn't say anything.

I spoke on another occasion at a conference in Kokkola, about 480 kilometres north west of Helsinki, on the coast of the Gulf of Bothnia. I was then less than halfway to Finland's northern border but well away from the concentration of population around the capital.

Myra came with me on this trip. On the way back we stopped at the town of Tammisaari. This is a pleasant resort town with houses dotted about. The properties had no walls or fences to demarcate whose property was whose. Being a fine day, people were walking about, on their own – and resolutely not talking to anybody. We also stopped at Tampere. This city, sometimes called the Manchester of Finland, is situated on a patchwork of lakes and rivers which in the nineteenth century provided water power for the cotton mills, the most prominent of which were set up by the Scottish company Finlayson. My father's cotton broking firm in Liverpool made its money in the early 1900s selling American cotton in Finland and Sweden. I had heard that during the First World War the firm was instrumental in establishing transportation by sledges pulled by horses and reindeer for their cotton shipments from Kirkenes. This town is close to Norway's border with Russia on the Arctic coast. The sledge transport to Tampere avoided the wartime blockade in the Baltic Sea. I checked this out in the public library in Tampere and sure enough the story appears to be true. I also found that one of my relatives was the manager of Finlaysons textile mill at one time and had been the honorary British Consul in the city.

I have a childhood memory of one of my father's Finnish clients, Mr Rautio, coming to our home near Liverpool. Our cat for some reason took the strongest possible dislike to him. For about fifteen Christmases thereafter Mr Rautio sent us a Christmas card, the same one each time, a picture of his house. We didn't

Transporting raw cotton in Finland in winter

tell the cat. It is a custom in Finland and certain other European countries for some people to send the same Christmas card, with a picture of their house on it, every year.

Back in Brussels, I attended a meeting of the board of the British Food Safety Agency, held in public in a conference centre in the city. The public could hear everything that was said and could see each member on individual television cameras. It was an interesting example of open government.

I attended a public consultation on EU food-labelling laws in the House of Lords in London, packed with enthusiastic British campaigners. Some of them seemed to me to be quite out of touch with ordinary people. I was reminded of the sandwiches at airports in Switzerland where the contents label is larger than the sandwich because of the amount of information provided, (thereby causing unnecessary use of paper, damnable in terms of environmental protection policy!). The green lobbyists and the consumerists were out in force at the meeting. One young man next to me went purple in the face in expressing his anger about what he believed was inadequate labelling of foods in the shops. He demanded that every cabbage on sale should bear a label declaring the plant's full nutritional characteristics. Of course, if he had had his way, there would have been protests from the ecologists about the trees cut down to make the paper for the large labels which would be necessary! He may have spoken for consumerists but not, in my view, for consumers.

One folly the Commerce Unit managed to prevent was a move to require declarations on every package of various products that they had not been tested on animals – or that any of the constituent parts of this type of product had *ever* been so tested. Imagine this on a small bottle of perfume! Displaying a notice on a store counter would surely tell people what they want to know – if anyone was interested. British journalists like to mock such rules which aim to get the right balance between competing policy aims and consumer protection; however, with all the inconsistency which they allow themselves, journalists will also call for better consumer information, protection of animals, safer products, clearer instructions and less waste and bureaucracy.

★ ★ ★

In this period of my life (1994 to 2002), I commuted from Manchester to Brussels, initially on the six thirty flight on Monday mornings. The availability of cheap tickets on these flights became more and more difficult – the cost came out of my own pocket – and I found myself having to travel on the early evening flights on Sundays. On Fridays I took flights between six o'clock and half past nine in the evenings from Brussels to Manchester. This was hardly a lifestyle to be recommended! Myra and I debated whether she should move to Brussels again but the costs involved, the upheaval of the children's education and her own activities as a Health Authority Chairman and as a magistrate meant that this was not the right answer. In the end I took a flat in Brussels within walking distance of my office in the European Commission.

Walking home, after working late in the office, necessitated taking a route free of dark corners and preferably frequented by other pedestrians; mugging and theft were not uncommon. Dealing with my personal laundry was a regular duty. On more than one occasion I put my clothes in the machine in the nearby launderette, went off to do something else and found the place had been closed for the night when I got back.

During my first couple of years back in Brussels I worked very long hours. When I left the office, the small shops on my way were closed so I could not buy any food. There was no convenient supermarket either. I got into the habit of buying a loaf of bread at Asda in Bromborough in Wirral on Sundays to take back to Brussels with me. The bread which stayed freshest was Irish wholemeal soda bread, which had been imported to England across the Irish Sea. When I did leave the office at a more reasonable hour, I would see Brits who were regular visitors to Brussels, business lobbyists and others, doing their shopping in a little convenience store. Looking in their shopping baskets, I deduced that a bottle of whisky and a packet of digestive biscuits was staple evening fare for many of them.

In 1998 Britain held the Presidency of the Council of Ministers. Tony Blair wrote in a pamphlet, "I am determined that the UK Presidency will show the constructive and innovative contribution Britain can make to European affairs." I and British colleagues were pleased that the Prime Minister took the trouble to produce this pamphlet although many doubted the accuracy of the sentiment expressed in it.

I made it a habit to attend a number of events in Brussels arranged for visiting British organisations to meet European Commission and European Parliament officials, even though it was not part of my own job. Knowing the ignorance of many in the UK about how the EU worked, I was able to clarify quite a lot of difficulties about how legislation was made and how grant-giving schemes worked. I also attended some British social events. One was a gala performance of Gilbert and Sullivan's *The Pirates of Penzance* by the Brussels British Opera Society. The then British Ambassador to Belgium was present; at the end of the performance, he gave a special rendering of an EU regulation to the tune of one of Sullivan's arias. The Eurocrats in the audience loved it.

Commission staff grades were indicated by letters and numbers. Grade A staff were graduates, grade B other administrative staff, grade C were secretaries and grade D drivers, messengers etc. My own final grade in the European Commission was that of Principal Administrator, grade A4. The A1 (Director General) and A2 (Deputy Director General) posts were appointed by the Commission in agreement with the relevant EU country's government. Some of the British quota was taken up by people previously working in Whitehall, as rising stars, "to sort the Commission out". Others were people Whitehall would not miss. Not all had any significant knowledge of the EU.

An A2 post in the Administration Directorate General was advertised for someone to be in charge of buildings, equipment and the organisation of conferences, activities well away from my own interests. A leaflet was circulated by one of the several trade unions operating in the Commission bearing a photo

Part of a leaflet claiming that I was being promoted inside the European Commission through British influence

of me with a large beard added to my features and looking like a Mafioso! This leaflet referred to me as a "subject of Her Majesty" and claimed that I would be the successful candidate supported by Whitehall. The union protested that the post should go to a career Commission official and not someone who had been an MEP. In fact, I had not applied for the job and was extremely doubtful whether Whitehall would have supported me if I had been tempted to do so, because I had never been "one of them". Someone else got the job.

I played no part in the 1994 Euro-election. But when the 1999 election came into view, I decided to be a candidate if I could. I was not dissatisfied with my job in the European Commission but this was just a job whereas being an MEP was a calling, a vocation, if that doesn't sound too pompous.

By this time, the system had been changed by the British government under Tony Blair from single-member constituencies to regional lists in a proportional system. In 1999 for the first time, voters in North West England were able to vote for any one of several lists of up to nine candidates. The main parties each submitted a list of candidates. Various individuals also offered themselves though these had, in practice, virtually no chance of being elected. The candidates elected from each party were those nearest the top of the list within the proportion of total votes which the party attracted. Voters were not permitted to vote for a particular candidate, only for the list. The Labour party laid down the order of the candidates from party headquarters. The Conservatives gathered its supporters in each region to a big meeting to decide the order of the list.

I attended the Conservative selection process at Bolton Football Club's stadium. The mood of the activists was very anti-European. Three local former MPs came out at the top of the list. I had been out of politics for ten years and was out of sympathy with the then current views of the party on Europe. When the party workers voted, I was too low on the list to have any chance of being elected.

I decided to campaign with an independent party, the Pro-Europe Conservative Party, which was set up to give resolute support for Britain's membership of the EU. Our party fought as well as we could but was soundly beaten, failing even to attract one per cent of the votes cast. The official Conservative and Labour parties each received about one third of the votes cast in the region, the Tories doing fractionally better than Labour.

Brendan Donnelly, who headed up our efforts in the Pro-Europe Conservative Party, explained the reason for setting up the new party: 'We cannot stand idly by while the anti-European interests in the Conservative Party, which destroyed John Major's government, turn the party into a mere lobbying group for Euro-scepticism. Like many Conservatives, we fear our Party has in recent years been turned into little more than a sect. The Conservative Party's European policy has been central to this process of degeneration.'

Under the earlier single member system, I was MEP for everybody living in the constituency, irrespective of whether they had voted for me or not. Under the new proportional system, citizens tend to address or be directed to an MEP of their own party, weakening the Member's claim to represent the interests of the whole of his or her patch. Moreover, Tory MEPs would be tempted to devote their best attention to the parts of the region containing their party's own supporters because it is these people who would decide the order of the names on the ballot paper at the next election. There would be similar pressures in the Labour party.

So I continued working in the European Commission. Most of the time I worked there, there was criticism from British and other national civil servants, including some from staff in the Permanent Representations (embassies of the EU countries) in Brussels, about the salaries paid to European Commission officials. The European Commission decided to carry out a survey of the pay and allowances (including expatriation allowances) of national civil servants posted to Brussels and compare these with the salaries paid to Commission staff. Its report of April 2000 concluded that the net remuneration of Commission staff was lower than the average net remuneration of comparable grades in the Permanent Representations of the UK, Denmark, France and Germany – people whose general working situations were similar to those of Commission staff.

Staff of the UK Representation (UKRep) can hardly have welcomed this information. As far as my own experience went, UKRep staff were not friendly or co-operative with the general body of Brits working in the Commission. In my early days, if I wanted to know how national civil services handled certain EU policies, I had to ask the Irish, the Germans or the Belgians because nobody in UKRep would help me. When I became an MEP, I complained to Douglas Hurd, then Foreign Secretary, about this. He said he would raise the matter with UKRep. Perhaps as a result, when I was again working in Brussels later on, I was occasionally invited to UKRep cocktail parties. My objective was not to have the free drinks but to get to know people and exchange information.

PART V

Thoughts, Afterthoughts and Perceptions

'Of course I'm not anti-European, bu

When I look back over my time in the European Parliament and the European Commission, I often recall attitudes within the Tory party in the 1970s – and wonder if they are that different today. A lot depends upon what we think is typically British (to be defended) and what we think foreigners are like (to be careful about). In fact, our understanding of these matters varies hugely from one person to another. It's all a matter of perceptions: what we *perceive* to be reality. The nineteenth century British statesman John Lubbock said: "What we see depends mainly on what we look for". This is pertinent to how many British people, guided by the media, view the EU today. The French novelist Flaubert said: "There is no truth. There is only perception". My personal experience has led me to perceptions of Europe different from those of many of my fellow citizens.

Mrs Thatcher led the campaign in 1979 to elect as many Tory MEPs as possible and most Conservative voters loyally fell into step. Yet most Conservatives, like most people, knew little about the EU or the people in the other EU countries at the time. Many feared it; even more disliked the very idea of it. Their attitude seemed bizarre to me and their lack of knowledge regrettable.

Some snippets of conversation at party events in 1979 illustrate the point. A retired colonel boomed across the room at a gathering at which the local MP was present that he had no doubt that "Brussels" really wanted to abolish the British monarchy. 'I've heard they want us all to speak French,' added the wife of a local landowner. 'They are trying to make us all French,' said the stout lady. 'I KNOW!' 'Do you feel yourself becoming a little French?' I asked. 'Not *me*,' she expostulated, chest thrust forward patriotically. 'But I know they are trying. I saw it on the telly.' 'The French *do* hate us, don't they?' said someone. I reflected that even if the French did not like us, which I do not believe to be true, I doubt they would devote much of their time to such feelings, having better things to do. A person ignorant of history would think that the Second World War had seen Britain and Germany pitted against France. Perhaps anti-

᠁ᄂ sentiment arises because so many of the interests and characteristics of ᠁e French nation are so similar to those of Britain. For whatever reason, anti-French sentiment was and is still strong.

'I've been told they want to shut down the Church of England', said a voice, not wanting to be outdone. 'They want us to drive on the right,' said one of the local worthies. 'I want out of the thing altogether.'

'I'm for Queen and country,' said the MP's wife, drawing her ample proportions up to their maximum in front of me. 'How about you?' Suspicion about my situation appeared at another event when someone commented: 'You *do* speak English very well.' 'Why should I not? I *am* English, born and brought up in Lancashire,' I replied. 'Oh, really,' she replied in a faint voice. 'I thought you had to be French to be an MEP'.

Suspicion of my motives took another turn one day. Some people thought I was not entirely serious in my candidature. 'Don't you *really* think Europe is a lot of nonsense?' another retired army officer asked me. 'I know you work there but isn't it really time now to tell the French to go to hell and get on by ourselves?'

'We should never have let the Empire go, you know,' said one stalwart at another meeting. By "Empire", I think he meant Australia, New Zealand and Canada rather than Nigeria, Jamaica or Bangladesh. I would not envy a British Foreign Secretary who had to summon the High Commissioner of, for example, Australia and tell him that we had changed our minds and that his country could not have independence after all! Australia had, quite reasonably, thrown in its lot with the US and other Pacific interests after the Second World War had demonstrated that Britain could not exercise much power in that region any more.

At one meeting, a Conservative Constituency Association Chairman demanded, in the presence of his MP, that Britain should get out of Europe and bring back Imperial Preference. This was the scheme created in the 1930s when reciprocal free-trade between Commonwealth countries was negotiated at a time when import tariffs on other trade were increasing. Re-establishing Commonwealth Preference, as it became known, would have hampered Britain's trade with America, Germany and many of our other main trading partners.

A burst of patriotism would sometimes bring forward references by constituents to St George, England's patron saint. I made attempts in the constituency to draw attention to England's national day, St George's Day, 23rd

April. Shakespeare had done his bit in making Henry V proclaim at Agincourt: 'Cry God for Harry, England and St George!' but very few people in England took any action to celebrate the saint. I suppose the fact that St George is believed to have been a Turk serving in the army of the Roman Empire, and is also the patron saint of Lithuania, and parts of Spain, Ethiopia, Venice, Greece, Russia and Portugal does not help our association with him.

Most of my constituents consumed continental products and went to the continent on holiday. It was strange how they could be so offended by the idea of our government working with continental governments towards a destiny which we shared. People would say they didn't want anything to do with Europe. I would reply: 'Have you no time for Mozart, Rembrandt, Verdi, or Ravel? For Mercedes, BMW, Citroën or Fiat? Do you not drink champagne, Guinness, Stella Artois or Mateus Rosé, or eat Gorgonzola, Manchego, Feta or Danish Blue?'

My mother (who was over the moon about my venture into politics) was a good, plain English cook. I tried to introduce her to more highly-spiced and garlicky Italian and other foreign dishes. 'I'm not eating all that foreign muck, herbs and spices', she declared on a number of occasions. But she would not eat roast lamb without mint sauce, roast pork without sage and onion stuffing or rice pudding without a sprinkling of nutmeg on it.

'Oh, yes,' the elderly Lancashire lady said to me when she heard of my adoption as a candidate for the European Parliament: 'Yes, I'm in favour of the Common Market. I like markets. My father used to take me to Ormskirk market every week'.

An example of ignorance about Britain's real position in the world after the Second World War came from a former Cabinet Minister in a conversation in the early nineteen eighties. I referred to the fact that the value of Italy's national production was about the same as Britain's (especially when measured against the then low pound sterling). 'Italy, as rich as us?' commented this VIP. 'Sounds a bit improbable to me. I remember when I was in the countryside out there. Most of 'em hadn't even got indoor lavatories!' I asked when that was. 'I think it was in 1944,' he said.

'I don't think we should have built that Channel Tunnel,' said one lady. 'We don't want all that rabies.' (At the time, dogs were subject to quarantine before entering the UK.) I asked whether she really believed that rabid dogs on the continent would walk through the twenty-two-mile tunnel, dodging 180 mph trains on the way. 'Yes', she said, 'I've known dogs to walk very long distances.'

I had visions of millions of rabid dogs in Poland, Romania, Uzbekistan and such places hearing about the opening of the Tunnel – on Sky TV? – and setting off for the Tunnel and Canine Eldorado in the UK. If I ever see her again I must ask the lady why rabies could not come on ferries and aircraft too.

Some people would insist that they were not European. I would ask: 'Then what are we – African, Asian or what?'

A general view was summed up by one party member. This man condemned Brussels, the Common Agricultural Policy, the European Parliament, the French, the Italians, the European Commission, Euro-junkets, MEPs' expenses, French apples, French farmers and so on, and then added, 'Of course, I'm not anti-European but…'

These views could not be ignored as being merely the views of Tory diehards in Cheshire or any other part of the country. These were among the people who raised much of the money which financed election campaigning at local level. Moreover, these were often the people who chose new Tory candidates to take the place of MPs who had retired or had quit the House of Commons for other reasons.

The words and actions of the government itself and its servants sometimes seemed to reflect the same views. When, in the 1970s, it began to look really likely that the Channel Tunnel would be built, the UK Immigration and Customs people began to think about how to manage their controls for passengers using the new facility. An early position of the British Customs was that they would need two whole carriages – *carriages*, not compartments – on each train using the tunnel so that passengers could be strip-searched if necessary! In the end, Customs control at destination was installed instead. At one time it was hoped that trains from the Channel Tunnel could go forward directly through London to the Midlands and the North of England. Whatever technical and financial problems there may have been, one major obstacle was that the Customs and Immigration people demanded that everyone would have to get off the train in London to go through the frontier controls. Just imagine the chaos and resentment this would have caused. (This was the case with through air services which ran for a while from Liverpool to Antwerp via London City airport; everyone had to get off at this Airport for passport and customs checks.)

I came across many more people in positions of influence than I expected who had little experience of travel or life abroad. Indeed, a good many constituency party supporters tended to take their holidays in Britain, in "Anglo" places such as South Africa or the Caribbean or, if in Europe, in places u͵ which foreign culture impinged on them only slightly. How else could th͵ behaviour of a London magistrate, commenting on a case of a man arrested for possession of imported drugs, be explained? He complained that Customs officers were clearly not searching travellers' luggage thoroughly enough. Did he really think that all passengers should be routinely questioned (or strip-searched)? Had he never seen the volume of passengers at Heathrow?

What would those good people back in 1979 have said if they had known how the EU would turn out? We have seen the EU playing a major role in the economic, military and political reconstruction of former Yugoslavia in the 1990s, co-ordinating a flotilla of warships to defend oil tankers against pirates off the coast of Somalia, leading economic development in the third world, eyeball to eyeball with the US in trade talks but partnering the US in standing up for peace and democracy in many countries. And the EU is operating a currency, the euro, since 1999, a currency which, despite all the doubts, is (at least, as I write in 2013) one of the world's big currencies, far outstripping the pound in importance.

Back in 1979, people said that the EU in general and the European Parliament in particular would never have any power. What would they have said if they had known then how both have grown in power and influence: that the EU would make a significant proportion of the *new* legislation applicable in Britain,[26] with the European Parliament at the centre of the legislative process; that individual MEPs now exercise as much influence on much new legislation as individual MPs (the latter being so constrained by the party whipping system in the House of Commons)? Now people complain that the European Parliament has too much power!

So the reality of the EU has changed much since 1979. But has the public perception changed? For years after 1979, people including businessmen would ask me questions such as when Germany would be joining Europe. Even in 2012, as I write this book, two examples of fear, ignorance and dislike came to me. One lady, to whom I was introduced as a former MEP, stepped back in fear,

---

[26] It is largely inaccurate to say, as some British newspapers do, that the EU has imposed much additional legislation on Britain. Much of the new legislation consists of the UK and the other EU countries bringing some of their laws into line with each other to permit people and goods to move around freely. It is therefore in many cases adjustment of existing laws, not the imposition of laws where there were no laws before.

was some sort of devil from whom she should be protected. This 2013! A man who had worked at board level in a major company was azed to be told that the European Convention on Human Rights (and its Court) was not part of the EU and that if, as he probably wished, Britain came out of the EU, it would not thereby cease to be a member of the Convention or cease to have to apply all of the human rights laws which causes so much controversy.

In my constituency newsletter in 1981 I wrote: "Have you heard the Common Market blamed for the weather? No? Well, I haven't either but it's about the only thing that it isn't blamed for nowadays. Let's criticise the bad things in the EEC but let's try to be rational about it and avoid pretending that the Common Market is responsible for everything that's wrong in life!" [27]

Those people in 1979, like many in the early twenty first century, chose to ignore the fact that the referendum held in 1974 approved Britain's membership of the EU. People now complain that what they thought we had joined was not what it has turned out to be. In the appendix, I summarise what we joined, which was there for everyone to see. There are none as blind as those who do not wish to see. "Determined to lay the foundations of an ever-closer union among the peoples of Europe" are the very first words of the Treaty of Rome. You can't be clearer than that!

---

[27] I am reminded of an Italian official in Brussels with whom I was discussing why Italy had joined the EU in the first place. Clearly, France and Germany had many reasons to come together. If they did so, it made sense for Belgium, Holland and Luxembourg to join them. But why Italy? My Italian friend opined that there were matters which Italy had to tackle but which its own parliamentary system could not come to grips with; it needed an external agency like the EU to handle it.

So what does "British" really mean?

Many of the people whose comments I have related above do not like foreigners, even fear them: *us* pitted against *them*. This supposes that we British all have the same likes and dislikes. It supposes that foreigners (in the context of this book, the citizens of other EU countries) are largely homogeneous and that one can like them or dislike them as a bloc. Neither of these suppositions is true. There are huge variations in how different people in Britain live and think and huge differences between the peoples who live on the continent of Europe. Here, first, are some snapshots of aspects of British life. They may help to resolve the question: "What really is the British way of doing things?" Or maybe it won't. Then follow some snapshots of life across in neighbouring countries.

One of our sons decided to do community work through the school instead of joining the school's army cadet squad. This, in his case, consisted of painting the houses of elderly ladies in north Birkenhead. The ladies probably didn't want their houses painted but welcomed the company. My son's friends told their parents about the sights, sounds and smells of where they had been: run-down houses, dirty houses, dirty streets, anti-social behaviour… Some of the parents were shocked and decided to pay their own visit to north Birkenhead. They went on their visits and were further shocked. Yet many of them had driven through the area many times (windows closed, air-con and stereo on) without understanding the conditions in which people lived. Most British towns and cities have areas like north Birkenhead but middle-class people don't usually go there.

I heard of a local burglar who would sit on the balcony of his high-rise flat, in Birkenhead, observing through binoculars who was going in and out of their house. He would phone his mates so that they could slip in and do a bit of burgling while the people were out. I heard of a pub in the neighbourhood where you could "order" a television or a video player. It would be "burgled to order" a day or two later.

Such conditions were not peculiar to Merseyside. In the 1980s, I went to look at an area of bad housing in the Blackhill council estate, of 1930s vintage, in north east Glasgow. One or two people invited me into their houses. In one house the wallpaper which had been put up three weeks earlier hung limply from the walls owing to the damp. The Corporation had been told of this umpteen times but no remedial action was taken. Residents only ever saw their councillors at election time. Less than twenty per cent of eligible citizens bothered to vote. I went into the police station. While I was there, an inspector came to carry out some routine paperwork procedure. The constable to whom I had been talking had to go outside and stand guard over the Inspector's car to prevent it being vandalised.

Prime Minister Harold Wilson used to talk of the "white heat" of technology, suggesting that this was to be the characteristic of British industry and commerce. I came across many examples of British industry that were completely unlike that, firms slumbering and quietly dying for want of good management. Perceptions in Britain about British industry were not always glamorous but I wondered how many people knew just how low our standards of efficiency and customer service really were.

An example of this occurred when Myra and I, then living in Belgium, needed a lawn mower. A combination of patriotism and the need for a good machine directed us to a manufacturer in the Thames Valley. We made a special detour to the factory while on a family visit to the UK. We arrived at two minutes past five just as the gates were being closed. I told the man that I knew the model I wanted, I would take it in my estate car there and then. I knew how much it would cost and had the exact sum ready in cash. 'Sorry, we're closed,' said the man. I said it would only take five minutes. 'We close at five. Can't do anything about it. You'd be lucky to get one in less than three weeks anyway,' said the man. We drove off – and bought a continental model when we went back to Brussels.

As an MEP, I went on an official visit to a sausage-making plant in the Midlands. We saw sausages being made in adjacent, clean, but not very modern, mixing-machines for different supermarket chains – the same meat "sludge" with a bit more pepper for this retailer, a bit less cereal for that. Then we went into another area full of bright new equipment. 'This is where we make meat products for export; EU standards of hygiene, you know.' It didn't seem to matter so much about the standards for what we Brits had to eat. "Where do you export to?' I asked. 'Japan?'

'No, the Japanese will only accept European meat products packed in Denmark and Ireland,' he replied.

If manufacturing had its defects at plant level, what about Whitehall and The City? I myself did not have occasion to contact people in London head offices very much when I first went to work in the European Commission. However I would often hear colleagues laugh at suggestions that anyone of any significance would be in their offices in London much before ten o'clock in the morning, UK time! True or false, this was the perception. How times have changed since then, especially in The City!

Another facet of British life, far removed from industry and The City, was the "country set". Some friends of ours lived in North Yorkshire, an area of considerable wealth in which resided a number of gentry. Our friends were invited for a meal one night shortly after coming to live in the area. "Dress: informal" said the invitation. Our male friend turned up in a pullover and baggy trousers, following what this dress code would have meant in London. To his great embarrassment, it turned out here that "informal" meant velvet smoking-jacket and bow tie!

Another friend went to a big house for dinner with his wife one summer evening. The custom was maintained for the ladies to withdraw after the meal while the men drank port. 'Anyone for a slash?' said the host, after the ladies had left the room. Heads nodded. The host led the way through the French windows on to the lawn in the middle of which stood a large yew tree. Nature's functions were performed by the assembled men standing in a ring around this tree.

London's club land (Pall Mall, not Soho!) is another facet of Britain. I was with a small group of MEPs, men and women from several countries, who were received by some high functionary in Whitehall. He was kind enough to invite us to his club in Pall Mall for lunch. He was one of the meritocrats which were then infiltrating the upper echelons of Whitehall, not a scion of some aristocratic family. After lunch he took us around the club. He explained that women were allowed in this particular room on certain days and in that particular room at certain times, all in reverent tones. He did not welcome or even understand the feelings of absurdity expressed by some of my French and Dutch colleagues about this discrimination against women.

Blackpool gives yet another perspective on English life, the Britain of thousands of working class people. I remember the story of a coach trip on a summer Saturday by the staff of the company I worked for in Teesside. After a convivial night out, the people made their way back to their coach. One man was very reluctant to board the coach and insisted on remaining in Blackpool. Unwilling to allow their colleague to be stranded in the resort, he was carried aboard and put on a seat, on which he fell asleep. When the coach got back to his home town, he asked where he was. 'You're back home,' said his colleagues. 'What am I back here for?' he cried. 'Well, you don't think we were just going to leave you in Blackpool, do you?' 'Hell,' he said, 'I'm in the middle of a fortnight's holiday in Blackpool with my missus. She'll be frantic!'

But Blackpool had a serious side too. For many years the Conservative Party held its annual conference there every two or three years. At party conference time, the tail end of the Illuminations was still in progress. Illuminated trams decked out as space rockets, cartoon characters and so on, jammed with visitors, trundled up and down the promenade. Takeaway fish and chips at rock bottom prices were on sale everywhere. The enormous pubs and bars were crammed with happy drinkers. In one bar, I once counted at least sixty serving staff. In those days conference delegates could enjoy going on foot from hotel bar to hotel bar, meeting political VIPs and attending the myriad fringe meetings. On their way to the Conference Ball, some, in their fur coats and ball gowns, would call into Yates' Wine Lodge. Here, happy, beery customers gazed hazily at notices proclaiming that "moderation is true temperance". Those who did not want beer could try draught "champagne" or a glass of Guinness with a port-wine chaser. Grander Tory delegates from the southern shires were either amused or shocked (or both) at this manifestation of mainly northern working class culture.

The Tory conferences were exciting, full of tension, especially when EU issues were discussed, and very well attended. LibDem conferences were different. I went to one, in Bournemouth, on behalf of Littlewoods. A colleague and I bought tickets at the door and went in. Being representatives of a company noted for its generosity to "good causes", we were able to talk directly with most of the LibDem leadership to put Littlewoods' views on certain current legislation.

To Blackpool – an odyssey

As an MEP, I went to the Conservatives' annual conference, or at least to part of it, every year from 1979 to 1989. One year in the 1980s, a Blackpool conference coincided with a plenary session of the European Parliament in Strasbourg. I travelled to Blackpool via Frankfurt, Dublin and Douglas, this being one of the few ways to get there on the day in question. On arrival at Blackpool airport, I rushed across the tarmac and got into one of the two taxis that were waiting. I had not booked accommodation so I asked the driver to take me to a B&B near to the Imperial Hotel where the party leaders stayed.

'It so happens that my wife has a B&B just around the corner from the Imperial. Nothing pretentious but nice and clean. Would it do?' he asked. I said it would. At the B&B the lady said, 'That will be ten pounds for bed and breakfast.' This was very cheap. I said I would have to leave very early the next morning before breakfast time. 'I'll leave you a thermos of coffee,' she said. 'Shall we call it nine pounds fifty, then?' I agreed. I went off to do the rounds of Conference fringe meetings.

In the morning, I watched some of the Today Programme being broadcast live from the lobby of the Imperial Hotel. Later on, having listened to some of the debates in the conference hall, I went out to find a taxi to the airport. I asked the driver how much the fare was. 'I don't really know,' he replied. 'How much do you think?' he asked. I told him what I had been charged on arriving in Blackpool. He said that amount would be fine. As I went into the terminal I noticed he was standing about. I asked a check-in agent why he was doing this. 'Probably an off-duty policeman doubling up as a taxi driver,' he said. 'Quite a lot of them do it. The police don't mind because it puts more officers on the streets for the conference and they are not being paid overtime for it.'

This visit to Blackpool had an amusing if embarrassing consequence. Two of my colleague MEPs and I were to travel back from Blackpool to Strasbourg in a chartered, four-seater plane. I sat in the front next to the pilot, the joystick moving about between my knees as the pilot steered the aircraft. The pilot handed out coffee cups and a thermos from a plastic bag. A little later, one of my colleagues said, "What time are we touching down in Luxembourg?"

'Oh, we are not stopping on the way,' said the pilot. 'But I need to,' said the colleague. 'Can't,' said the pilot, 'not in the flight plan.' Silence for a while and then sounds of desperation. The plastic bag was passed back. It was the first thing to be unloaded when we got to Strasbourg.

A Yorkshire interlude

During my second period working in the European Commission, a speaking engagement at a conference took me to York. Yorkshire people sometimes claim that their county is really a separate country and not, in the full sense, part of England. (Yorkshire may have a claim to have played an important role in that earlier European

Union, the Roman Empire. The Emperor Septimus ruled the Roman Empire from York between about AD 208 and AD 211. Constantine assumed the position of Emperor in York after Constantius died there in AD 306.)

On my way to the conference and not far from York, I spent the night at a motel on the A1. I went out for a walk after arriving in the early evening. I asked a couple who were doing their garden where the nearest pub was. 'No pub here,' was the reply. On observing my disappointment, the man said 'Well, I think there may be one down there over the bridge.' There was, about a quarter of a mile away in a mining village which the gardeners obviously did not think was part of the same world. The lounge bar in the pub was almost empty when I got there. There were three men in it, well into their fifties, one being the landlord, all wearing cowboy hats. The landlord was trying to mend the firing pin of some kind of hand-gun which was to be used for firing blanks during a country-and-western music session which was to begin shortly.

A thin chap next to me turned out to be the artiste for the evening. An hour later he began to sing, accompanied by an electronic rum-titty-tum machine to complement his tenor and falsetto renderings. It turned out that one of the other "cowboys", with a grey beard, was also a country-and-western singer; 'But I do commercials as well', (whatever that might mean) he added.

'I'm from Wakefield,' said the artiste. Wakefield was about ten miles away. 'Which part of Wakefield?' asked greybeard. 'Normanton.' 'That's not Wakefield, lad! Which part of Normanton?' 'Alltofts.' 'That's not Normanton!' said greybeard.

More customers arrived – large, middle-aged, muscular miners with ramrod straight backs and beer bellies; their wives were bigger still. A huge plate of door-step sandwiches was offered round. This may have been to ward off imminent starvation or so as to comply with one of the idiocies of the British system of pub licensing at the time which required that, if a bar was to stay open after normal closing time, supper must be served. The artiste sang on.

'Does anyone like Slim Whitman?' he enquired of the rather meagre gathering. 'Yes, Joe does,' said the landlord, pointing to an elderly, inoffensive little man who took fright at the limelight now thrust upon him. 'Do you know The Yellow Rose of Texas?' someone else asked. 'No, I don't know that one,' said the artiste. We got Slim Whitman.

During the interval, the landlord and the locals reminisced. 'We've had one stabbing, one suicide and a Doncaster Rovers' supporter thrown through the window in the last six weeks,' said the landlord. One by one each of the locals at the bar capped this tale of brawn and bravado. Then they fell into silence savouring these memories of Yorkshire grit.

'Aye,' said the artiste after a while, 'but it's nowt like my trip to Huyton in Liverpool the other week. That were rough!! All them junkies banging their heads against the wall. I was real scared. The cigarette machines have welded iron bars fixing them to the wall. They don't sell matches because folk might try to burn the place down. I was glad to get back to Alltofts, I can tell you.'

(Talking about Yorkshire reminds me of a Dutch customs officer with whom I worked in the European Commission. He told me he was stopped one day by two burly Yorkshire traffic policemen on the A1. One of the officers motioned to the Dutchman to get out of the car. The Dutchman complied. The officer also got out and lectured him on keeping below the speed limit. The Dutchman feigned ignorance of English and waved his arms about – as some English people believe all foreigners do. The officer began to get his notebook out. Time for desperate measures, thought the Dutchman. He took the officer by both arms, kissed him fulsomely on both cheeks, got back in his car and drove off, leaving the officer covered in embarrassment over these unmanly foreign habits and hoping that his colleague in the car had not seen the episode.)

British food is part of being British. What is "normal" British food and drink is open to question. Even everyday expressions have different meanings in different parts of Britain. Try ordering a Scotch or a pint of bitter in a Scottish pub! Better to ask for a whisky or a pint of heavy or eighty shilling ale and you will be served. In Tyneside pubs, "scotch" is served in pints, scotch being the local word for everyday beer. Depending upon where you are, a bread roll can be a bun, a batch, a barm or a stottie cake.

Seeing the pleasure and pride that foreigners took in their food, I regretted that back in the 1980s very little pride was taken in our own food in Britain. This has changed a great deal in more recent years. We now have splendid and distinctive food in Britain such as Scots porridge and Scottish shortbread; Lancashire hot pot; roast beef and Yorkshire pudding; Cornish afternoon teas with clotted cream; Welsh lamb, and last but not least, fish and chips. I must not forget scouse, Liverpool's "national" dish, a stew of different cuts of meat with potatoes and other vegetables, usually served with pickled red cabbage. (I bought a tin of German *Labskaus* in Hamburg. In a restaurant it may be served with a fried egg on it).

We British don't always recognise what is special. I was served *paté en croute* in Strasbourg by a proud restaurateur as something very special. It was a pork pie! It was only in 2008 that Melton Mowbray pork pies became a protected brand. As regards beer, a proud host in lager-drinking Bavaria offered me what was, for him, a very special beer. It was similar to English brown ale!

★ ★ ★

Wales has its own language. Scotland has its own legal system. Scotland and Northern Ireland have their own banknotes. There are different television programmes in Scotland, Wales, England and Northern Ireland. The Queen is head of the Church of England but not of any Church in Scotland, Wales or Northern Ireland. Scotland, Wales and Northern Ireland have their own national and international soccer teams. Northern Ireland and the Republic of Ireland field a joint team in the Six Nations rugby championship. The English, Welsh, Scottish and Irish rugby teams combine in some international matches as The British and Irish Lions. Cricket is one of England's 'national' games but not widely played in Scotland.

So what, then, with all these variations, does 'British' really mean? Most British people will have sampled some but by no means all of these and many other variations of the British way of doing things. What is the *real* Britain, the *real* British interest, the Britishness which should be projected in Europe?

Those Continentals

There are just as many differences within and between individual EU countries as there are between the different parts of the UK. Here are some snapshots-in-words of the various habits and customs I have seen in that variety of disparate places often lumped together as "the Continent".[28]

One misunderstanding that often arises is the term "continental Sunday", by implication more "open" than Sunday in Britain. Yet many British shops are now open for six hours on Sundays whereas most shops in Germany and many in France, Belgium and elsewhere are closed on Sundays!

Some of the other EU countries, notably Spain, Germany and Belgium have regional government systems – as the UK is beginning to have. For example, some Germans feel almost as strong a loyalty to their *Land* (province) as to the Federal Republic. There are different types of provincial government in Germany. Hamburg, Berlin and Bremen, known as "City States", combine City government with *Land* government. In the other thirteen *Länder*, City and *Land* are separate. Despite moves towards standardisation in the 1990s, there are still differences in the powers of German Mayors vis-à-vis the members of their municipal councils, some of the differences having being imposed by the British and American occupying powers after the Second World War in accordance with their own respective national systems. Each *Land* has its own policing system, its own radio network, local transport system etc.

The inclusion of religion within constitutional arrangements varies from one country to another. Whereas in the UK the head of state is head of the Church of England and twenty six Anglican bishops sit in the Houses of Lords, France and the Netherlands are officially "lay" countries.[29] In a number

---

[28] In travelling around, I have often been struck by the amount of British involvement in continental countries there had been over the last centuries, from the Middle Ages through to Victorian and later times. This rather puts the lie to the sometimes-heard view that our involvement with our continental neighbours is something which only started when we joined the EU – although two World Wars should be enough proof that this is far from the truth.

[29] Separation of church and state in France was officially confirmed in 1905

of EU countries there is a limited access for churches to public (including EU) funding, most often for maintenance of ancient buildings or cultural events in church properties; in some countries governments make contributions towards the salaries of clergy on behalf of consenting church members. There may also be government grants where churches are engaged in the running of schools.

The acceptability of Muslim traditions and dress varies considerably from one EU country to another. France has banned certain types of Muslim dress in public places. The wearing of the Christian cross has been challenged by certain schools in Britain although the Sikh turban may be worn by Sikh motorcyclists instead of the crash helmets which everyone else has to wear.

Constitutions in the EU's other countries vary. Some are kingdoms, others republics. Some heads of state play an active role in government; some do not. Voting systems vary from "first past the post" to proportional systems. Many have legal systems on the Napoleon Code. Law in England, Wales and Northern Ireland is mainly common law. Ireland, Scotland, Cyprus and Malta mix common law with other traditions.

The attitude towards social issues such as the status of women in society, recognition of the rights of gay men and lesbian women, the disciplinary environment in which young people are raised, the treatment of corruption and other criminality, the protection of animals and respect for the natural environment vary greatly from one EU country to another.

★ ★ ★

I had not been to Spain before I was elected, but as an MEP I went there many times. I enjoyed the food there but never got used to the lateness of the hour at which the Spanish, including children, have dinner. After Spain joined the EU in 1986, Spanish MEPs of the *Alianza Popular* joined the British and Danish Conservatives to form the European Democratic Group. This meant that some of our group meetings took place in Spain, usually in the offices of *Alianza Popular* in Madrid. On one occasion, a Group meeting was held in the city of León. European Commissioner Leon Brittan joined us – in León with Leon!

While Britain has had an, at least partially, democratic system for several centuries, modern Spanish democracy only goes back to 1978 when a new constitution was introduced three years after the death of the dictator, Francisco

Franco. While democracy is now well embedded in Spain, political and architectural reminders of the *falange*[30], the dictatorial regime that Franco came to lead, are still present.

I visited El Escorial to the north west of Madrid. Here King Philip II had created a burial place for Kings in accordance with the wishes of his father, Charles V, who ruled most of continental Western Europe apart from France. (Philip married England's Queen Mary, known as "bloody Mary", daughter of Henry VIII and half-sister of Elizabeth I, in 1554 and became King Consort of England and Ireland until Mary died in 1558. He himself died in 1598 in the palace he built at El Escorial.)

Near this palace, the dictator Franco ordered a 150 metre-high stone cross to be built to commemorate the fallen of the Spanish Civil War of the 1930s. There was also a burial vault in a tunnel below it. These were constructed and dug by 16,000 forced labourers. When the burial chamber was dug, it was discovered that it would be bigger than St Peter's in Rome so part of it was left unconsecrated in order not to outshine St Peter's in terms of consecrated space. It was named as a basilica by Pope John XXIII in 1960. In the end only Franco, who died in 1975, and José de Rivera, the creator of the *falange* movement, were buried there. The tunnel leading into the burial chamber is rather like a railway tunnel (but of course clean!) What a contrast with the final resting place of his fellow fascist, Adolf Hitler, whose body was burned outside a heavily bombed bunker near the Brandenburg Gate in Berlin in 1945! The memorial has been something of a rallying point for modern day Spanish right wingers.

Bull Runs

Bullfighting and bull runs (corridas and encierros), troubled me. I took part in calls to the Spanish authorities from a group of MEPs to ban these activities.

One day, I hired a car at Madrid airport intending to go to Coria, a town where a bull run was to take place. I drove through the night and I reached my destination at around half past four in the morning. Coria is a small, picturesque town with a medieval wall around it. All the ancient gates were blocked for the bull run. I surmounted the wall through a bar-cum-restaurant which sat on the top of it. "El Ingles," (the Englishman)

---

[30] Literally, phalanx formation

said someone looking in my direction. I never discovered how they knew I was coming to visit.

The bull was chased about the streets for several hours by young men with sticks, swords and knives. The doors of all the bars were blocked by tightly fixed vertical wooden poles. The younger men could quickly squeeze between the poles to escape if need be. The bull, of course, could not get in, which was the whole idea.

Most of the participants were very drunk. Several of the drunken braves were trodden on by the bull because they simply fell over in its path. Every now and again, the bull charged its attackers, sometimes ending up with a thud as it projected itself past them and hit a door or a boarded-up window. Around seven o'clock in the morning the bull was shepherded into the town square which was surrounded by temporary seating. A hundred or more young men then poked and pushed it, stabbed it and lashed at it, some of them being butted or knocked over in the process.

I sat in my seat, some distance from anyone else. A radio journalist came directly to me and asked me for a comment and he was followed by a representative of the Mayor. This worthy gentleman asked me to witness the bull being shot, which was carried out neatly through its head. Several young men jumped on the carcass, slit its throat and jumped and fell in the blood as it spilled out. They then demonstrated to me that the beast's testicles were still in place when it died; these were then hacked off and brandished in the air. The crowd then started to rampage around so the Mayor offered me sanctuary in the medieval town hall, the crowd pounding on the door. Then he offered me breakfast with the local Chief of Police before I drove back to Madrid. I was saddened to be told later that the large scale bullfighting which took place elsewhere in Spain would not be commercially viable without the support of tourists from northern Europe.

What had all this to do with an MEP? Legally speaking, absolutely nothing! But politics is about persuasion and in this case, I and one or two other British MEPs were trying to help Spaniards who opposed this cruelty in their own country. Some of the Spanish opponents of bull runs were physically afraid to make their position known in public.

I made a statement about all this on Spanish national radio from Oviedo in northern Spain. One of my MEP colleagues told me that the King of Spain had heard the broadcast.

The Spanish newspaper El Pais reported my activities on 25 June 1987: 'I asked myself whether people who participate in these festivities are completely civilised.' This was thrown back at me time and time again: but I meant what I had said!

In this campaigning, I was sometimes in touch with Vicki Moore, of Southport (near Liverpool), who was later gored in Coria. She subsequently died of cancer and her husband, Tony, keeps her campaign going in Southport under the name FAACE (Fight Against Animal Cruelty in Europe).

Press coverage of part of my campaign against bull runs

NEWS FILE

Boycott plea over bulls

A EURO MP last night called for a British boycott of all Spanish imports — "right down to their oranges" — as a protest against last week's ritual bull torture.

Two bulls a day are tortured and killed during the five-day fiesta in Coria, Spain. Andrew Pearce, Euro MP for Cheshire West, said he had driven 200 miles to the town, and arrived "when the brutality was in full swing." He added: "Some of the people were blazing mad that I was there. They were very hostile and aggressive."

Un eurodiputado británico pedirá la suspensión del festejo del 'Toro de Coria'

EFE, Cáceres

El eurodiputado británico Andrew Peace pedirá ante el Parlamento Europeo la suspensión del festejo del *Toro de Coria*, que se desarrolla en esta localidad cacereña coincidiendo con la celebración de las fiestas de San Juan, por considerar que se trata de un espectáculo "bestial y sádico".

Peace, que se encuentra en Coria para comprobar la supuesta brutalidad cometida contra los toros que se utilizan en estas fiestas, ante la denuncia realizada por la Asociación para la Defensa de los Animales (ADA), ha manifestado que informará al Parlamento Europeo sobre la crueldad de éstas.

"Me pregunto si las personas que participan en este festejo son seres completamente civilizados", dijo Peace.

★ ★ ★

It was through our Spanish colleagues that our Group was invited to meet the King of Spain. We stood around in a polite circle in his palace. One of our Spanish Members gave a short speech in Spanish. The King then translated it into English for the benefit of the British Members!

Received by the King of Spain. Poul Møller, a Vice President of the European Parliament, in the background.

Much later, I visited the vast, open-cast copper mine at Las Minas. This was run by the British Rio Tinto Company until Franco nationalised it in 1954. Birmingham-built steam locomotives had hauled trucks laden with ore along the rail tracks which spiralled round the huge hole up to ground level. It was the biggest mine in Europe but production had more or less ceased as lower-cost mines in other continents were developed and sales of copper were hit by increased use of glass fibre for making cables. The Anglican Church in Las Minas, reminiscent of a Yorkshire village church, and the houses built for the eighty or more British staff with their British-style chimneys (quite unnecessary in the Spanish climate) paid tribute to this Victorian investment and the British people who made it work.

★ ★ ★

Myra and I visited Gibraltar on holiday. The place is full of history and felt

278

thoroughly British but we found it overwhelmed by fish and chip shops, picture postcards and duty-free goods stores.

The British captured Gibraltar from the Spanish in 1704, not for themselves but for the Austrians, with whom Britain was in league against the French. The transfer to Britain was agreed by the Treaty of Utrecht in 1713. The fact that this treaty is written in French caused a few difficulties in the House of Commons when discussions about the territories were held as talks about Gibraltar's future got under way in 2002.

There was always a certain tension in the European Parliament when Gibraltar was mentioned, both before and after Spain joined the EU in 1986. Gibraltar was part of the EU from 1973 when the UK joined. Four British MEPs were appointed to represent the territory's interests in the Parliament, although Gibraltarians had no electoral say in which MEPs were given this role. Whenever the Spanish demanded that Gibraltar should be handed back to Spain, I would recall that the territory had been under British rule for over 270 years compared with 251 years under previous Spanish rule. Spain's claim on Gibraltar was weakened by its own presence on the coast of Africa in the enclaves of Melilla and Ceuta, set into the territory of Morocco.

★ ★ ★

I had been to Germany several times before becoming an MEP, including a couple of times before the Berlin Wall was built. At the time of my first visit, there was just empty space and a mound of earth around the Potsdamer Platz in Berlin. I stood on top of this mound and looked around. When the Wall was built by the Russians and the East Germans in 1961, to prevent further escapes of the inhabitants of the Soviet sector, at this point it followed a more or less straight line except for bulging around this mound. I learned later that the bunker in which Hitler died was close to this spot. Since the Wall has been removed, the subway station for the new high-rise Potsdamer Platz complex of shops and apartments covers part of the site.

In the cold war period, the Brandenburg Gate separated the two parts of Berlin and formed part of the Wall. What had been, prior to the last war, a major traffic thoroughfare was at that time so quiet that rabbits played on the verges and dallied on the road itself – under the eyes of the East German guards with their binoculars and Alsatian dogs. While the Wall existed, I went over to the East sector every time I was in Berlin, almost as a point of principle to show the flag. I still don't understand why so few West Germans did so, if only to show the flag of democracy.[31]

One day I crossed into East Berlin via Checkpoint Charlie on my own. I registered my passing through the Checkpoint at the US Army office and, by telephone, with the British Army, hoping that if I didn't come back by curfew time, ten o'clock in the evening, they would come and rescue me. I went into a local public library and looked for English language books on the shelves. I spotted a book with a passage about Liverpool, the purest of propaganda. It dwelt on the supposed horrors of the treatment of the poor by the cotton "barons" (i.e. the brokers in the Cotton Exchange, like my father) in the city. The book claimed that it was a current occurrence for the poor to line up outside St George's Hall for food parcels. I copied out the passage by hand onto a piece of paper, as it was so totally inaccurate. The librarian came to see what I was doing. I told her how wonderful it was that Germans could read about my city. She did not know whether to be pleased about this or to call the police. I finished as quickly as possible and left with profuse thanks. I had the text reprinted later in the *Liverpool Daily Post* as an example of Communist propaganda.

I ended up having a few drinks in a noisy bar just behind the Wall. I was given to understand that the Soviets allocated apartments in this area mainly to trusted people, but the drinkers I met on this occasion were forthright in their condemnation of the Soviets and all their works. When they found out that I was British, the general conversation gradually turned into a small conference about the woes of life under the control of the Soviets, with me as the central point of the discussion, despite my inadequate command of German.

I had to leave to get back to West Berlin before the curfew. As I walked among the silent bombed-out buildings around the French and German Cathedrals, I heard footsteps behind me. Each time I looked around, there was nobody to be seen. Was I under police surveillance? What would have happened if the person following me had caught up? I shall never know. This was a new experience for me but fairly normal I suppose in a communist police state like East Germany.

As an MEP, I and some colleagues visited the British Embassy in East Berlin. The room in which we met was on an upper floor of a building forming part of

[31] The Soviets did not accept that West Berlin was either a separate country or part of the Federal Republic (i.e. West Germany) so West Berliners, stateless according to this thinking, were not admitted to East Berlin even though West Germans were.

a terrace of rather grand style. I was told that the volume of electronic beams emitted by Soviet and East German espionage teams on both sides of the embassy was such that staff could not work there for more than a certain length of time.

On one official visit with colleague MEPs to the Soviet sector in a coach, we were accompanied by a British Military Police Colonel in uniform. At Checkpoint Charlie, the protocol was that we stayed inside the coach and showed four pages of our passports through the windows to one of the *Vopos*, the East German People's Police (*Volkspolizei*). Our Colonel exchanged smiles with a female *Vopo* officer. He told us that a few days previously he had gone with a group of visitors into the Soviet sector but for some reason had stayed behind for some time after the rest of the party had left. This completely confused the *Vopos*, who arrested him and detained him for a short time while the matter was sorted out. The person who arrested the Colonel was the female officer whom we could now see at Checkpoint Charlie.

The ACP-EU meeting which I attended in the city (see above) took place in the old Reichstag (Parliament) building, in West Berlin, which was burned out shortly after Hitler came to power. The building had been partially brought back into use by this time and was fully restored in the 1990s to the designs of British architect Norman Foster. It is said that in the cold war period every room in the Reichstag, after it was brought back into use, except one, was penetrated by electronic eavesdropping equipment situated just a hundred metres away, over the Wall, in the East sector.

On some occasions, such as when committees of the West German Parliament met in the Reichstag building, Soviet tanks (which were routinely permitted to enter West Berlin just as western troops were permitted to enter East Berlin)[32] set out to block the route from the airport. On these occasions, the French and British armies, in whose sectors the airport and the old Reichstag building lay, had to have the Soviet vehicles shifted.

After one visit to Berlin, I decided to come back by train through East Germany and stay in Magdeburg on the way. I had equipped myself beforehand, as was obligatory, with a rail ticket and a hotel voucher. As I stayed overnight in that drab city with its boarded-up churches, my passport, lodged at the hotel

---

[32] After the Second World War, Germany was divided by the Allied Powers into British, American, French and Soviet Zones, apart from Berlin which was within the Soviet Zone and occupied jointly by the four Allied Powers. Under reciprocal agreements, military personnel of the four Powers in uniform had freedom of movement throughout Berlin.

reception office, was stamped by the police with the date of my stay, the only time I have experienced such a procedure in a hotel. As the train came to the border with West Germany, it pulled up between barbed-wire fences which separated the tracks from each other. The idea was that police dogs could run up and down between the fences. This was to catch anyone trying to flee to the West who jumped out of, or had concealed themselves underneath, the train's carriages.[33]

I was in Berlin with Myra and the children soon after the Wall came down in 1989. Along with many other people, I hired a hammer from a man in the street – five Deutschmarks for thirty minutes – and hacked off some lumps of the Wall for myself as a souvenir. I saw short lengths of barbed wire supposedly from the top of the Wall on sale to tourists, but as I happened to see a lorry arrive from a West German steel works containing brand new wire apparently destined for this trade, I did not buy any.

On this trip, my family and I had gone by car. We turned off the main autobahn from Helmstedt to Wernigerode in the Harz Mountains, where there was an old steam railway. We looked around for somewhere to stay and got rooms over a pub. I am sure we were the first western tourists to visit that pub, judging by the looks of incredulity we were given. On arrival in Berlin, we found it very difficult to get accommodation and ended up in a very posh hotel just off the tree-lined boulevard, *Unter den Linden*. We took a different route back and once again had great difficulty in finding somewhere to stay. Eventually we found a hostel with 1,600 beds where we could stay very cheaply for a couple of nights so that we could visit Dresden and some of the nearby industrial towns under their clouds of soft-coal smoke. The hostel had meals at fixed times but we never discovered when they were. We bought snacks in a local shop and ate them in our rooms.

We stayed in Potsdam, near which we visited the Sanssouci palace, the answer of Germany's Hohenzollern kings in the nineteenth century to France's Palace of Versailles. The Potsdam conference in 1945 between President Truman, Joseph Stalin and Winston Churchill (who was replaced by Clement Attlee after the general election) was held in the Cecilienhof building in the Sanssouci Park. Its design was said to be inspired by Little Moreton Hall in Cheshire. Fancying an evening glass of beer, I strolled into

[33] Most countries have fortifications of some kind to keep unwanted people OUT. It is worth noting that the Berlin wall and all this barbed wire was the attempt by the Soviets and their East German vassals to keep their own people IN!

My son Edward hacks a piece off the Berlin Wall.

the main street of Potzdam. Nearly everything was closed. The town was more or less in darkness. It seems that it was not much of a fun place in the, then recent, Communist times. We also visited the Glienicke Bridge over the river Spree, famed for exchanges of prisoners between the Russians and the western powers during the Cold War.

We called at the Wartburg Castle where Martin Luther, pioneer of the Protestant rebellion against the power of the Roman Catholic Church, translated the Bible into German. This was a bold move in the face of Rome's opposition to making the Bible available in languages which ordinary people could understand. We also visited Colditz castle, made famous in a film about its time in the Second World War as a prison for Allied officers.[34]

In Munich, I visited the Bürgerbräukeller, the beer cellar where Hitler jumped up onto a table waving a pistol in 1923 and proclaimed a revolution and the formation of the Nazi party. (He was put in prison for this and only came to power in 1933). Another site linked to the 'thirties is the Hofbraühaus. Here,

---

[34] Another remarkable castle I visited on another trip was Neuschwanstein, perched on a hill in Bavaria. This was the inspiration for the Disneyland's Sleeping Beauty castle.

you can have mountains of sauerkraut and cold sausage but the main thing is to drink a litre of beer; smaller measures are not served! The beer is served by female staff who carry four litre-full tankards in each hand. The sinews in their arms stand out like piano wires! You are regaled by a splendid "oompah band", all female on my visits, who play the same repertoire of five or six Bavarian tunes every fifteen minutes, including the favourite *Ein Prosit, ein Prosit, gemüdlichkeit; einz, zwei, drei, Suffa!* – Cheers! Cheers! Comradeship; one, two, three, knock it back!' Serious-looking Japanese tourists pass through, photographing everything and everybody at close quarters but not eating or drinking anything.

As an MEP, I visited the prison in Stammheim near Stuttgart. The prison had been specially built next to a court house where the Baader-Meinhof gang were tried. Double-locking electric doors and other high-security precautions were much in evidence. The purpose of my visit was to try to help a man from my constituency who had worked in the building trade in Germany. He had been arrested in Hamburg for being in breach of requirements to pay social security taxes for the men he employed. He was transferred to Stammheim, the trip (he said) taking nineteen days with stop-overs at local prisons en route. I was asked by relatives to do what I could to have him freed. The man said that he had not been told exactly what act he was accused of; only that he was in breach of a particular section of the German penal code. I offered to do what I could. I had to empty my pockets for the guards on the way out. I appealed to the German authorities to tell the man the details of what he had allegedly done or release him. He was released some weeks later.

On another visit to Germany, I visited the former prison camp at Belsen, where human hair torn from the bodies of the Nazi's victims can still be seen. The sight of modern German teenagers, watching aghast a film about what had gone on there in 1943 and 1944, is a potent memory.

★ ★ ★

Strasbourg was obviously the French city which I visited most often. However, arriving in the Parliament building at around half past eight in the morning and leaving any time between seven and ten o'clock at night did not leave much time for visiting the magnificent cathedral, wandering through the streets lined with hall-timbered buildings or along its canals. These canals link with the mighty river Rhine which has major port facilities and is the fourth busiest port in France.

Across the Rhine is the German city of Kehl. People on the two sides of the river crossed from one side to the other far less frequently than is the case where both banks of the Rhine are in Germany, as they are for many miles as the river flows northwards towards the North Sea. When I first went to Strasbourg in 1979, there were long queues of trucks at both ends of the bridge waiting to fulfil customs formalities. And this was supposed to be a common market!

France is a country with centralised government structures, as is Britain. Hundreds of years ago the French kingdom expanded outwards from Paris and found natural borders of the English Channel, the Atlantic Ocean, the Pyrenees and the Mediterranean. Just as the British look back with nostalgia at the period of The British Empire ("When Britain really ruled the waves", as W. S. Gilbert put it), the French look back to those days when their country was Number One in Europe.[35] Whereas the British can maintain a feeling of major importance in the world through the adoption of English as the world's language, the French find it hard to accept their lower status in world power play and in particular the fact that Spanish and German are probably as important languages in the world as French.

Many British people suppose that France is a Roman Catholic country (whereas, as I said earlier, it is officially lay). Casual observation suggests that, in terms of attendance at church services, France is no more a Christian country than Great Britain, although the whole legal and social structures of both countries is based on the actions and standards of Christian churches over the centuries.

On one of our holidays, Myra and I made a small intervention in Church affairs in France. We went to a tiny Romanesque church in south west France. I chatted to the church warden before the service. When he read out the parish announcements at the end of the Mass, he said how nice it was to welcome representatives of the Church of England. This was the only time I have ever been taken to be an international representative of my Church.

★ ★ ★

[35] Emperor Charles V ruled, from 1519 until his abdication in 1556 (in Brussels' Grand' Place) over most of the territories surrounding modern France. This was followed by a period when France was the major power in continental Europe, from the reign of Louis XIV (The Sun King) to the time of Napoleon.

Having Danish Conservatives in the European Democratic Group meant occasional political visits to Denmark, mainly to Copenhagen.

The Danes like to display their national flag and need no particular festival or other special reason to do so. They are fiercely proud of being Danish and of their monarchy and have no difficulty in combining loyalty to the crown with their strong brand of social democracy. Some ten per cent of the population of Denmark are not of Danish origin; they are mainly Norwegians and Swedes plus a number of east Europeans, Asians and Africans.

The meetings of our European Parliament Group (the EDG) in Denmark were held in the Danish Parliament building (unlike our London meetings where we usually met in Church House, the headquarters of the Church of England)[36]. Our Danish Conservative colleagues usually arranged for us to meet some of the Danish government Ministers, who, at the time, were also Conservatives. One evening we were invited to go from the Parliament building to the private residence of the Prime Minister. I missed the coach from the Parliament which had been arranged to take us there, so I took a taxi. I arrived at the Prime Minister's house with no trouble only to find that I was the first to arrive. Unknown to me, the coach had taken a roundabout sightseeing route. The Prime Minister received me alone and we chatted for three-quarters of an hour before my colleagues arrived. Better than the tour! If I had arrived early for a meeting at 10 Downing Street, would I have been invited to chat with Mrs Thatcher?

I have been reminded several times in Denmark that the Danish Vikings were the last people to colonise England. It is true that the Normans took over the government of England after 1066, but they came as an occupying force, a ruling class which took over from the native Anglo-Saxon aristocracy, rather than as a mass settlement of people. The Danes came and settled here in numbers. Blood group A, associated with the Vikings, is still very prevalent around England's east coast estuaries where the invaders landed. At least one of the major UK retail chains stocks an average range of women's clothing in places such as Tyneside, one whole size larger than elsewhere in the UK because of the predominance of taller women, presumably due to Viking genes.

---

[36] In view of the antipathy of the House of Commons, as an institution, towards anything to do with the European Parliament, at least when the Conservative party was in power, I find it ironical that the prestigious building in Smith Square, close to the Palace of Westminster, which formerly housed Conservative Central Office, is now the UK base of the European Commission and the European Parliament and known as "Europe House".

A feature of Copenhagen in the 1980s was Christiania, a former barracks then occupied in summer by hippies of many nationalities. They had divided the barrack blocks into "rooms" by hanging up curtains and carpets from the roof beams. Some of the hippies, men and women, went about half-naked. Some had children with them, others touted hash quite openly. I was told that the police found it better to have this going on where they knew about it rather than push it underground and out of their sight.

I went with the European Parliament's Environment Committee to visit a waste incineration plant some distance from Copenhagen. The plant, we were told, was technologically avant-garde. We flew to the nearest airport, arriving there at about eight o'clock in the morning, were ushered into the plant's boardroom and invited to sit around a large table. There were little Danish flags and bottles and glasses. 'Have another beer,' said our host. Another? Another? At eight o'clock in the morning?

In the nineteenth century, Denmark was a major net importer of coal and manufactured goods from the UK. The Danish authorities decided that the trade balance should be corrected by boosting exports to the UK of butter, bacon and canned pork products, at which they have been very successful. They insist on the products being of high and consistent quality and consistency. While much British bacon was of splendid quality, some of it, at that time, was not. The Danes have found that their hams do especially well in America, their bacon sells well in the UK and the fattier parts of the animal are welcome for making sausage in Germany. Every part of the Danish pig finds its market. British farmers had not always had the advantage of such sophisticated marketing strategies. Considerable progress has nevertheless been made, despite, or perhaps because of the fact that the common agricultural policy does not provide production subsidies for pigmeat. I visited a new plant from where some of the pigmeat was canned in the form of chopped pork. No expense had been spared in its construction. I have never seen so much stainless steel in my life!

When discussing the ban on herring fishing, then in place in certain parts of the North Sea, and commenting on how most fishermen, except the British, ignored the ban, we were told that what we were eating had in fact been sold on the Danish market by British fishermen!

In the 1980s a family holiday took us to visit Michael, a relative of Myra, who lived in Aalborg in the north of Denmark. He took us to a stretch of sand dunes on the west coast of Jutland, facing the North Sea. Hundreds of large wooden cabins had been built behind the dunes, sheltered from the wind.

People stay in them in the summer months. Being Denmark, where there seemed to be a rule for everything, regulations stated that people were not allowed to stay there during the winter months. There were still reminders of tensions between Denmark and Germany. 'For many Danes, Germans are not welcome to own summer houses here,' Michael told us. 'A few Germans do rent places here but they are not liked,' he said.

We have all heard complaints about Germans putting down their towels to reserve the best bits of Mediterranean beaches. We were told that elsewhere in Denmark, Germans have been known to dig a hole in the sand, put their towels in it and stick a German flag up to reserve their piece of sun, sea and sand! This may have been a joke but it accurately reflected the opinion of some of the Danish population (in the 1990s, at least) for whom the brutalities of German occupation were a matter of personal or family experience.

The city of Aalborg is a clean functional place. *Akvavit,* a Danish spirit somewhat akin to gin, is distilled here. I tasted one of the other local potions, *Gammel Dansk,* which was said to be good for hangovers. It is the result of centuries of Danish tradition, "bringing together the skill and history of a fine people", it is said. However, it tasted to me like a mixture of petrol and cough medicine! I suppose, though, it makes a hangover seem relatively agreeable.

The John Bull pub in Aalborg sold Boddington's ale, roast beef lunches and English football scarves. One of the principal restaurants in the city was called Penny Lane. (This Liverpool street was named after John Penny, an eighteenth century slave trader.)

I asked Michael about incomes in Denmark. He said that the income and allowances of an unemployed person were about two-thirds those of the after-tax salary of a bus driver. A managing director of a business in the town might get nearly double the bus driver, after tax. This relatively small differential of after-tax salaries is compensated by good quality schools and medical treatment which is mostly free.

★ ★ ★

I went with my director in the European Commission to an office of the Italian Customs in the suburb of Rome called Roma-EUR. The construction of this complex of buildings was started by the dictator, Benito Mussolini, in 1935 for a World Fair – *Espositione Universale di Roma* – to be held in 1942. The fair was to celebrate twenty years of fascism but was never held because the Second

World War intervened. It was later used as an extension to the business and residential areas of Rome.

My director and I had left Brussels on a very early flight. We found that some twenty Italian officials had been lined up to meet us in the office on an upper floor of a tall building. Midday came; no coffee. One o'clock came; no coffee and no sign of lunch either. About half past two, they asked would we like coffee. We said 'Yes, *please!*', wondering if they served biscuits with it. They said we would go downstairs and round the corner for it. The whole party went down the lift, which only took four people at once, meaning that it took several trips for us all to get down to street level. Out into the street, round the corner, down another street and then, hey presto, into one of those little stand up coffee bars. We were each given an espresso, a dribble of very strong coffee in a tiny cup; delicious, but nonetheless just a dribble. No biscuits. Then back into the street, round the corner, into the building and up the lift, in relays again. Lunch was up to my director and me to arrange for ourselves after we left the Customs office around half past four in the afternoon.

Cheese gave me some insights into Italy: *la bella Italia,* as one of the German MEPs who knew three words of the language kept saying. Mozzarella cheese is required for pizza and is also served cold with basil and tomato. It is sold stored in lumps in cold water. Mozzarella is produced from milk with a high fat content and some of the best Mozzarella is made from buffalo milk. We saw water buffalo imported from India on a farm in the shadow of the famous Monte Cassino monastery, situated on a mountain south of Rome. The German MEP was so overwhelmed at seeing them that he was muttering '*Wasserbüffel! Wasserbüffel!*' in awe-struck tones all the way back to the hotel.

Near Monte Cassino, the EU had part-funded the building of a plant for grading and packing fruit. One of the problems of Italian farming at that time was that, while the farmers could grow good quality fruits and salad vegetables, they were ill-equipped and ill-trained in sorting the top quality items from the indifferent and in packing the produce well enough to be acceptable for international markets.

Another visit to Italy took members of the Conservative Group of MEPs to meet the Pope. We were introduced one by one to His Holiness and a photograph was taken of each of us individually as we shook the Pope's hand. The Vatican City has long had its own stamps and coins. The coins circulate locally on a small scale and were similar to, and interchangeable with, Italian currency at the time. When the euro was introduced, the Italian Central Bank forgot to clear with the European Central Bank that it intended to make a similar arrangement for Vatican City euros. All euro coins have the same European design on one side but a national design on the other, varying from one EU country to another. Feathers in the European Central Bank in Frankfurt were ruffled when it was discovered that the Vatican had an image of the Pope on the "national" side of its coins. There were protests, especially from France and the Netherlands and that this was introducing religion into politics and should not be allowed.

★ ★ ★

Amsterdam is a beautiful city with its museums, canals, bridges and old houses. There was another side, however. I watched the dirty, haggard junkies gathering when it was time for the day's ration of drugs or drug substitutes such as methadone to arrive. Not a pretty sight. In the entrance of the main railway station of Amsterdam were posters which indicated, with very little need for decoding, where to buy cannabis. The "cafés" concerned usually displayed green plants or had pictures of green plants on display. There were menus on the counter showing the prices of the different kinds of cannabis available. I was told that those in the know could tell which establishments sold heroin and cocaine.

The authorities in Amsterdam had a bus which went round dispensing methadone to junkies as a supposedly non-addictive substitute for heroin. I visited a chapel by one of the canals which gave shelter to addicts. The pastor there shouted with rage at what he saw as the folly of this dispensing of methadone, which he said was addictive. 'It takes longer to become addicted to methadone than it does to heroin and longer to come off it', he said.

Another view of Amsterdam came when I took the suburban train to Bijlmermeer, which must have been a pleasant garden-city when it was new, not so long before. Under the arches beneath the station, the passengers heading for the bus stops outside followed me and each other, for safety, past the old builders' huts used as drinking dens. Fear was evident. What it was like at night, I can't imagine. I was told, though I have no official confirmation of it, that junkies had been moved out there from the central part of Amsterdam by the police because their presence in the centre was bad for tourism.

On 17 October 1986 the *New Statesman* reported: "Amsterdam is the cesspit of Europe, huffed Tory MEP Andrew Pearce at a press conference on October 1. The poison from here has spread around. It's like one man with a foul smell in his garden. I believe the Dutch government ought to be looking to their consciences." Strong words, but if you don't use strong words you don't get your view across.

Referring to the production and transport of drugs, I was quoted in *Conservative News* of November 1986 as saying: "The Commission has the ability to tie aid to their position on the drugs problem and there is increasing evidence that drugs are being channelled to Europe through African, Caribbean and Pacific countries which benefit from EU aid."

A Chester local paper quoted my views on drugs on 14 October 1986 as: "Drug taking is the greatest scourge of our time and must be stamped out if possible. I wholly welcome the proposed get-tough policy on drug traffickers and the call for better coordination of prevention and rehabilitation programmes."

A Dutch MEP, Hedy D'Ancona, thought I was being unfair to the capital city of her country. In a plenary debate in 1986 she invited me to be her guest for a weekend in the city. I replied: 'I am grateful to Mrs D'Ancona for her kind invitation to spend a weekend in Amsterdam. I have to tell her that this is the second offer I have had from a lady in Holland to do just that. If there are other bids I would prefer they be communicated to me in writing because if I get too much of this across the microphones I shall be in trouble with my local newspapers'.

An interesting little fact I discovered about Amsterdam was that the owners of some of the sex establishments paid for their streets to be swept frequently; street litter was thought to be bad for that kind of business. Such schemes were I suppose forerunners of today's Business Improvement Districts in British cities where retailers contribute towards the cost of keeping city streets clean and tidy.

★ ★ ★

The first time I went to Athens, in 1959, was as part of a group of university students studying economics. Our group was received by the Lord Mayor of Athens and partook of his *retsina* and *ouzo*. This had a disastrous effect on one of our Swedish colleagues who assured us he was fine because he was north European! We believed him until we noticed him head-down in his plate of food on the table of the open-air restaurant below the Acropolis where we went for dinner later on.

In the 1990s, the European Commission sent me to speak at a tourism conference at Halkidiki in the north of Greece. In the evening, what we thought would be a short tourist trip was proposed. This was to take us by coach to some ancient ruins we had never heard of. When we had been going for some time, someone asked how far it was. 'About two hours each way,' was the answer! In fact we were being taken into Greek Macedonia or Makedonia. The idea was to impress on us politically that this territory in the north west of Greece was really Greek and populated by Greeks. The neighbouring country called Macedonia, previously part of Yugoslavia, made claims both to the territory and to its name. There has been endless friction about this since Yugoslavia broke up. The Greek government had particular worries during the Bosnian conflict, later on, over the stationing of American troops in Greek Macedonia because of the territorial pretensions of the Macedonian state.

The word *Yugoslavia* means the southern territory of the Slavic people. The country was created in 1918, after the end of World War I under pressure, particularly from US President Wilson, from fragments of the Turkish and Austrian empires which had been on the German side in World War I. It comprised various peoples, or ethnic groups, each of which has a strong sense of its own individuality.

In the world of *haute cuisine,* a "macédoine of vegetables" is a collection of small cubes of carrots and potatoes mixed together with peas and other vegetables. The name reflects the ethnic mix of several Balkan countries where you find a village occupied by people of one ethnic group and down the road a village populated by another ethnic group. Albanians, Greeks, Bulgarians, Hungarians, Romanians, Serbs and others are sprinkled across the map and often suspicious of each other. It is extraordinarily difficult to know which national state should own which territory.

★ ★ ★

A similar mixture of people existed in Cyprus before 1973 when the Turkish Army invaded the island in response to provocative comments by Archbishop Makarios and the Greek government. Greeks and Turks had lived in Cyprus in neighbouring streets and villages, and even in neighbouring houses, often in a state of mutual loathing and with precious little practical contact between them. In 1973, disorder between the two ethnic communities caused the Turks to flee the south of the island. Divided Cyprus was born the following year. The British Army finally divided the two sides. Their commander drew a line on a map of Nicosia to divide the two sides. Unfortunately this line was not very well drawn and went through the middle of several buildings.

I visited the Turkish part of the island, the people's Democratic Republic of Northern Cyprus, with my family, as guests of the government. This was long before Cyprus became a member of the EU. I had heard much about the atrocities on both sides at the time of separation. I had also heard about the attempts of the government of the Greek-speaking part of Cyprus to gain control of the Turkish part of the island by economic pressure – and maybe worse. They planned to do this with the help of their allies, the military dictatorship then in control of Greece.

The Turkish Cypriots were at pains to show us the sites of the atrocities which they said were committed by the Greek Cypriots in 1973. They talked, over ten years later, as though the terrible massacres had only just happened. Perhaps the Greek Cypriots told the same stories, but the other way round, on their side of the border.

I dined with President Denktash, head of the Turkish Federation of Northern Cyprus. Many of the citizens of this territory had an agreeable life but the authorities of the Greek part of the island imposed many irritations. The Greek Cypriots attempted to prevent shipments of fruit and other exports from Turkish Cypriot ports by taking up the entire EU quota set for exports from the whole island (Cyprus not yet then being a member of the EU.) They also prevented commercial flights and ordinary mail coming to the island except from Turkey itself. My family and I had to take a flight officially bound for Ankara. In fact, we sat on the plane at Ankara and it went on to northern Cyprus. Mail for the northern part of the island had to be addressed to a post office box in Turkey, for onward transmission.

We went to Nicosia and looked at the frontier between the two sides with three tracks running between the broken buildings along the dividing line, one track each for the Turkish soldiers, the United Nations soldiers and the Greek Cypriot soldiers. I noticed how well clad, indeed suave, many of the UN troops looked, notably the Scandinavians, unlike the British soldiers who provided much of the logistics for the UN – and who had distinctly workman-like appearances.

The British Army invited me to fly in a helicopter along the dividing line between the two parts of the island and we landed at one of the British bases. These military bases are sovereign British territory, not under the control of either of the Cypriot governments and played a very important role in electronic surveillance of the southern flank of Russia and other parts of the former Soviet Union. They are also an important staging post for military flights to the Middle and Far East. The pilot of the helicopter was a sergeant who came from Everton, a Liverpool suburb and the site of the city's other football team. I am sure it is not necessary to say what we talked about!

My family and I went to the Anglican church service in Kyrenia on the Sunday of our visit. The chaplain invited us and some of the ex-pats who lived there back to his flat which overlooked the charming harbour. We went on to the beach at Famagusta, a long curve of luxury ten-storey hotels – all empty since the partition of the island.

I was never invited to the Greek part of Cyprus, nor did any of their diplomats in Strasbourg ever approach me. This was probably because I was known to take an interest in the Turkish part of the island and often spoke or put down parliamentary questions about the situation there. However, that interest did not mean that I necessarily supported their side of the feud.

★ ★ ★

After I had left the Parliament, Myra and I made a day trip from Helsinki to Tallinn, the capital of Estonia. What a sad place at that time, after years of Russian occupation! It was a problem that nearly a quarter of its 1.3 million people are not ethnic Estonians but Russians. This situation was a relic of Moscow's efforts to bring the country, once and for all, under Russian suzerainty. The Estonians feel cheated out of their country and the Russians there feel homeless.

Estonia was for centuries a trading centre and fortress at the entrance to the Gulf of Finland. The EU was about to lavish money on it to bring its citizens up to West European living standards and to lever in private capital. Most obvious signs of the West, as usual, were the German banks and the representative offices of the German *Länder* (provinces) poised to help their companies do business there. There were lots of well-suited Italian businessmen there too.

★ ★ ★

This is our Europe, they are our fellow Europeans, with all their similarities and differences. What variety! Long may it remain so!

Time well spent?

At the end of 2002, being sixty-five, I retired from the European Commission and have lived near Liverpool ever since. I have only been back to Brussels once and to Strasbourg once.

I have certainly had an interesting life. But was it useful? I had to keep many balls in the air, like a juggler. Was I able to achieve something?

Much in politics happens by accident. As Harold McMillan once famously said as an explanation of a government crisis, 'Events, dear boy, events'. I had no early training to be an MEP nor any particular education to help me to fulfil that role. As an MEP, I was what my very varied experiences, outlined in this book, had made me. I expanded my knowledge by personal exploration and observation and by asking questions – better than reading a hundred tomes of political theory. I wanted to represent Britain and British people as they really were, especially those in my own part of the country.

I have fallen out of sympathy with certain current Tory policies because these policies do not seem to deal with the interests of ordinary people, at least those in my part of Britain. I have to wonder why a party seeking to represent the British people selects so many of its leaders from such a narrow range of school, social and geographical backgrounds. Maybe some of the LibDems come closer to being typical of modern Britain. However, their party still has to shed an image of not clearly standing for anything in particular and of espousing off-beat, minority causes. As for Labour, leaving aside the weakness of Ed Miliband's leadership, questions of policy remain outstanding. Is the party socialist or not? Is it in thrall to the Trade Union barons?

I waved the flag for Britain in the EU institutions. I campaigned against socialism, then (and now?) such a threat to Britain's prosperity and quality of life. I spoke up for democracy, respect for human rights and private enterprise in all countries and, in particular, in Africa as the only means of making the lives of people there better. I sought help for businesses in my constituency, especially in the face of the concentration of so much of our national wealth in London. I worked with the MPs in my patch on policies benefitting local people. I firmly defended, and still do, the rightness of Britain being in the EU, hopefully at its centre where its policies are decided. To answer the MP's wife whom I mentioned earlier in the book: 'Yes, I'm for Queen and country'. The best way to exercise this pledge is through building a strong, democratic and prosperous Europe with Britain at its heart.

It is not the way in politics for anyone to be able to say "I achieved this or that on my own". Even Prime Ministers credited with great achievements have been helped by many people in arriving at their decisions. At my level, I do not claim that I created world-shaking political actions. I *do* claim that many matters, some small, some more important, would have turned out a little differently if I had not acted and spoken as I did.

I enjoyed my time. I conclude by saying that whatever I did achieve I would not have achieved without the support of a loving wife who provided a stable family background for me.

Yes, for me it was time well spent.

Myra with, in clockwise order, William, Andrew, Edward and Sarah – in Northern Cyprus.

APPENDIX

APPENDIX

The European Union:
A simple account to how it works

In 1973 Britain, Ireland and Denmark joined Belgium, France, Germany, Italy, Luxembourg and the Netherlands in what was then known as the European Economic Community (EEC). The EEC had been created by the Treaty of Rome in 1957. The EU countries collectively are formally known as the Member States. The EEC was renamed the European Union by the Maastricht Treaty, signed in 1992. In this book, for the sake of simplicity, the term "EU" refers to either the European Economic Community or the European Union, which ever was in existence at the relevant time.

Legislative decisions in the EU are mostly made jointly by the European Parliament and the Council of Ministers. The Parliament's role has grown considerably since 1979, it now having the power of "co-decision" in many matters.

The Council of the European Union (formerly known as the Council of the European Communities) takes decisions either by unanimity or by "qualified majority" voting, according to the topic. Votes are weighted roughly according to the population of each Member State. At its meetings, the Council is composed of the Ministers of each of the EU countries for the activity in question – agriculture, third world development, budgets etc. The heads of state of the EU countries have occasional meetings as the European Council, at which broad policy is determined.

The European Parliament, formerly known as the European Assembly, became directly elected by the peoples of the EU countries in 1979. As well as voting on legislative proposals from the European Commission, the European Parliament has a role of questioning the actions of the Commission and monitoring its expenditure. The voting system for elections to the European Parliament in each EU country is laid down by the government of the country concerned. In 1979 there were 410 Members (MEPs). The number rose to over 700 MEPs by 2012.

Proposals for legislation are made by the European Commission, which also has the task of implementing the decisions that have been made. The Commission was formerly known as the Commission of the European Communities. Since 1967 it is responsible for the administration for all matters arising from the Treaty of Rome and also for those under the European Coal & Steel Community Treaty (1952) and the Euratom Treaty (1958). In this book, the term European Commission includes its predecessor, the Commission of the European Communities, where relevant. The term "European Commission" can refer specifically to the Commissioners. There were eleven of them in 1979, two from each of the four big countries, one each from the five smaller ones. In 2012 there were twenty seven Commissioners, one from each EU country. The Commissioners vote like a cabinet on legislative proposals to be sent to the European Parliament and to the Council of Ministers. Their remit is to support the interests of the EU as a whole, not only those of their own particular country. The Commission's staff work in about thirty Directorates-General (DGs), which are rather like Whitehall Ministries but not nearly as big. The Commission's staff in 1979 numbered about 20,000 of whom perhaps a quarter were fully occupied in interpreting between the languages used in meetings or for translating documents. English has superseded French as the principal working language but French is still quite widely used. Final versions of formal documents are printed in all twenty three EU working languages.

The EU is based on the rule of law. Every action the EU takes must be within powers granted by the Treaty of Rome, by amendments to that Treaty or by legislation made under them.

EU laws mostly consist of Directives, Regulations and Decisions. A *Directive*, having been approved by the European Parliament and the Council of Ministers (and after a long and broad-based public consultation process), has to be put into national law by the government of each EU country, usually within two years. *Regulations* are directly applicable throughout the EU. These tend to be mainly technical or administrative, sometimes putting flesh on legal instruments already enacted. *Decisions* are addressed to particular persons or organisations on specific matters.

Other EU bodies include the European Court of Justice, the European Court of Auditors, the European Central Bank and the European Investment Bank.

The European Court of Justice (part of the structure of the EU) should not be confused with courts set up by the Council of Europe. The Council of Europe was set up in 1949 and now comprises forty seven Member States.

Britain was a founder member. The Council of Europe is the parent body of the European Court of Human Rights, which came into operation in 1953. The Council of Europe and the European Court of Human Rights are entirely separate from the EU. British MP and lawyer Sir David Maxwell-Fyfe guided the drafting of the Convention. All of the EU countries are among the signatories of the Convention. The UK has eighteen parliamentarians in the Parliamentary Assembly of the Council of Europe, about one third of them being Members of the House of Lords.

The euro was introduced in 1999 and replaced the national currencies of 17 EU countries. It is a tradable currency with notes and coins. It replaced European Units of Account (EUAs) and European Currency units (ECUs) which were, previously, accounting measures but not currency. In mid-2012, the euro was worth about eighty pence in UK currency.

The Treaty of Rome laid down its task in Article 2 as: "the establishing of a common market and progressively approximating the economic policies of Member States, to promote throughout a harmonious development of economic activities, a continuous and balanced expansion, an increase in stability, an accelerated raising of the standard of living and closer relations between the States belonging to it."

Article 3 of the Treaty laid down eleven activities to be pursued. Among these were the aim of setting up a common market for trade in goods (including the approximation of laws to permit such trade), the abolition of obstacles to free movement of persons, services and capital, the prevention of distortion of competition and the application of procedures for co-ordinating the economic policies of Member States and for remedying disequilibria in their balance of payments. Many of these objectives have been achieved but others, such as a common market in services (i.e. free movement of services such as financial services), have not.

There were also provisions in the Treaty to establish common policies for agriculture and transport, to set up a European Social Fund and a European Investment Bank. There were measures to co-ordinate and promote overseas trade and development.

The Treaty of Rome has been amended, by agreement of all Member States, several times, by means of the following treaties (date signed followed by date of entry into force): the Treaty of Brussels (1965/1967), the Single European Act (1986/1987), the Treaty of Maastricht (1992/1993), the Treaty of Amsterdam (1997/1999), the Treaty of Nice (2001/2003) and the Treaty of Lisbon (2007/2009).

The treaties were also amended by measures to bring into the EU the UK, Denmark and Ireland (1973) Greece (1981) Spain and Portugal (1986) Austria, Finland and Sweden (1995) the Czech Republic, Cyprus, Estonia, Hungary, Latvia, Lithuania, Malta, Poland, Slovakia and Slovenia (2004) and Bulgaria and Romania (2007). Croatia joins during 2013.

Both the European Parliament and the European Commission have websites. They also have offices at 32 Smith Square, London SW1P 3EU and in other cities around the world.

Acknowledgements

I am grateful to Robin Bird of Wallasey for giving me permission to use several of his photos and also to Robert Owen and the British Embassy in Brussels for permission to use their material. I acknowledge the granting of permission for use of the photo on page 41 by *The Daily Telegraph* and permission to use the photo on page 157 by *National Museums Liverpool* (the Stewart Bale Collection in *Merseyside Maritime Museum*).